S0-BYW-655

# An Actual Man

## *Michael Murphy and the Human Potential Movement*

EDITED BY JAY OGILVY

Minuteman Press
Berkeley, CA

*For Michael Murphy on his 80th birthday*

AN ACTUAL MAN. © 2010 by Jay Ogilvy. All rights reserved.
Printed in the United State of America.

© 2010 cover photograph, Daniel Bianchetta

ISBN 978-0-9819945-7-4

Design and layout by Margaret Copeland, Terragrafix

Cover photograph by Daniel Bianchetta

Library of Congress Cataloging-in-Publication Data is available upon request.

# Contents

Introduction and Acknowledgements  *Jay Ogilvy*  1

## The Early Years

*The New Yorker* Profile of Michael Murphy  *Calvin Tomkins*  7

To Hell With Russia, To Michael With Love  *Keith Thompson*  45

Ahimsa, Indeed  *Sara (Sukie) Miller*  55

An Experiment  *Mary Catherine Bateson and Nora Bateson*  57

From *Education and Ecstasy*  *George Leonard*  71

## The Russia Connection

Michael Murphy: Quintessential American  *Vladimir Pozner*  77

Moonshots Are Us  *Joseph Montville*  81

Putting It to Use  *Lizbeth Hasse*  87

## Adventures in the Paranormal

Michael Murphy and the Extraordinary in Human Life and Experience  *Stuart Kauffman*  109

Michael Murphy and the True Home Field Advantage  *David Harris*  113

The Myth of Michael Murphy  *Sam Keen*  125

From Luke Skywalker to the Corps of Discovery: The Sursem CTR Series  *Emily and Ed Kelly*  129

The Innkeeper's Work  *David Presti*  139

Protecting Me from the Dreaded Murphy  *Charles T. Tart*  141

The Next Great Work: The Enneads at Esalen  *Robert McDermott*  145

For Our Friendly Neighborhood Innkeeper  *John Cleese*  157

## And Seriously...

Michael Murphy and the Two Realms  *Robert B. Reich*  161

Applied Hope  *Amory B. Lovins*  165

Michael Murphy and Embodied Practices  *Robert N. Bellah*  169

Synoptic Flag Burnings  *Don Hanlon Johnson*  175

The Moral Arc of History  *Robert W. Fuller*  185

The Evolution of Experiential Education  *Gordon Wheeler*  205

## Love Letters

Dear Michael  *Nancy Lunney-Wheeler*  225

Homage to the Youngest Octogenarian  *Stan and Christina Grof*  229

Dear Baba  *Ken Dychtwald*  235

Mother Mike  *Chris Price*  237

Dancing Mind Embodied  *Chungliang Al Huang*  239

To Be Continued  *Allan Badiner*  242

Once More With Feeling  *Mary Ellen Klee*  245

## The Religion of No Religion

Tribute to Michael Murphy  *Huston Smith*  249

Michael Murphy, A World of Friendship  *Zentatsu Richard Baker*  251

An Exemplary Human Being  *Ken Wilber*  257

Michael Murphy in the Land of Oz  *Jeffrey J. Kripal*  259

## And More, Always More...

Appreciating Mike  *A. Lawrence Chickering*  275

Michael Murphy: The Person, the Legacy  *Richard Tarnas*  277

Your Legacy  *Riane Eisler*  279

Acknowledgement  *Stephan Schwartz*  280

Eleven Theses on Murphy  *Jay Ogilvy*  281

# Introduction and Acknowledgements

In Europe it is the custom that when a scholar of distinction crosses one of the higher decade birthdays, colleagues contribute to what the Germans call a *Festschrift*—a volume of essays in honor of the celebrant. Like book revues that don't mention the book under review until the sixth paragraph, such volumes are often composed of pieces that do more to honor their writers than the honoree. Bristling with footnotes, they can be death marches of pedantry. Not so these essays in honor of the very lively Michael Murphy. It is a testimonial to Michael's vast range of interests that the following essays are so various.

Almost all of these essays have been written for this volume. Except for Gordon Wheeler's essay much of which appeared in *Here & Now*, an excerpt from George Leonard's book, *Education and Ecstasy*; my essay which appeared in *ReVision*; and Calvin Tomkins' essay which appeared in *The New Yorker*, all of the other essays are completely original. Summoned in early 2010 to write something in honor of Michael, all of these busy individuals put aside the rest of their lives and sat down to write about Michael Murphy.

Talk about eight blind men and an elephant! Here we have forty visionary people all focused on one human being: A being so remarkable that the rest of us do well to take his measure. And who better to take his measure than the remarkable contributors to this volume?

We begin with Calvin Tomkins' *New Yorker Profile*, published in January, 1976. If you've never read this essay, you'll enjoy it now lo these decades later. If you have read this essay, it was probably some time ago. Read it again today. It speaks well of Michael, of course, but also of Calvin Tomkins who saw such promise so soon.

Reading Tomkins' essay shortly after it was published, Keith Thompson was so impressed that he had to seek out this Murphy fellow. Sukie Miller and the sisters Bateson, Nora and Mary Catherine, add to our sense of "the early years," as does the excerpt from the late George Leonard's *Education and Ecstasy*.

The next group of essays address "the Russian connection"—historic in its significance. Vladimir Pozner, Joseph Montville and Liz Hasse have all played crucial roles over decades of citizen diplomacy.

Of the following section, "Adventures in the Paranormal," let it be said that some of these essays are quite sober; Michael's abiding interest in the survival of bodily death is a serious quest in what philosopher William James called "radical empiricism." Some of the other essays in this section are less serious. You won't want to miss David Harris's hysterical account of Murphy's profound influence on the fate of the San Francisco 49ers. Nor do we expect a somber note from John Cleese.

But seriously…it is a very great honor when the likes of former Secretary of Labor, Robert Reich rises to toast the Master. Likewise when MacArthur Award winner and energy guru Amory Lovins finds Michael a paragon of "Applied Hope." Next, one of our country's greatest sociologists, Berkeley Professor and White House Medal winner Robert Bellah adds his appreciation of Michael's interest in "Embodied Practices." Don Johnson, Robert Fuller, and Gordon Wheeler then add substantial original essays, with footnotes, that bring the book as close as it gets to a classic *Festschrift*.

Then a change of pace: a series of shorter "birthday cards"—briefer essays just brimming with love for our remarkable friend. This book could end right there and its subject would be duly honored, but of course there's more. Not only is Michael a philosopher, a golfer, a novelist, a football fan, and the co-creator of the remarkable piece of social invention we know as Esalen…he is also a mystic. While they are way too smart to try to eff the ineffable in their paeans to Michael, Huston Smith, Richard Baker, Ken Wilber and Jeff Kripal are the people who can speak best, if obliquely, to this side of Michael's many-dimensional character.

Not surprisingly, essays on Michael Murphy are bound to break the mold of any set of neat categories or section headings. We conclude with a grab-bag of pieces that, fittingly for Michael, don't quite fit anywhere else.

Many thanks to all of the authors who rose so quickly to the challenge of writing these essays in honor of Michael. And thanks also to Daniel Bianchetta, longtime resident of Esalen and official "court photographer," for the picture on the cover. Thanks to my stepson, Wiley Marooney, for keyboarding Tomkins' essay which was written on a typewriter rather than a computer. And thanks to Fred Fassett and Margaret Copeland at Minuteman Press in Berkeley for their help in designing, printing, binding and publishing this volume.

But thanks most of all to Michael Murphy, an actual human, who walks and talks and runs and stands as an example of just what the human potential movement can produce. In trying to take the measure of this man, one cannot help but be impressed by the length and breadth and depth of his achievement—the sheer scale. We live in an age when the great work, the *magnum opus*, is out of fashion. We live in a postmodern age where grand Hegelian meta-narratives are rare. We suffer too many narrow specialists, cautious experts, and critical critics carping at one another across academic barricades.

Several of the authors of the following essays are sensitive to the grandeur—not the grandiosity—of Murphy's vision. Jeff Kripal comments: "The simple truth is that Mike thinks, imagines, and envisions big. *Really* big." Gordon Wheeler concludes his essay, which is about much more than experiential education: "This work of transformative individual and social development is ultimately a spiritual quest. Its ultimate meaning is transpersonal. This is politics in the highest sense. In the transcendent, deeply revolutionary spirit of Esalen's founder Michael Murphy, let us all dedicate and rededicate ourselves to this great work."

We would do a disservice to our subject if we took the following essays as a series of disconnected dots, or as so many thank you notes from forty grateful fans. Taken as a group, taken as a whole, taken holistically, they portray a magnificent vision. Behind the humor, beneath the love, beyond the fun stories of outlaw escapades, there is a philosophy of human existence, a new psychology of hope, and a politics that can carry us beyond enmity. Michael Murphy's vision of our human potential, when seen in full, is nothing short of inspiring. Read *all* of these essays, beginning to end, and you will be a better person. Convince your friends to read them and we will have a better world.

# The Early Years

# The New Yorker Profile
# of Michael Murphy

CALVIN TOMKINS[1]

It is somewhat ironic that the Esalen Institute, in Big Sur, California, should have acquired a reputation mainly for encounter groups, public nudity, and a general spirit of emotional letting go. When Michael Murphy and Richard Price started the Institute in 1962, neither of them had ever heard of an encounter group, and Murphy, at least, now has serious reservations about the ultimate value of the encounter process. It is true that encounter—which has been described as a way of achieving personal growth through the exploration of feelings among people gathered together for that purpose—owed a great deal of its vogue to the development it underwent at Esalen, and it is also true that the attacks on encounter therapy that now come with increasing frequency from the psychiatric profession usually single out Esalen as the fount of heresy. The fact of the matter, however, is that encounter groups have never accounted for more than a small percentage of the Esalen program, which includes lectures, workshops, and seminars on a seemingly limitless variety of subjects, from God in the Secular City to Mountain Aesthetics Along the Big Sur Coast.

"Mike Murphy never had a hard intellectual fix on any philosophical position," according to William Irwin Thompson, an author and teacher, who founded a more specifically spiritual learning community, Lindisfarne, on eastern Long Island. "That's what made Esalen different

---

[1] This essay first appeared in *The New Yorker*, Jan. 5, 1976, under the title, "New Paradigms." It is reprinted here with the kind permission of Calvin Tomkins.

7

from what it would have been under someone like Buckminster Fuller or Paolo Soleri. He didn't put his stamp on the place—which meant that Alan Watts and Abraham Maslow and Fritz Perls and the others could come and use it for their own purposes. But Esalen wouldn't have happened without Mike. It all had its origin in his sensibility and his spiritual quality."

What Esalen did become, under the careful non-guidance of Murphy and Price, was an extremely influential center of the human-potential movement—a somewhat amorphous but rapidly growing effort to tap unsuspected resources of energy or sensory awareness in all of us. Humanistic and transpersonal psychology, psychosynthesis, transactional analysis, gestalt therapy, encounter, sensitivity training, and a panoply of "body-awareness" techniques are aspects of the movement, along with such mass-market packagings as Transcendental Meditation and Erhard Seminars Training (EST). Carried far enough, the human-potential idea leads to speculation about the transformation of man and society. According to Murphy and others, we are on the verge of tremendous social changes—changes as great as those that accompanied the evolution from hunting and gathering to farming and stock raising in the Neolithic age, or from feudal to modern society during the Industrial Revolution, the difference this time being that evolution has accelerated to such a degree that we can be aware of the changes as they are taking place, and can to some extent prepare ourselves for the post-industrial world that is in the process of being born. What is needed, the transformationalists say, is new paradigms—new models for looking at the nature of man and the universe. Talk of paradigms and paradigm shifts is often a clear sign that one is in the presence of a transformationalist.

Recent developments in scientific research have lent reinforcement to some aspects of the human-potential idea. Brain researchers how have established that linguistic skill and analytical thought are associated with the left hemisphere of the brain, while the right hemisphere seems to handle the perceptual modes that we have thought of as intuitive, have opened up new perspectives on the so-called creative process.

Through galvanic skin response and other "biofeedback" indicators, it has been shown that man can become aware of his own internal processes, such as blood pressure, nervous tension, and brainwave patterns, and that by becoming aware of them he can learn to control them—as Indian yogis have been doing for centuries. Experiments of this sort have made it possible for scientists to take an interest in areas of human experience that were formerly considered fit for study only by humanists or divines. In fact, it is beginning to be thought that telepathy, clairvoyance, mystical transports, and other altered states of consciousness may be latent in most, if not all, of us, along with psychic powers and dominions not yet demonstrated. Is some revelation at hand? In a society whose institutions all seem to be crumbling, in a cosmos that has expanded lately to include antimatter and quarks and black holes, it grows easier to conceive that anything is possible. The myths of antiquity recur; the new journey, one hears, will be inward, into the depths of our conscious and unconscious powers. The new science will be closer to religion than to technology.

In a small, tidy studio on Telegraph Hill, with a view of San Francisco Bay from the Golden Gate to the Oakland Bay Bridge and beyond, Michael Murphy does a lot of thinking about such matters. The studio is upholstered in books—books on Tibetan Buddhism and Vedanta and Christianity and Islam; the complete works of Sri Aurobindo and Sri Ramakrishna; the Upanishads, in various translations; Meister Eckhart, St. John of the Cross, St. Theresa; Freud and Jung; Coleridge, Blake, Joseph Campbell, Plotinus, James Joyce. A whole library of the human potential, past and present. Alone in his studio, Murphy practices yoga meditation and works on his second novel. His first, "Golf in the Kingdom," published by Viking in 1972, concerned the mystical aspects of Murphy's favorite game. The new one has to do with a contemporary artist whose preoccupations, like his Basque ancestors, are very similar to Murphy's own.

There is also another, less solitary Murphy, who lives with his new wife in the attractive suburb of Mill Valley, goes to all the home games of the San Francisco 49ers, runs five miles a day, and continues to serve as chairman of the board of the Esalen Institute. For the last year or so, he has been trying to extricate himself from the day-to-day operation of the Institute. He spends as little time as possible at Esalen's San Francisco office, on Union Street, and he seldom goes down to Big Sur. Dulce Murphy, the attractive, subtle, and highly competent girl he married last July, and who is director of the San Francisco office, does her best to shield him from excessive demands on his time, but it is a frustrating job. In addition to his other gifts, Murphy is endowed with a warm, responsive nature, extravagant good looks, and a wild Irish charm. His studio has an unlisted telephone number. Most of the time he is working there, he keeps the telephone unplugged. But sometimes people simply come and ring the doorbell until he answers.

Sam Keen, a writer and lecturer and one of Murphy's closest friends, said recently that there had been a real change in Murphy during the last three or four years—a sort of coming down to earth. "He's more of a friend than he used to be," Keen said. "There's more ordinary humanity, more of the sloppy side of friendship. He's more willing to come out and have a coffee with you at the Trieste. Also he can get angry now—before, he was always a little disembodied. Mike is a joyous mystic, you see. It's the ecstatic side of the religious nature—very rare these days. The danger in a person like Mike is that he's unmarked by life; he lives on such a high plane that he may not know what other people are going through. But this is changing."

Murphy himself said not long ago that what he really wanted to do was to live the life of Jacob Atabet, the central character in the novel he is writing. "Atabet discovers that the body is an opening into the secrets of time, a sort of evolutionary star gate," he said. "In it, the universe is remembered, level upon level. And so his lifelong voyage is back to the birth of the universe through this bodily descent. I really do believe that evolution is becoming conscious of itself in man, and that man is on the verge of a transformation. There's a great opening up, a synthesis now going on between intuition and intellect, body and mind, matter and spirit, East and West, and terms like 'human potential' and 'transpersonal psychology' and 'altered states of consciousness' are emerging to deal with it. The new maps are all provisional of course. But I think of this as the most exciting adventure ahead of us, and it's what I want to do for the next forty years."

When Murphy was growing up—in Salinas, about forty-five miles from where the Esalen Institute is now—he alternated between wanting to be a doctor and wanting to be a minister. The doctor idea came from his grandfather, Henry Murphy, who was the town's leading physician. Dr. Murphy, born and raised in Bristol, Tennessee, did so well with his practice in Salinas that he was able to build two hospitals there. He delivered a great many of the babies born in town—including John Steinbeck, who is said to have used Michael and his younger brother Dennis as models for the two brothers in his novel "East of Eden." Murphy sometimes dreams about his grandfather. "Gramp lived in a big house, and he was such a figure in town," he says. "He didn't have any business sense at all, but my grandmother did. She was a very strong character—forbidding at times—and she took over their business affairs quite early, and invested in real estate, and did pretty well with it." She also took Michael and Dennis to church for the first time, in 1944, when Michael was fourteen—their parents were not churchgoers. The Episcopal service made little impression on twelve-year-old Dennis, but Michael was enthralled by it. He went to church every Sunday after that, eventually becoming an altar boy. That summer, he spent a month at an Episcopal Church camp and came back saying he had decided to be a minister. This went on for several years—each summer he would go to church camp and opt for the ministry, but then, over the winter, to his parents' relief, he would tilt again toward Grandfather Murphy and medical school.

Both Michael and Dennis Murphy where bright, popular, and sports-mad. Good at most games, they both excelled at golf—their father, who was a lawyer and a golfer, started them off early. By 1946, Michael was playing in junior tournaments around the state. That same year, Dennis shot a 2 on the notoriously difficult par-4 tenth hole at the Pebble Beach Golf Links, overlooking Carmel Bay—an event that is still remembered with awe in the local pro shop. Sports counted for a lot in the Murphy family, where life had its ups and downs. "My parents had an enormous capacity for having a good time," Michael recalls. "My mother in particular had this gift of buoyant joy, which I like to think came from her Basque parents; her father had been a sheepherder from a town near Pau, in the Pyrenees. There was a lot of tension in the family, too. Stormy days and sunny days, light and darkness. But through it all my parents' fidelity to each other and to us held the pain and the joy together and contributed, I think, to my sense of a happiness and a meaning behind all the contrary appearances. Denny and I had very different strategies for coping with the dark side of things. He would plunge into the middle of the troubles; I would always withdraw. When I was about fourteen, I began deliberately to work out a philosophy to deal with this. It became a kind of daily ritual to work at it while I walked to school—to try to come to terms with this incredible sense I had that joy was *lurking*, that there was such richness and beauty laid up at the core of life, and at the same time there was all this pain and unhappiness. I worked out some kind of naïve theory about emanations—that there were emanations of something that was descending, trying to come into being, and that the basic thing to do in life was to help that happen. I also started reading a lot then—Will Durant's 'The Story of Philosophy,' Emerson, and especially Jung. I actually used to go around spouting Jung in high school, and I had just about decided to become a psychiatrist." None of this seemed to bother his classmates at Salinas High, where he was a valedictorian of his class, president of the student body, and captain of the golf team.

Rather introverted as a young child, Michael had become a "raging extrovert," as he puts it, in high school, and he continued in that vein during his first two years at Stanford. (He had turned down a scholarship to Harvard in favor of Stanford—largely, he now feels, because of the happy memories he had watching football games there with his parents.) His career as a campus hot dog came to an abrupt halt, however, in 1950, in the second semester of his sophomore year, when he wandered by accident into Professor Frederic Spiegelberg's opening lecture on comparative religion. Spiegelberg was a great figure at Stanford—a world-famous Asian scholar and a mesmerizing lecturer. Murphy, who had been going through the traditional sophomore atheist phase, found his spine tingling as he listened to Spiegelberg discourse on the five-thousand-year-old beginnings of Hindu religion. "He opened the course with the Rig-Veda—the Vedic hymns—and with this early version of the Brahman, the divine spirit. Spiegelberg had been a great friend and colleague of Paul Tillich, and, like Tillich, although he had all that scholarship, his real gift was being able to transmit his own intuitive hold on a subject. When he said 'Brahman,' it was a sacred utterance!"

The meeting of East and West, prophesied in F.S.C. Northrop's famous book of that title, was very much in the air at this period, particularly in California. Paramahansa Yogananda, the first "grand master" from India to settle for a long period in the West, had established himself in Los Angeles as early as 1924; others had followed, among them Swami Prabhavanda, who became the teacher of the transplanted Englishmen Aldous Huxley, Gerald Heard, and Christopher Isherwood. Spiegelberg himself had recently been to India and had met the great yogi Ramana Maharshi (whom Somerset Maugham had visited in 1936, later drawing on the experience for his novel "The Razor's Edge"), Aurobindo Ghose, and other religious leaders. (In 1951, Spiegelberg became the first director of the American Academy of Asian Studies, in San Francisco. The Academy attracted many important scholars, including Haridas Chaudhuri, from India, and Alan Watts, the former Episcopal chaplain of Northwestern University, who became an authority on Zen Buddhism and exerted a compelling influence on the Beat Generation poets and writers. It also attracted Murphy, who took courses there while he was still in Stanford.) Spiegelberg's lectures seemed to Murphy to be supercharged with personal meaning, and toward the end of the semester, when Spiegelberg got to Aurobindo, he felt an almost overwhelming surge of recognition. Sri Aurobindo

(1872-1950) was, in Spiegelberg's view, the master spirit of our age. "He thought that Aurobindo and Heidegger were the two greatest philosophers of the twentieth century," Murphy says, "but that because Aurobindo had come to knowledge through his own experience and through yoga, he had more depth than Heidegger, who had come to it out of intellectual genius. Actually, I started reading Aurobindo's 'The Life Divine' before Spiegelberg got to him in the course, and it had an incredible impact on me. Aurobindo's stuff about the evolution of consciousness here on earth fitted right in with my own very primitive and naïve notions. There was a tremendous feeling of everything falling into place."

That autumn, Murphy took Spiegelberg's course in Indian religion, and joined a group of students who met twice a week to discuss "The Life Divine." Walt Page, a graduate student with a streak of white hair running down the middle of his head, was the group's animating spirit. Page had a powerful, precariously balanced mind and a pressing need for disciples. Murphy resisted becoming a follower—when six of the group went away with Page during Christmas vacation to form a sort of commune off campus, he was not among them. ("Gradually they all came back," he recalls. "One of them told me they'd got into a convoluted and rather sordid situation, but he was still so much under Page's spell that he could hardly talk about it. Several years later we heard that Page had committed suicide.") By this time, Murphy had made a final decision not to go to medical school. He stopped taking money from his parents, feeling that he had disappointed their expectations; what spending money he needed he earned by waiting on tables at his fraternity house. He dropped out of all extracurricular activities and saw few people outside class. That spring, Dennis Murphy, after hitchhiking across the country, stopped by to say hello to his brother. He found him in a small room at the top of a tower, deep in a meditative trance. "I poked him in the chest," Dennis says, "and he opened his eyes, and said, 'I've been expecting you.' That was the first time he became Jesus."

✤ ✤ ✤

When Murphy graduated from Stanford, in 1952, the Korean War was still going on. He was drafted into the army and sent to Puerto Rico, where he spent the next two years interviewing draftees to check for malingering (he found only two possible cases), and reading a great deal of history. He also wrote a letter to the Aurobindo ashram in Pondicherry, asking permission to go there when he got out of the service. The first reply was affirmative, but a little later another letter arrived, telling him not to come. After completing his Army service, he went back to Stanford with the idea of taking a doctorate in philosophy, but something was wrong. "I began developing weird symptoms— obsessional thoughts that I was going to have an epileptic fit. I was studying pre-Socratic philosophy, analyzing ideas, making charts—all that left-brain stuff—and inwardly I kept thinking I had to go to India. One night, I woke up and felt I was going to disappear. There was just going to be nothing left of me. I dressed, went outside, and started to run. I ran for two hours, trying to get my body back. A few nights later, the same thing happened. I really thought I was going crazy. But I had enough insight to know that I was just doing violence to what I really wanted, and so in 1956 I went to India. I went to Europe first. Because of all that history I'd been reading, I wanted to see places like the Forum in Rome, Reims Cathedral, London, and Edinburgh—the Edinburgh trip later became the basis for 'Golf in the Kingdom.' And, oh, Christ, I was being chased by this girl! It was so funny—I was a virgin until the age of thirty-two. In high school, everything was so innocent, and then, getting into religion when I was so young…. Anyway, I met this girl on the Ile-de-France going over; she was about five years older than I was, and it was like a French farce. I was determined to keep my virginity until I got to the ashram! Finally, she got disgusted and took off. All my symptoms disappeared on the trip. I went to Rome and made such a commotion at the Indian Embassy, saying I would wire Nehru direct, that I scared them into giving me a visa in one day. I went on to Egypt, and had a great time with the pyramids and all that, and then I traveled around India for a while before going to Pondicherry. The ashram had heard I was coming—I knew a couple of Americans who were staying, and I'd written to them. So I just presented myself, and they let me stay."

The life and works of Aurobindo Ghose are still not widely known in the West. Born in Bengal but brought up and educated in England, Aurobindo began his political activity in the cause of Indian independence in 1902, some fifteen years before Gandhi appeared on the scene. The British arrested him as a terrorist, and while in jail he had a profound religious experience that altered his life. Released in 1909, he retired soon afterward to the French colony of Pondicherry and, with a group of disciples, founded the ashram where he spent the rest of his life working out his philosophy of the evolution of human consciousness. Aurobindo believed that mankind had come to a "crisis of transformation" comparable to the prehistoric appearance of mind in living creatures. Through the discipline of yoga he explored and charted in himself the successive stages of ascending consciousness, leading to the moment when the Supramental consciousness would descend and transform man's nature and, with it, the terrestrial world. From 1926 on, Aurobindo pursued his quest in seclusion, seeing only a handful of followers.

Over the years, Aurobindo's ashram grew to be the largest in India, accommodating nearly two thousand people. The members grew most of their own food crops and lived together as a nearly self-sufficient community, under the direction of a remarkable Frenchwoman, Mme. Paul Richard, who had appeared on the scene, with her husband, soon after Aurobindo arrived. Paul Richard was a politician who had come out to run for the French Chamber of Deputies as the candidate from Pondicherry; both he and his wife became fascinated with Aurobindo, and they founded a journal, *Arya*, to publish his writings. The outbreak of the First World War forced them to leave India. Later, they were separated, and in 1920 Mme. Richard returned alone to Pondicherry to devote the rest of her life to Aurobindo. She took over the management of the ashram, saw to its continued growth, and served as the principal link between Aurobindo and the world. Aurobindo died in 1950, but the Mother, as Mme. Richard had come to be known, was still there when

Murphy arrived. She was in her late seventies, and she was a formidable woman, whose spiritual force Murphy soon experienced at first hand.

An American girl at the ashram was behaving very strangely. She had fallen in love with a boy whom Murphy had known at Stanford, but the rules of the ashram forbade intimate relationships (as well as alcohol, tobacco, and politics). The boy had gone off alone to the Himalayas, and the girl was in great distress. Every evening, the members of the ashram gathered in a large open space for *darshan*, when they would file by the Mother and each person would experience an individual, momentary transmission of her presence, symbolized by the giving of a flower, perhaps, or a few words. One night, the girl was seen standing beside the Mother throughout the ceremony—a breach of etiquette that scandalized the devout. A few nights later, someone came running to Murphy's room to tell him that the girl was going to kill herself. She was standing on the roof of the highest building in the compound, the one called the Golconda, and she had a rope around her neck. Murphy went up on the roof and managed to coax her down, but afterward he thought he had better have a talk with the Mother.

"It was quite a juxtaposition for me," he said. "I had seen the Mother in this numinous way, and now here I was face to face with her, talking about this situation. I could see she was very upset by what had happened. An Englishman had killed himself three months before at the ashram, and there were two other Westerners who'd had psychotic breaks that same year. It was one of the reasons they were saying no to Western applicants. Anyway, the Mother said that I would have to stand by the girl and be very watchful. It happened again about a week later. I looked up, and there on the roof of the Golconda, silhouetted against the sky, was a ghostly figure standing right at the edge. It was a drop of about sixty feet, down to a concrete walk with reflecting pools. I went straight to the Mother, who was just getting ready for the evening *darshan*. I could see her sort of shudder all over. She said, 'I will use you as my agent. Go up and be with her.' So I climbed up to the roof. I sat down some distance away, sensing that if I made any kind of sudden move toward her she would really go over. I started to meditate. And, with that, I felt this incredible—it was like billowing *waves*. It's hard to believe that it could have been just suggestion. Pretty soon, I forgot all about the girl. But gradually she came toward me and sat down, and eventually I got her to come downstairs. Soon afterward, we managed to get her into a hospital, and from there she went back to New York."

In spite of his experience on the roof, Murphy never did become one of the ashram's true believers. Aurobindo's teachings had acquired since his death a rigidity that they did not have when he was alive, and the Mother tended, according to Murphy, to make dogmatic pronouncements. Murphy disliked the cult atmosphere, but he liked most of the other aspects of life at the ashram very much. Somewhat to his surprise, he found that great emphasis was placed there on the body—on physical well-being and sports. In addition to hatha yoga and some of the Asian martial arts, there was soccer, cricket, track, basketball, and swimming. Murphy himself introduced softball, which was taken up enthusiastically by several of the Asian members. Afternoons at the ashram were given over mainly to sports, and the mornings, at least in Murphy's case, to meditation and study. There was no formal instruction in Aurobindo's philosophy; relatively few of the Indians there, Murphy discovered, had even read "The Life Divine." The arts were encouraged—nearly everyone wrote poetry (Aurobindo had also been a poet), and the Mother herself wrote didactic plays, which Murphy found awful. His own life there came to center more and more on meditation. He could meditate for four and five hours at a time. There are dangers to this sort of total immersion, as he found out two years later, back in the United States, when he tried to imitate Ramana Maharshi's feat of meditating while gazing at the sun. Murphy gazed at it for half an hour. Afterward, he felt strangely depressed, and that night the street lamps looked blood-red to him. He went to an eye doctor, who asked what he had done, and then called in three colleagues to look. The doctor told him to come back in a week. His eyesight improved a little during the week, and when he went back for his appointment the doctor said he was very lucky—he had come so close to losing his sight, and there was nothing that anyone could have done about it.

☖ ☖ ☖

After a year and a half at the ashram, Murphy went back to Palo Alto. He took a room in the same house he had lived in as a graduate student and continued his life of meditation and study, working two days a week to support himself. He took gardening work, and he was a bellhop at Rickey's Inn, where the Green Bay Packers stayed when they came to the West Coast (Murphy was delighted to carry their bags.) In the summer of 1960, learning that Haridas Chaudhuri, one of Aurobindo's leading disciples, had set up a center in a big old house on Fulton Street where students could live and study and meditate, he moved to San Francisco. It was at this point that he met Richard Price. Although Murphy and Price had been in the same class as undergraduates at Stanford, they had not known each other there. Price, who came from a well-to-do Illinois family, had majored in psychology at Stanford; he had no religious leanings, and he was interested mainly in social anthropology. After graduating from Stanford, he took a year of graduate study in clinical psychology at Harvard and then went into the Air Force, where he had what the military considered a nervous breakdown—to Price it seemed more like an ecstatic experience. He spent the next six months in military hospitals, after which his family had him committed to the Institute of Living, a private hospital in Hartford, Connecticut, which Price came to regard as a private prison. (Murphy sometimes says that Esalen is Price's revenge on mental hospitals.) In 1960, Price was in San Francisco, "waiting for the world to come around," as he puts it. At the suggestion of one of his friends, he went to visit the Chaudhuri center on Fulton Street, where he found Murphy. Price moved into the house soon afterward. In their thinking, Murphy said not long ago, "Dick and I found we were in very similar places."

Murphy supported himself in San Francisco by working two days a week for a shipping-news journal. When the editor told him he would either have to work full time or quit, he quit, and suggested to Price, more or less on the spur of the moment, that they go down and look at some property his family owned in Big Sur. Murphy's grandfather, the Salinas physician, had bought the land in 1910—three hundred and seventy-five acres of rugged mountain and coastline—with the idea of developing it into a health spa on the European model. Hot mineral springs flowed out of the rocks on a cliff overlooking the Pacific— springs that the Esalen Indians had bathed in for centuries before the white man arrived. Dr. Murphy had built bathhouses over the springs and installed bathtubs, which had to be brought in on a fishing boat and derricked up the cliff, because there were then no roads in Big Sur. He had also built a large house and one or two smaller ones, but he had died before the spa idea came to fruition.

When the Murphy boys were growing up, their parents used to take them to Big Sur on weekends and in the summer. Dennis loved the place; Michael, who didn't care for hunting or fishing, often felt that he would rather have been home playing games with his friends. Grandfather Murphy had wanted the property to remain in the family, and his widow had respected his wishes. When Michael and Dick Price went down to look at it in 1961, however, some fairly peculiar things were going on there. Michael's grandmother had appointed a friend of hers, a Mrs. Webb, to act as caretaker of the property, and Mrs. Webb was using one of the buildings as a meeting place for the First Church of God of Prophecy, an evangelical sect to which she belonged. The evangelicals coexisted on somewhat uneasy terms with the assorted types who went down to use what was then known as Slate's Hot Springs, after the original homesteader on the property. Henry Miller was living in Big Sur then, and he and his friends used to go over to the baths occasionally. A much rougher crowd, known collectively as "the Big Sur Heavies"—people who camped out in the mountains for a variety of reasons, not the least of which were said to be drug dealing and the cultivation of marijuana—also used the baths, and so did a growing number of male homosexuals, some of whom came from as far away as San Francisco and Los Angeles. Murphy and Price were appalled by the goings on at the baths. The situation had clearly got out of hand, and it occurred to Murphy that maybe he ought to do something about it.

Why not, he thought, take over the family property and start a center to explore their own interests in philosophy, psychology, social anthropology, and the more esoteric disciplines? "It was as simple as that," Murphy recalls. "I'd had something like the same idea when I was in India, but nothing had come of it. Now, though, there was a good deal of pressure building up from my family for me to do *something*—here I was thirty and still just meditating." Price liked the idea. He had a small income of his own, and was not tied down to anything in particular. Seeking further guidance, they drove to Santa Monica to discuss the plan with Gerald Heard, the writer and mystic, whom Murphy had met through mutual friends at Stanford. Heard gave them a lot of encouragement, and so did Heard's friend Aldous Huxley. "Suddenly, everything was charged with meaning and excitement," Murphy says.

They next went to Salinas to talk things over with Michael's grandmother. She was in her late eighties then, still vigorous and not easily won over. The idea sounded faintly reminiscent of Dr. Murphy's dream of a European health spa, and it appealed to her for that reason, but she was dubious about her grandson's ability to run any sort of enterprise. Finally, she consented to let them have it on a long-term lease. "I can't give it to you, Mike," she said. "Because I know you'd just give it away to some Hindu." She also insisted that Mrs. Webb remain in control of the property until the end of her lease, which had three months to run.

Murphy and Price decided to wait out the interval at Big Sur, where they were looked upon with considerable suspicion. Word of what they were planning got out, and nobody liked it. They put up a steel fence around the baths, with a gate that they locked at night, but night after night the lock was either picked or broken. Michael's grandmother had hired a guard, a Kentuckian in his early twenties named Hunter Thompson (the future gonzo journalist), who lived in the main house on the property and was charged with keeping out intruders. One night, a bunch of aggrieved homosexuals ambushed him and nearly succeeded in throwing him over the cliff. Calling the police was no solution; the nearest town, Carmel, was forty miles up the coast, by a slow and winding road. Murphy and Price were not entirely without allies. Besides Hunter Thompson, they could count on support from Joan Baez—not yet famous as a folksinger—and her boyfriend, and from two other young couples, friends of hers, who had rented shacks on the property from Mrs. Webb, and who were building a trimaran that they planned to sail to Tahiti. Heavily outnumbered as they were, the future proprietors decided to provoke a showdown.

On what came to be known as the Night of the Dobermans, Murphy and Price locked themselves in at the baths and sat down to wait. Almost immediately, they heard a thunderous commotion on the path leading down to the hot springs; and moments later they were joined by about a dozen young males in T-shirts and blue jeans. A retreat seemed advisable at this point. Murphy and Price walked back up the hill, to the accompaniment of loud taunts and jeers, and set out to round up their cohorts. Murphy went to where Joan Baez and her friends were living, and got the men to come out and bring their dogs—three young Doberman pinschers on short leashes. The assembled home forces then headed back toward the baths. On the way the two male Dobermans got into a vicious battle over the female. Dobermans are noisy fighters—no silent bulldog grips for them. The owners finally got the dogs apart and continued down to the baths, but nobody was there. They came back up the hill to find the invaders regrouped in the main parking lot. They were about thirty strong by then, menacing but dogless. The male Dobermans had another set-to at the edge of the parking lot, and again the night air was rent by sounds of unimaginable savagery. The owners got them separated again just in time to see the last of the enemy jumping into cars and lamming it up the road.

That was the end of the homosexuals, and also the First Church of God of Prophecy. Mrs. Webb and her frightened followers moved out a few days later. Murphy and Price took over the property, posted guards at the entrance, and negotiated a compromise with Big Sur Heavies— the baths would be open to anyone, gratis, every night from midnight to 6 A.M. By and large, this is still the situation. Esalen guests are advised not to visit the baths after midnight, and those who do are presumably prepared for what they may find there. Murphy himself feels that the somewhat lawless, Wild West atmosphere surrounding the baths has played an important part in the development of Esalen's unique character. "I think a lot of the atmosphere of the place came from this outlaw element, having these people around," he has said. "It may have contributed to the kind of try-anything spirit of the place. For a while, we tried to make rules and have separate sides of the baths for men and women, but that kept breaking down, so finally we just said the hell with it."

One of the amazing things about Esalen is that its founders never did have a clear plan for the place. Both of them wanted a center where people from different disciplines could meet and exchange ideas. They liked to think of their approach as Taoist—letting things develop naturally, even if that led (as it did) to continuing chaos and a certain degree of mismanagement. They would not impose their own thinking on others. Murphy sometimes says (a bit ruefully) that he has never yet been able to get anyone at Big Sur to read the works of Aurobindo.

Price took over the administrative side of the operation, while Murphy threw himself into programming and promotion. His enthusiasm seemed boundless. "I've sometimes thought that the tremendous energy with which I plunged into Esalen came from the submerged extrovert who'd been in the closet all those years," he observed recently. "It just seemed to come rushing out." He and Price spent the first year working on the grounds and buildings, planning, and lining up people to lecture or give seminars. One of Murphy's earliest supporters was John Levy, a onetime engineer whose interests had turned toward psychology. (He later became the guiding spirit and executive officer of the Association for Humanistic Psychology, in San Francisco.) "I felt quite confident that Mike would make a go of it, mainly because of his combination of self-confidence and humility," Levy said a while ago. "A lot of people in this area have plenty of self-confidence and enthusiasm, but they can also be pretty arrogant. Mike never came on as somebody who knew he had the message, and that in itself was impressive." Certainly Murphy seemed to have no trouble persuading people to come to Big Sur. Aldous Huxley, Gerald Heard, Alan Watts, Arnold Toynbee, Frederic Spiegelberg, Ken Kesey, S.I. Hayakawa, Linus Pauling, Paul Tillich, Gary Snyder, Norman O. Brown, Rollo May, Bishop James A. Pike, Carl Rogers, B.F. Skinner, Carlos Castaneda (then a graduate student at U.C.L.A.), and a host of others who might seem to have had little in common gave lectures or seminars or just dropped in during the first years of Esalen's existence, and paying guests arrived in sufficient numbers to finance a steady expansion of the facilities.

At first, Murphy and Price and a few paid employees did all the work. One of their more remarkable assistants was a Chinese-born financier named Gia Fu Feng, who had gone to Wharton School of Finance and Commerce, at University of Pennsylvania, and had worked for a while on Wall Street. Feng had more or less decided to go back to mainland China in 1960, but when he got to San Francisco he met Alan Watts, discovered Zen and other aspects of his Oriental heritage, and decided that perhaps Mao's China was not the place for him after all. Watts introduced him to Murphy and Price, and Feng offered his services. For a while, he was the chief cook at Esalen; he also kept the accounts, on the abacus, and taught Tai Chi Chuan.

Esalen was certified as a nonprofit educational institution, and, thanks in part to the general inefficiency that prevails there, it has always had difficulty staying out of the red. From the outset, though, the omens were highly propitious. Murphy and Price were eager to meet Abraham Maslow, the real father of humanistic psychology, whose work had struck them as a natural bridge between the psychiatric establishment and all the new trends that were emerging. One foggy night in the summer of 1962, Maslow and his wife happened to be driving south on the precipitous coast road through Big Sur. Seeing a light and thinking it might be a place where they could spend the night, they pulled into Esalen's parking lot, knocked on the door of the Main house, and introduced themselves to a group of astonished people who had read Maslow's books. Their hosts insisted that they stay. Maslow returned many times after that to lead seminars and his friendship was an important factor in the Institute's growth.

Although Maslow later became president of the American Psychological Association, he saw his own humanistic psychology as a "third-force" alternative to strict Freudianism and its offshoots, which ruled the psychoanalytic profession, and to the behavioristic psychology that had become dominant in most university psychology departments. Freudian analysis has traditionally been focused on the pathology of human behavior. Maslow and his followers shifted their attention to the enormous and largely unsuspected possibilities for human growth in so-called normal people—the untapped human potential. And in place of the behaviorists' mechanistic concept of human nature as a network of conditioned responses, Maslow posited a human nature that is partly species-wide and partly unique. Most of us, according to Maslow, are capable, moreover, of what he termed "peak experiences"— breakthrough moments of deep emotional understanding or intensity, the most dramatic examples of which are the spiritual revelations of saints and mystics. "My thesis is, in general, that new developments in psychology are forcing a profound change in our philosophy of science, a change so extensive that we may be able to accept the basic religious questions as a proper part of the jurisdiction of science, once science is broadened and redefined," Maslow has written. The very first program at Esalen, offered in the fall of 1962, was a series of four seminars on "The Human Potentiality;" the opening seminar dealt in detail with the work of Maslow. The human-potential movement has been the focus of a great deal that has taken place at Esalen since, although neither Maslow nor anyone else could have felt easy about some of the experiments carried out there in its name.

Looking back now on the early years, Murphy and Price sometimes wonder how they managed to surmount the multiple disasters. Several of the first group of seminarians (as Esalen quaintly calls its paying guests) witnessed a nearly fatal attack on Dennis Murphy in 1963. Dennis, who had published a best-selling novel ("The Sergeant") in

1958, and who was living in a house of his own on the Big Sur Property while working on his second, got into an argument with a local artist, and before anyone realized what was happening the artist had stabbed him nine times with a knife. Dennis survived. Michael got him to the hospital in Monterey, spent a sleepless night, and came into his room the next morning to find Dennis sitting up in bed smoking a cigar and trying to blow smoke through his wounds. (Dennis subsequently left Big Sur for Los Angeles, where he became a successful screenwriter.) A couple of the early employees at Esalen were arrested on drug charges, in spite of strict anti-drug regulations laid down by Murphy and Price, and undercover narcotics agents often prowled the premises. But in the main the seminarians were getting high on experiences that had no connection with drugs. The most popular programs were the various body-awareness and encounter groups, in which almost anything could happen.

The basic principles of encounter and some of the techniques had been worked out as early as 1946 by the psychologist Kurt Lewin and his associates at the Massachusetts Institute of Technology. Lewin's "T-group" methods were designed mainly to help people perform more effectively in groups—in the Army, in business, in scientific laboratories—and to minimize tensions by being more honest and straightforward with one another and by letting their suppressed feelings come to the surface. Lewin's work led to the founding of the National Training Laboratories, with headquarters in Arlington, Virginia, many of whose clients are industrial corporations. It was soon discovered, however, that the process of taking part in small group sessions of this nature often led to extraordinary emotional reactions among the participants. The power of a group to elicit such responses was hardly a new discovery; primitive shamans knew about it, revivalist preachers make use of it all the time, and group therapy has long been an accepted aspect of psychiatric practice. But the idea of using the group as a lever to bring about emotional breakthroughs in normally healthy individuals seemed to touch a highly sensitive nerve in America in the affluent nineteen-sixties. The eminent psychologist Carl Rogers, who popularized the term "encounter," has called it "the most rapidly spreading social invention of the century, and probably the most potent." New group techniques proliferated in the sixties—particularly on the West Coast. Encounter, sensory awareness, gestalt therapy, transactional analysis, marathons, psychodrama, and other shortcuts to "personal growth" blossomed in suburban community centers, in churches, and even in private houses throughout the land, together with the more esoteric practices of Sufism, Zen, and yoga. It is probably true that all this would have happened without Esalen, but it is also true that Esalen was for several years the narrow neck of the funnel—the place where many of the new methods were tried out and developed before they spread into the larger community. It was the laboratory, and there were occasions when it appeared to be on the brink of blowing up.

The danger, of course, lay in its great appeal to mad scientists. Murphy and Price kept a sharp eye on the leaders of the early encounter sessions. There was no real training course for such leaders, and no agreed-on credentials except sensitivity, intelligence, and a high degree of self-awareness; psychiatric training, with its doctor-patient orientation, often seemed to be the worst sort of preparation for the subtle give-and-take of effective group process. Murphy attended almost every one of the seminars given at Esalen in the first four years—more than two hundred in all, about ten of which were straight encounter groups. If he felt that a leader showed signs of cruelty or insensitivity, that leader was not invited back. But what was one to do with a mad genius like Fritz Perls?

Frederick S. Perls visited Esalen for the first time in 1964, and two years later he returned there to live. A lot of people were scared to death of him. He spoke with a heavy German accent, he had a very large head with intense, penetrating eyes and a beard that went in all directions, and he wore a sort of jump suit with heavy bead necklaces. Dennis Murphy once dreamed of Perls as a huge, room-filling head with hairs coming out of his nose and ears and brushing against the walls on either side. In his younger years in Europe, Perls had studied with Max Reinhardt, and his methods were nothing if not theatrical.

Gestalt therapy, which Perls developed in the fifties (and which is not to be confused with the experimental science of Gestalt psychology), proceeded on the assumption that under proper conditions and with proper techniques the neurotic symptoms that prevented people from realizing their own true natures could be brought to the surface in relatively short order, without months or years of analysis. One of Perls' techniques was to gather a group of people and call for a volunteer to sit beside him in what he called "the hot seat" and to relate a recent dream. Perls maintained that every part of a dream—an inanimate object, an animal, a gesture—was a projection of the dreamer. He would make the person in the hot seat act out all these aspects—if the dream had a chest of drawers in it, the subject would have to become the chest of drawers. In the process, Perls would notice something about the subject, something that was being unconsciously avoided or repressed, and he would proceed step by step to bring it out, forcing the subject to a final stage that he called "the impasse"—an emotional climax followed, with luck, by a cathartic recognition. "Fritz had the most fabulous clinical mind I've ever seen," Murphy recalls. "He could spot where the problem was, and he had a genius for pushing it to the surface—that's why he was so scary. And with Fritz the therapy game was going all the time; he was that way at lunch or in the baths." Once, when Perls thought the leader of a certain seminar was being pompous, he crawled the length of the room on all fours by way of protest. ("This is beginning to look like sickness," Abraham Maslow, who saw the performance, murmured to Murphy.) Although Perls terrified people, his seminars were always crowded, and there was never any lack of volunteers for the hot seat.

Another game that Perls played to the hilt was one that Murphy and Price called Capture the Flag. He wanted to make Esalen over in his own image—to get rid of the religious and mystical aspects, and turn it into the world center of gestalt therapy. Perls himself became quite famous while he was at Esalen; his book on gestalt therapy was worshipped by college students, and all sorts of people were attracted to Esalen by his powerful presence. Ida Rolf, a therapist who had developed her own theory and method of "structural integration" of the body through deep massage (called "Rolfing"), soon came to Esalen at Perls' invitation and became a part-time resident. Several other younger psychologists came to study with Perls, and Price, who had begun by disliking him, went on to study under him and to become, after four years, an exceptionally gifted gestalt therapist and, in a sense, Perls' successor at Esalen. Perls never did manage to take over the place, and in 1969 he left to form his own therapy center on Vancouver Island. He died in the spring of 1970.

For a time in the sixties, Perls' principal antagonist was William C. Schutz, the field marshal of encounter. Schutz, a psychologist who had taught at Harvard and Berkeley, came to Esalen in 1967 at Murphy's invitation. His approach to encounter was eclectic and experimental. He had led or participated in all kinds of groups and had studied all the new methods—bioenergetics, psychodrama, psychosynthesis, Rolfing— and while he used elements from most of these in his own work, he was also willing to try anything else that suggested itself during the group process. Schutz's idea was always to seek out the trouble spots in a group and go right into them. If two people hated each other, Schutz might get them to wrestle then and there. (Fistfights were discouraged, but they sometimes happened anyway.) If a seminarian seemed to be uneasy about his or her body, Schutz might try to get that person to strip and show it to the others. The popular success of Schutz's book "Joy," published the year he arrived at Esalen, which described many of these methods, and the frequent appearance of Schutz on television talk shows to discuss his work contributed no little to the growing fame of Esalen, and also helped to form the popular notion that Esalen *was* encounter—and Schutz's form of encounter, at that. Perls resented this. Schutz and Perls stopped speaking to each other after a while. No one suggested that the two of them wrestle.

When Schutz arrived, Esalen was in the early stages of what George Leonard calls its "big-bang period." Leonard, a senior editor of *Look* and one of Murphy's closest friends—his thinking and writing about Esalen and the human-potential movement have had a strong influence on Murphy's own—was a frequent group leader or participant in seminars at Big Sur during the late sixties. "We really thought we were on the verge of vast breakthroughs that would change the world," he recalls. "The atmosphere in the lodge at mealtimes was just electric with new discoveries; people couldn't sit still through a meal, the vibes were so terrific. I remember once, soon after the media had started to run stories on Esalen, a guy from one of the networks was there wanting to know what we were all about. I talked to him for a while in the dining room, and then I saw Mike Murphy and called him over, and Mike talked, but we weren't really getting to him. Gia Fu Feng came in, and I called *him* over to the table. "What is Esalen really about, Gia Fu?' I asked. Gia Fu pointed at Mike and at me and at Dick Price, saying, 'I see God! I see God! I see God!'—and walked away. Gia Fu was just unbelievable. Another time, he came tearing into the dining room at lunchtime and said, 'Two women in my group have spontaneous orgasm!' It was like that all the time in those days."

Much of the excitement in the fall of 1966 centered on the residential program for fifteen carefully selected Esalen Fellows, who had agreed to spend nine months at Big Sur. The premise, roughly, was that if people could be brought to heightened states of consciousness in weekend or five-day seminars, what would happen if you gave them nine months of Esalen's battery of psychic stimuli? The fifteen psychic astronauts had been selected from more than two hundred applicants, by the well-known family psychologist Virginia Satir, who was the director of the program, and a good many of those she had chosen were graduate students or college teachers in psychology or sociology. The program was repeated the following year with twenty-two residents, and was then dropped.

"It was such grandiose thinking," Murphy said recently. "We had seen these things happening in groups that were epiphanies of some sort of immense power, and we really wanted to see how far we could go with that. The residential program coincided with the whole hippie thing in 1967—the 'summer of love' in San Francisco. It was very much in the spirit of the sixties, when everybody sensed these enormous possibilities just around the corner. There was a kind of drunkenness in the air then. The program was certainly a failure in the sense of not realizing our original intentions. It was just impossible to sustain that level of expectation. Bull Schutz disagrees with me; he still thinks the program was a huge success. It's true that some of our most creative group leaders here came out of it—people like John Heider and Steve Stroud and Stuart Miller. But I think a lot of it was destructive. It shook hell out of people. Of the thirty-seven people in both those seminars, two committed suicide within a year. One had been through a lot of rocky times before she came to Esalen, the other was a psychologist who stayed with us only three months. Of course, there are suicides at the Aurobindo ashram, and on college campuses, too. There definitely is a risk element in any kind of opening-up process. But, to me, our program didn't have the sense of center—the balance—that you have to have if you're going to go very deeply into personal transformation. It was too wild and chaotic. Some of the residential Fellows would take people down to the baths and get them plunging between the hot water and the cold water, and they'd start to hyperventilate in between, and it was as powerful as taking hallucinogenic drugs. People would start barking like seals! We had to close the baths while this sort of stuff was going on. One week, they tried what they called a 'symbo group,' everybody staying together in physical proximity for a whole week, except to go to the bathroom, and more or less pooling their separate identities—there was no me-you language allowed. The power of this kind of group hypnosis is just astonishing. It can take people to very far-out states. But I have very serious reservations about the long-term results."

Murphy himself took part only intermittently in the residential program. He had had enough of group process after four years, and, anyway, he was too busy with other things. Esalen was growing in all directions, very unsystematically. The building program that today provides accommodations for seventy guests plus a large staff was in full swing. Murphy was away from Big Sur about one week in every four, trying (with little success) to get foundation grants, speaking at colleges and universities, investigating new aspects of the human-potential movement. There was also the Esalen center in San Francisco, which Murphy started in the fall of 1967. Like the residential program, the San Francisco center had messianic overtones. Only a small number of people could come to Big Sur—the facilities were limited, and the costs (about a hundred and fifty dollars per person for five days' room and board) tended to make for a clientele that was middle-aged and relatively affluent. Believing strongly that their discoveries held great importance for the larger public, Murphy and some of his colleagues wanted to make the Esalen experience available in a much broader and younger social milieu, and San Francisco seemed the natural place to find this. The Esalen San Francisco center held its first lectures and workshops in Grace Cathedral, thanks largely to the good offices of Bishop James A. Pike, who was a friend and admirer of Murphy's and had lectured at Esalen. (Pike had left the active ministry in 1966, under threat of expulsion for heresy; his former chaplain at Grace Cathedral, David Baar, became the first director of Esalen's San Francisco programs.) Later the center moved, much to the relief of the Episcopal diocese, to its own quarters, on Union Street, where it was soon offering more than a hundred and fifty programs a year, in everything from aikido to an "awareness workshop for dental professionals."

Tremendous events were impending; everybody at Esalen felt it. The transformation of consciousness was *at hand*, here in California, where the natives seemed ripe for conversion to altered states. Esalen was even solving the racial problem. Black-white "confrontations"— encounter sessions organized by Price Cobbs, a black psychiatrist in San Francisco, and George Leonard, the former *Look* editor, who was now Esalen's vice-president—were being held at Big Sur and in San Francisco. Participants of both races were learning to bring out their hidden racism and their suppressed rage and fear, and were establishing in the process a new paradigm (indispensable word!) for dealing with the troubled situation between the races everywhere. But then Esalen developed a racial problem of its own. An assistant director of the San Francisco center, a white man, got into a heated argument over the telephone with Ronald Brown, a black psychologist and one of the program leaders. Brown felt that he had been insulted. Leonard, Cobbs, and several others in the program decided that the assistant director was a secret racist, and that something would have to be done. A summit encounter session was set up in the office of Cobbs, and Murphy, who was in New York, was summoned back to attend it. Murphy cancelled a trip to the Menninger Clinic, in Topeka, where he had been scheduled to speak at a conference on altered states, and flew straight to San Francisco.

About a dozen people came to the encounter session, which went on for several hours. The embattled assistant director kept insisting that he had helped to lobby the 1965 Voting Rights Act through Congress and didn't need to prove himself to anyone. After two hours had gone by, they took a ten minute break, and when they reconvened their target was no longer among them. The group then zeroed in on Murphy. "It wasn't enough to be on the firing line in those days," Murphy recalls. "You had to confess your unconscious racism. God, the language that flew around that room! Maybe if I'd really let fly with my own anger at the whole silly situation it would have been better, but in that kind of situation I just got catatonic—numb. 'What are you going to do about this man?' they kept asking me. I'd ask if they wanted me to fire him, and they'd say no, they wanted him to be emotionally reeducated. They wanted him sent down to Big Sur for six weeks, to 'get in touch with his anger,' and all that. I agreed to that, finally, and everybody left exhausted but happy. But then I got back to the San Francisco program leaders. All the phones were ringing at once. So the next morning I called George Leonard to tell him what was going on. George, who had felt all along that the situation would prove impossible to deal with, gave up at this pint. He said, 'Wait a minute, Mike,' and left the phone, and then he came back and said, 'Mike, I'm resigning.'"

Leonard's resignation as vice-president was immediately followed by the resignations of the black program leaders and the collapse of the program. Price Cobbs, Ron Brown, and another of the black program leaders, named Michael Brown, have since started a highly successful consulting firm in San Francisco, which specializes in organizational development and race relations. All three of them remained friends of Murphy's, as did George Leonard. The controversial assistant director did go to some group-process workshops at Big Sur, but a few months later Murphy fired him anyway. The whole incident could have been averted, Murphy feels now, if he had only handled it a little more skill-fully. It just proved to me the failure of encounter," he said recently. "The whole idea that you can solve anything by shouting at people in a group is ridiculous."

According to George Leonard, the racial Donnybrook really marked the end of Esalen's big-bang period. The transformation of society was not, perhaps, quite as imminent as had been thought. A new spirit of moderation was growing at Big Sur, which over the years had begun to seem less like an encampment of gypsies and more like a well-planned, well-tended, and rather expensive resort. Some of the extremists there were distressed by the calmer pace. Perls left in 1969 to establish his gestalt-therapy center in Canada. In 1970, a group that included sev-eral of the alumni from the residential program went down to Chile to work with Oscar Ichazo, whose Arica movement, heavily influenced by the teachings of Gurdjieff, was preparing to transform society right away. Price was devoting his time mainly to leading gestalt-therapy groups, while a succession of managers struggled to bring order out of the administrative chaos. (Although Big Sur was filled to capacity virtually year-round, the place nearly went bankrupt in 1971.) Murphy spent less and less time at Big Sur. He was busy with the San Francisco center (which consistently lost money), and he was trying to bring some order into his personal life as well.

The past ten years had been a bruising period for him, emotionally and spiritually. Murphy had even plunged into marriage at one point, much to the dismay of his colleagues. According to Price, the two events that really caused Perls to leave the country were the election of Richard Nixon and Murphy's marriage, both of which seemed to him to presage the coming of Nazism. The girl was older than Murphy, beautiful, and twice divorced. They met in an Esalen seminar, had a stormy two-year affair, and got married on the spur of the moment one night in 1968 after seeing "Zorba the Greek." "We drove up to Carson City, Nevada, where we were married by a midget," Murphy recalls. "He stood on a box, and he looked just like Bucky Fuller, and I knew it couldn't last." For three months afterward, Murphy insisted on keeping the marriage a secret—which did not help relations between the couple. "We had the most tremendous battles," he says. "And meanwhile we were getting therapy from a psychiatric community that stretched for three thousand miles. Abe Maslow, Rollo May, Bill Schutz, John Levy—we broke the best therapists of our time on the prow of the marital ship. Finally, we just wore each other down." They were divorced at the end of 1969.

In a sense, Murphy was also trying to divorce himself from Esalen. The place was his creature—"Esalen is Mike Murphy," Schutz often says—but it had grown to be too successful and too complex and too demanding. Murphy strenuously resisted the efforts of a number of "personal-growth centers" in various parts of the country to associate themselves with Esalen; he was willing to give them all the advice and help they wanted, but he felt that Esalen was big enough already and that to make it the nucleus of an institutional network would endanger its value as a laboratory. Besides, Esalen's imitators often seemed bent on commercializing and vulgarizing the model. There were "growth centers" in California whose program seemed to consist mainly of nudity and recreational sex. Esalen had its share of both, of course, but they were more or less incidental to everything else, in spite of the impression given by a filmed documentary, "Here Comes Every Body," that dealt with an Esalen encounter group; the film was made under the general supervision of Schutz, at a time when Murphy and Price were both away, and it gave rise to a lot of ill will at Big Sur.

Price and Julian Silverman, an experimental clinical psychologist who came to Big Sur from the National Institute of Mental Health, really ran the operation down there while Murphy ranged farther and farther afield. In 1970, he went to Europe with Stuart Miller (a former Esalen residential Fellow) and Miller's wife, Sara. They held conferences on the human potential in London and spent time there with the psychiatrist R.D. Laing. Laing had been invited to come to Agnews State Hospital, in San Jose, California, by Price and Silverman, who had initiated a three-year experimental program, influenced in part by some of Laing's ideas, to work with schizophrenics—a sort of "break-out center," where patients undergoing schizophrenic crises would be treated not as madmen to be restrained but as individuals going through difficult and possibly creative experiences. (Laing declined, but the Agnews project was carried out, and has attracted considerable attention.) From London, Murphy and the Millers went to Rome to meet Roberto Assagioli, the Italian psychiatrist, who was the founder of psychosynthesis. Assagioli's work had seemed to Murphy to be remarkably close in spirit not only to that of Maslow and the other humanistic psychologists but also the thinking of Aurobindo. "What Aurobindo called yoga, what Abe Maslow called self-actualization, what Fritz Perls called organismic integrity, Assagioli called psychosynthesis," Murphy said recently. "All these share basically the same idea—that there is a natural tendency toward evolution, toward unfoldment, that pervades the universe as well as the human sphere, and that our job now is to get behind that and make it conscious. But the disciplines that emerge to deal with this unfoldment have to reflect the many-sidedness of the human psyche, and this is why psychosynthesis is so valuable. Assagioli himself was really a man of very wide European culture. He was the truest sage I've ever met."

The following year, Murphy and the Millers traveled together to Russia. They had heard reports that the Russians were doing a lot of research on parapsychology (extrasensory perception and other psychic phenomena). "A lot is happening there, but it's hard to know how much of it is government-sponsored," Murphy reported afterward.

"One theory is that the Russians thought the Americans were getting into parapsychological research with the idea of exerting influence at a distance, and so they set up a number of laboratories of their own. The person who seemed to be the impresario for parapsychologists, Edward Naumov, was pathetically eager to impress us and work with us, but also to find out everything we knew. We decided he must be some sort of agent, because he had freedom to travel anywhere—whenever we'd change our plans, he would be free to come with us, and he would insist on coming. But then this curious thing happened. We had an invitation to go to Friendship House, in Moscow, which is where they entertain all the big shots. Naumov heard about it, and started pressing us to arrange a convocation of parapsychologists and scientists at Friendship House, and we did—we got the thing set up for about three hundred people to meet there. The day came around, we went to Friendship House, and the director, who seemed very nervous, took us on a tour of the place. After the tour, we asked whether it wasn't time for the meeting to start. The director said that the meeting had been cancelled. He said that Naumov was a charlatan and would be a disgrace to Friendship House. We never could figure the thing out. Later, apparently, Naumov was arrested and imprisoned for two years."

While Murphy and the Millers were in Russia, they also set up an intercontinental experiment in telepathy, which was carried out soon after their return. Murphy, sitting in his studio in San Francisco, concentrated on "sending" a series of images to a Russian telepathist, who was sitting in his room in Moscow, under supervised test conditions, to "receive" them. The Russian did "receive" with remarkable clarity the first image that Murphy sent—a toy wooden elephant from a photograph in a dictionary—but the over-all results of the experiment, Murphy says, were statistically inconclusive.

The two sides of Michael Murphy's nature were again in conflict. Esalen and the human-potential movement continued to make large claims on his attention, but the other Michael Murphy, the closet extrovert, was knocking authoritatively to get out. Murphy spent more of his time in his studio on Telegraph Hill, writing and meditating. He was working on "Golf in the Kingdom," a philosophical novel about a Scottish golf pro named Shivas Irons, who quotes from Pythagoras and the Hindu scriptures and scores a nocturnal hole-in-one on the thirteenth hole at "Burningbush" (read St. Andrews) by relying on the force of "true gravity." For the character of Irons, Murphy drew upon several people he knew, including the charismatic Stanford graduate student Walt Page, and the portrait is a lively one. It seemed entirely natural, moreover, for the author to approach philosophy and mysticism by way of sports. Writing the book brought on his own readdiction to golf, which he had been too busy to play for several years. It also strengthened his long-held suspicion that sports could be seen as an American yoga, a path to a true harmony of body and spirit.

Soon after the book appeared, in 1972, Murphy began hearing from people, some of them professional athletes, who had what Maslow called "peak experiences" similar to those described in "Golf in the Kingdom." One was John Brodie, the highly successful quarterback of the San Francisco 49ers. Brodie, a firm believer in Scientology, had many unusual experiences to relate, including one about a key pass he had thrown in a playoff game with the Washington Redskins in 1971. Even the game films, he said, seemed to show that just as the pass was about to be intercepted by Pat Fischer, the Redskin cornerback, it rose up, above Fischer's outstretched fingers, and (without being deflected) settled into the arms of the 49ers' fleet wide receiver Gene Washington, who ran with it for a touchdown to tie the game, which the 49ers eventually won, 24-20. Brodie had been impressed by "Golf in the Kingdom," and he wanted Murphy to collaborate with him on a book about his own career in football. Murphy readily agreed. He was an ardent Brodie fan, and the thrill of spending time at the 49ers' training camp and seeing their games from the bench was almost too great to bear. Unfortunately, the manuscript was nearly complete before Murphy let Brodie read what he was writing. Murphy had set his imagination to work on the material that Brodie provided him, and the result was another philosophical novel, with a culminating scene in the Vatican. Brodie wanted no part of it. He subsequently engaged another collaborator, who produced a book, "Open Field," with virtually no mystical overtones; even the story of the miraculous pass to Gene Washington, which had already appeared in *Intellectual Digest* in the version that Murphy wrote, was stripped of any supernatural suggestion. Murphy was disappointed, but he remains a fan of the 49ers, who have been having quarterback trouble since Brodie retired.

Sports as yoga—the idea plucked at Murphy's extrovert nature and led to plans for an Esalen sports program. Although for financial reasons the program is still relatively undeveloped, instruction in "tennis flow" and cross country skiing and distance running has now joined aikido, Tai Chi Chuan, and energy-awareness workshops in the Esalen curriculum. Murphy himself has taken up distance running. In 1973, at the age of forty-three, he started training with Mike Spino, once a nationally ranked marathon runner, and within a year he ran the mile in five minutes twelve seconds, and the marathon distance, twenty six miles, in three hours and thirty nine minutes. Spino says he has never seen anything like it. For Murphy, running has become another form of meditation. He runs at least five miles a day, along the waterfront to the Golden Gate Bridge and back.

For a time in 1974, Murphy thought he had finally escaped from all administrative responsibilities at Esalen. His good friend Richard Farson, a psychologist and the co-founder of the Western Behavioral Sciences Institute, at La Jolla, California, took over as president of Esalen, and Murphy began spending virtually all his time working on the new novel. Just as he was getting well into it, though, Esalen problems boiled up and over. Personality conflicts at Big Sur led to Farson's resignation, and Murphy had to step back in temporarily and assume control. He was immediately faced with the need to make drastic cuts in the San Francisco programs, which had lost more money than usual that year, and to reconsider Esalen's whole future course. Since then, profits from the Big Sur operation have mounted steadily.

Most workshops are fully booked months in advance, long-term debts are being paid off, and the place has become so respectable that corporations regularly send their employees there for emotional loosening up. Esalen, in fact, is no longer really at the cutting edge of the New Consciousness movement. EST, Arica, and Transcendental Meditation are more in the news at the moment, and a host of newer and perhaps stranger disciplines are undoubtedly slouching toward California to be born.

Counter-revolutionary forces have also surfaced here and there. A couple of years ago, some California legislators wanted to introduce a bill to make encounter groups illegal unless they were led by a licensed psychiatrist. Murphy, called to Sacramento to give his views, pointed out that such a law would be practically unenforceable—for one reason, because so many encounter sessions these days take place in churches: how could you prove that the group wasn't discussing the New Testament? The proposed bill died, but the attacks from both the behavioral psychologists and the orthodox psychiatrists continue. Encounter, with its here-and-now orientation and its emphasis on the exploration of spontaneous feelings, is accused of being anti-intellectual and anti-scientific; the spontaneity of the group is seen as spurious, and the group pressure as incipiently Fascistic. A significant percentage of encounter-group participants, it is said, come away emotionally damaged in one way or another, and relatively few draw any lasting benefit from the experience.

A recent, widely circulated study of encounter-group participants at Stanford claimed that sixteen of two hundred and six volunteers suffered psychological injury. Schutz, in a published reply, called the study wholly misleading and blatantly unscientific, and pointed out that a large proportion of the participants actually took part in group processes that had nothing to do with encounter. "The basic principles of encounter are honesty and responsibility," Schutz often says. "What could be more homey?" Murphy agrees that the "casualty rates" of encounter have been exaggerated, but he sees some truth in the persistent criticism. The original error, he sometimes feels, may have been to think of encounter as therapy. People came to groups, went through emotional changes, and left thinking that the new insights would carry over into their regular life; when this didn't happen, they got depressed and discouraged. Perhaps it would have been better if they had approached the experience more for its own sake. Both Murphy and Price suspect that the experience of encounter may be closer to that of theatre than to that of therapy. One can be emotionally stirred by a performance of "Hamlet" without expecting life to be different afterward.

"People sometimes come away from Esalen and leave their jobs, get divorced—things like that," Murphy said not long ago. It was after dinner at the Murphy's house in Mill Valley, a cool evening, the light from a fire the room's only illumination. "This is a part of our reputation that's true. Naturally, it's offensive to the medical viewpoint that is oriented toward fixing people up so they'll be well adjusted to their own society. Esalen has been subversive toward that kind of psychiatry. Some psychiatrists also mistrust us because we use lay people as group leaders—even though recent studies by the National Institute of Mental Health show that lay people very often have more talent for therapy than professional psychiatrists. A great many psychiatrists are interested mainly in keeping the door that Freud opened from opening any wider. The psychiatrists' reduction of the mystical was a theme of the Salinger stories that had such a huge effect on me in the fifties. I read 'Franny' when I was at Stanford, and, God, it hit me like a ton of bricks. What resonance! Salinger was a great ally in those days. A lot of people really thought I was crazy then, and I wasn't too sure they weren't right—I needed reassurance. What happened in the sixties was this incredible comeback of the whole mystical side of things. Esalen certainly had role in that, along with the drug scene and the counterculture. Now there are signs that maybe the medical establishment is opening up a little. For example, Stuart and Sara Miller have started a three-year project to expose a limited number of doctors and nurses to some of the work we've been doing at Esalen—psychosynthesis, gestalt therapy, encounter, massage, biofeedback techniques to alleviate pain, and so forth—with the idea of making medical practice more humane.

The project started at Esalen, but now it's independently funded, and still being run by the Millers. Sara also started a teacher-training project in connection with the University of California at Santa Barbara, under a grant form the Ford Foundation, on more or less the same basis—getting these new ideas and methods into education. The thing is just spreading everywhere you look."

After a pause, Murphy said, "There's no question about it. We're going to explore mind. We come into it as adventurers, sometimes as drunken sailors, and some aspects of this thing get very crazy, and even demonic. The power of group process is almost limitless, and it can be very, very dangerous. I'm aware that we're assuming responsibility for human lives in much of what we do at Esalen, and that there's a big risk in encouraging people to transcend themselves. I'm aware that Madness Gulch is right around the corner. But it's going to be done. The hunger for this sort of thing is simply enormous, and the risks are worth taking. Of course, one of the things I really hate is encounter as a religion. I love Bill Schutz for his solid strength—he's very comforting to be around—but because he's made out of India rubber and keeps bouncing back from every kind of confrontation I think he underrates the dangers. To run an encounter group or a gestalt-therapy group for nine months is just not the answer. Esalen has been great for these opening-up exercises but not for the long haul. The problem is to find sustaining ways of life, sustaining disciplines, and, to me, Roberto Assagioli's psychosynthesis points toward the kind of comprehensive spirit that's needed. You can't live on encounter. Encounter is like an initiation ceremony, a way of crossing a boundary and looking at what's on the other side. I feel that in future disciplines encounter groups as we have known them will have a very small place, while meditation techniques and approaches like psychosynthesis will have a very large one. The human-potential movement as a whole has its own inherent logic, it seems, that is corresponding more and more with the great contemplative traditions of the past."

Murphy was quiet for a while, gazing into the fire. "Vision's still dawning," he said. "The instinct for transformation has existed since

Paleolithic times, and has developed in many ways through shamanistic and religious traditions. But now we have a chance as never before to draw from all these traditions and learn from both their weaknesses and their strengths. Nearly all of them have been limited in one way or another—neglecting society, like some of the ascetic Indian yogas, or belittling the body or failing to integrate the mind. Aurobindo was one of the pioneers in this kind of integration. And now there's an incredibly strong impulse to bring the body back in. At Esalen, for example, the body came into things immediately—it was all around me right away. I think that the physical body and the social body go along together, and that the transformation has to involve them both. From our modern vantage point, we can develop broader and more sophisticated disciplines, I think, and throw back the horizons for the next stage of human ascent."

Asked how he foresaw the transformation as taking place, Murphy said that he saw both a horizontal and a vertical direction to it. "The horizontal one is that more and more points of access into this richness are becoming available. The human-potential thing is spreading all through the culture. Old-age groups, hospitals, schools, prisons, community centers—there are a million ramifications. There's also the factor of necessity—closing time in the gardens of the West. The ecology movement is helping to spread the idea that transformation is possible and necessary, and so is the breakdown of so many of our traditional institutions. I think there will be pioneers—pirates of the spirit, like Jacob Atabet. It's the thing I want to do for the rest of my life. I think that as people appear who make these voyages into the interior, into inner space, each voyage will be an inciting act. Just like Lewis and Clark opening up the West: My God, now there's all that to discover! I think I'm going to have to take about a year and go back and do what I did in the fifties—meditate eight hours a day every day—to see where I am now. Have these last thirteen years loosened things up to allow me to get to spaces I couldn't get to before? I owe myself at least that experiment. If I push too hard or too fast, I'll wreck myself. We each have a kind of right speed. There's still going to be the intensity and excitement. It may even be greater now, without all the wild storming of the gates that went on in the sixties, and all the bad trips. There will still be bad trips, too, of course; a lot of experiments of this kind will end badly—some already have. The space program is a good analogy. To go really far, you have to be well organized. For my own part, though, I think there's going to be plenty of room for adventure."

# To Hell With Russia,
# To Michael With Love

KEITH THOMPSON

Dear Michael,
I can easily say the day I was introduced to you, 33 years ago, still ranks as one of the supercharged experiences of my life. Before this goes to your head, I'd better qualify that you weren't even present at the time. Whether this says more about your amazing charisma at a distance or my preternatural talent for projection is an open question. Either way, Jay Ogilvy's invitation to contribute to this volume of affection gives me the happiest opportunity to ponder the myriad ways your intellect, warmth, humor, creativity, generosity, athleticism, and activism have informed, guided, amused, encouraged, and inspired me for more than three decades.

By way of overture, I'd like to set forth certain numinous—I use this word quite advisedly—details leading up to the day we actually met in person. It strikes me your novelist psyche might enjoy the back-story of a particular character (namely myself, early 20s, intellectually restless, ready for Something Big) as that story leads into the larger story or plot, roughly: You and I—and several like-minded collaborators—bent on exploring life's mysteries, proceeding with appreciation for the groundwork of the world's great wisdom traditions but with an audacious sense that those traditions conveyed by no means the final word on the human adventure. Most importantly: tribesmen determined to have a rollicking good time in the process, with no chance of apologies or surrender at any point.

As to my being introduced to you before we actually met, this refers not to anything occult or paranormal but to the 1976 *New Yorker* magazine profile through which I came to know of the trajectory of your life and work, chiefly involving a place called Esalen. I'm struck by that phrase, "came to know." Strange thing about the process called cognition. They used to think ("they" being those who get to be called authorities about what's true) that knowledge is passively received through the senses—just show up, open up, and thou shall receive. Piaget, following Kant, famously turned that one on its head by demonstrating the "operations" through which the knower actively builds up ("constructs") knowledge through experience.

You proceed on a certain path until you get to a clearing. And everything makes sense, including the fact that you wouldn't have gotten there if it weren't for other clearings you reached earlier on the same path. The psychedelic moment comes when you stop and realize you're not going down any predetermined path at all. We make the path by walking, as the poet Antonio Machado said.

This is to say the *New Yorker* profile that made such an impression on me might never have come to my attention but for two significant prior experiences. I'll start with the one in church.

Like you I was raised in a family where faith wasn't top priority. You might say we were nominally religious and de facto secular. Still, my mother felt it proper for her four sons to have some relationship to the Episcopal Church in which she had been a member all her life. As an Episcopal acolyte during my teens, I grew to love the sequence beginning after all the congregants had settled and stopped hustling and bustling. There followed hushed, pregnant silence leading into the sheer grandeur of the pipe organ that inaugurated the weekly procession up the sanctuary aisle. The juxtaposition of stunning silence and organ music that literally rocked the cells of my body seemed the very essence of church. Then, the organ would stop, the acolytes would extinguish their candles, the minister would mount the podium, and with his first utterance of mundane church-speak, the strangest thing would happen. Every hint of the holy evaporated like so much morning mist. This happened week after week.

More than once I wondered if that result—the effective banishment of the sense of the sacred—might be the actual goal of church, or whether it was more like an accidental byproduct, due, perhaps, to a really boring minister. Ultimately the question didn't matter because about this time I discovered that the solace of sacred silence was not a church-specific reality. I can still vividly remember the summer evening I climbed up the ladder-like TV antenna outside our house—strictly forbidden by my father—and spent the whole freaking night on the roof decoding the stars (twinkle-dit-twinkle-dash-twinkle-dash-dash-twinkle-dit). No one even knew I was gone. It didn't get much better than that.

By the time our family drifted away from churchgoing I hadn't begun studying for confirmation; thus I departed before getting introduced to church doctrine. So in a very real sense the actual content of my childhood religious life was each week's vibratory collage of soulful quietude, triumphant sound, pervasive incense, and light refracted through stained glass. From my frequent sojourns to the roof came an abiding sense of divine spaciousness that made me feel at home in the universe each time I snuck back down the antenna into consensus reality.

Flash forward to the summer prior to my senior year as an undergraduate, studying Renaissance literature at New College, Oxford University. One fine afternoon I decided to split off from the usual pub rounds with fellow students. No specific plans, mostly just wanted to be by myself. I walked along Broad Street and stopped at Blackwell's bookstore where I proceeded to meander up and down the cloistered aisles. At the time I tended toward fiction and political science, but this day I took a fateful turn into new territory, marked "Philosophy." With curiosity that surprised me, I started leafing through books about meditation and yoga until my eye caught a particular title: *In My Own Way*, the autobiography of Alan Watts, a writer I had never heard of. I made my way through half the book right there in the store. I found particularly amusing Watts' description of a Stanford professor named Frederic Spiegelberg:

Several years ago the students of Stanford voted him the best teacher on the faculty, which must have enraged his colleagues because you cannot maintain proper status in an American university without cultivated mediocrity. You must be "academically sound," which is to be preposterously and phenomenally dull.

But this—and I know you will understand why, Michael—was the passage that mesmerized me:

> When I first met Spiegelberg he wore a hat with an exceedingly wide brim, spoke English with a delicate German accent which always suggests a sense of authority and high culture, and was propagating the theory that the highest form of religion was to transcend religion. He called it the religion of nonreligion. I call it atheism in the name of God; that is, the realization that ordinary everyday life and consciousness is what the Hindus call "*satchitananda*," and which I translate as "the which than which there is no whicher." … Spiegelberg and I have always regarded ideas and conceptions of God, as well as compulsive and schedule notions of the "right way" of spiritual culture, as forms of idolatry more confusing than any amount of material images and icons…. No sensible person ever confused a crucifix or an image of the Buddha with the divinity itself, and as for techniques of spiritual development, "The ways to the One are as many as the lives of men."

The incendiary ideas in those sentences accomplished two amazing things for me simultaneously. First, they provided a conceptual framework (a core rationale and foundation) for my childhood reveries in church and on rooftops. Second, they kindled my latent interest and desire, plus a certain fearlessness, to explore the possibility of directly experiencing states, or modes, or simply *ways* of being, related to "the which than which there is no whicher." Could it be that there was something (or perhaps "no thing") infinite waiting to be experienced in the confines of ordinary life? Something not merely available but possibly constituting the *summum bonum*—the greatest or supreme good—of life itself? Heady thoughts for a college senior from northwest Ohio.

I bought Watts' book and spent much of the rest of my summer at Oxford practicing meditation (out of sight of my college peers) and attending Bach organ recitals (of which there were many, Oxford being Oxford). Returning to college several weeks later, I quickly realized that the new life burning inside me wouldn't make for casual conversations at the student union. Ohio State University in the mid-70s was not by any stretch a hotbed of diverse spiritual activity. There was one group, however, that seemed promising: the local chapter devoted to teaching Transcendental Meditation. The pitch was simple: for a nominal charge you could be introduced—*initiated* was the word—to a simple method of meditation involving the silent recitation of a Sanscrit term called a mantra. I went, I paid, I received.

And then I beat a hasty retreat. For though I had not yet heard the word "cult," there were more than a few signs this was not a healthy group. For one thing, TM initiates were told not to tell their mantra to anyone. What was *that* about? And we were instructed to meditate twice daily, 20 minutes per session, just that much. This raised the inevitable question: "Who says?" The answer was visible in all directions; the TM center was filled with photos of Maharishi Mahesh Yogi and floral altars devoted to praising his unquestioned divinity. Did I mention that the teachers and senior students all seemed to be zombies? The whole scene reeked of a narrowing rather than a broadening of self. As an English major, I had had too much glorious exposure to Whitman ("I am large, I contain multitudes..."), Thoreau ("Only that day dawns to which we are awake. There is more day to dawn..."), and Emerson ("Plunge into the sublime seas, dive deep, and swim far"), to want to hang out with suburban middle class refugees for whom the brain-bypass operation that goes with guru worship was the necessary cover charge of Enlightenment. I was glad to leave with a meditation technique to practice on my own, but mostly just glad to leave.

Looking back, Mike, I have to think my impulse to run from that scene was related to the fact that I had recently taken up recreational running, the satisfactions of which did absolutely nothing to reinforce any idea that the worlds of consciousness and matter were on some tragic collision course. (Within a year, I completed my first marathon, a four and a half hour ordeal on a brilliant May morning with starting temperature and humidity both above 80. Advice: If you meet the Buddha on the road, check electrolyte levels immediately.)

Which brings me, finally, to the chase. The year is 1976. I've just graduated from college. I'm 22. I go to see one of my favorite people in the world, a family friend my mother's age. Marge Reid is a marvelously heretical thinker who called me up one day out of the blue—I didn't even know her—to congratulate me for writing a controversial letter to the editor. Introducing me to the works of Faulkner and the iconoclastic journalism of I.F. "Izzy" Stone, Marge never tired of encouraging me to extend my mind in every conceivable direction. It gave me enormous pleasure to comply with this directive. On this particular day, I'm regaling Marge with dispatches about Alan Watts, Aldous Huxley, Abraham Maslow; none of whom we had previously discussed. Suddenly she opens her eyes wide and raises both hands with palms facing me, as if telling me to stop. Had I struck a nerve? "Wait," she says, then scurries out of the room. Ten minutes later she's back with a magazine, which she flips through until just the right page.

"Read the long article about Esalen," Marge says. It turns out to be the January 5, 1976 issue of *The New Yorker*. Marge thought she handed me a magazine that day. I left with a manifesto.

*The New Yorker* described an educational institute in Big Sur, California wedged beneath stark mountains and above the rugged Pacific Coast. In launching this center with his friend Dick Price, a young man named Michael Murphy was influenced by Aurobindo's vision of the full development of human nature, joining the West's focus on the development of the physical, material and mental areas of human life, with the spiritual development and philosophical directions developed over thousands of years in the East. I had never heard of Aurobindo but his emphasis on the full flowering of human nature (matter as the densest form of spirit; spirit as the subtlest form of matter) seemed a perfectly welcome departure from the either/or exclusivity of traditional materialist and spiritualist worldviews. If human nature consists of physical, emotional, mental, and spiritual dimensions, it made perfect sense that there should be ways to educate, evoke, and inspire the fullest expression of each aspect, but free of the dogmatism common to groups organized around a single idea or charismatic leader.

I was thrilled to learn the brilliant Frederic Spiegelberg had been a crucial influence in your intellectual development and your decision to start Esalen. I could only smile when I read that you, too, had started out in the Episcopal Church; that you had developed a grand passion for running; that your quest to penetrate life's secrets had started early in life. Particularly I was struck that your visit to the Aurobindo ashram to practice meditation had left you as wary of the guru model as had my brief intersection with TM cult. And I cheered your commitment to keep any particular teacher from "capturing the flag" at Esalen, though I had no doubt your vigilance on that would be an endless, exasperating, thankless, but inevitably worthwhile mission.

I took my first Esalen workshop in 1976. Believe it or not, I showed up in a taxi. I had arrived in Monterey too late to catch the shuttle to Esalen, so I hailed a local cab. "Let me get this straight. You want me to drive you to *Big Sur*?" Esalen's gatekeeper assured me I was the first person to arrive that way.

The following year I moved cross-country to California, where I've been ever since. I got to know George Leonard in Mill Valley, where we both lived within walking distance of one another. We met for coffee one morning. "You know, George," I began, "I've been thinking I'd really like to meet your friend Mike Murphy." I can still see George cocking his head slightly, as if taking my full measure. "You know, Keith, I think Mike Murphy would like to meet you, too. Write down your phone number."

You called within a few days and suggested we go for a run—our first of many up Blithedale Canyon, then along the winding streets near Cascade back down to Lovell. Afterwards we talked for hours about psychology, politics, the meeting of East and West, the widespread appetite for transformative experience, the necessity of smart, open-ended theories and practices that foster integral development of unique individuals. I stayed for dinner with you and Dulce. Months later I heard about a small rustic cabin for rent within waving distance of your patio. The cabin became my hermit's abode during the enchanted years our wild and crazy gang (you, Dulce, Jim, Mary, Steve, Bruce, Ed, Moore, Anne, myself, and various others) trained together for marathons, practiced meditation, read the works of Plotinus and other Greek philosophers and mystics including Saint John of the Cross and Saint Teresa of Avila, held informal seminars to discuss these works, often talking late into the night over meals with wine and plenty of laughter. Plato's *Symposium* had nothing on us, dude.

The alchemy of all this had a hugely magical dimension. There's no way we could have created this grand alliance systematically if we had set out to. What's clear, all these years later, is that a genuine integral impulse truly seemed to guide the enterprise: tough athletic workouts in the spirit of achieving our best rather than winning over anyone; contemplative practice to cultivate interior capacities free of heroic efforts to achieve particular outcomes or confirm any specific philosophic perspective; the study of remarkable books in search of wisdom for everyday living. Most of all: an abiding spirit of friendship, mutual respect and high regard, and deep gratitude for the miracle of existence. All within a context that the quest for vision is far from over, that the instinct for transformation continues, and that widespread cultivation of extraordinary human capacities could very well open new possibilities for our evolution as a species. Hence the challenge to constantly evaluate truth claims in a way that keeps the amazing adventure moving forward.

And having a blast in the process. Thanks especially for that, Mike Murphy. Thanks for being a fantastic mentor, an inspired teacher, an intrepid fellow athlete, a phenomenal father to your beautiful son, and an extraordinary friend. The sheer delight you bring to everything you do is just contagious.

I'll never forget the day I took you to see a Cheech and Chong movie. You had never heard of these clowns, and you were still laughing hours after we left the theater. I was thinking the other day: it's going to be fun to know you when you get old. By the way, when do you plan to start that? No time soon I hope.

All best,
*Keith*

# Ahimsa, Indeed

SARA (SUKIE) MILLER

One of my early, holographic memories is of a sunny afternoon when Stuart Miller, Mike and I were meeting cross legged on the floor in our two room San Francisco "office" planning the next Esalen catalogue...how many pages was it then? Maybe 10?

All the new ideas and old ideas and crazy ideas and non-ideas floated through the room as we talked and exclaimed and I chain-smoked, carefully putting my ashes in the loveliest of bowls which Michael— always a bit fastidious—would immediately empty. On we jabbered, and on I smoked, as we planned those immediate and distant futures. It was only late in the day that Michael—apropos of I do not remember what—told us the story of some wonderful set of blessed bowls that the then newly or about to be anointed Dick Baker had specially brought to Michael from Japan. "Did we notice their subtle beauty?" he asked. "Look, Sukie, you have one right next to you!"

That day, long ago, in that sweet office, I learned the Hindu word *ahimsa*, which I came to understand to mean (mere) ignorance or being without knowledge. A gentle word.

When I look back over the glorious years we have had, dear Michael, traipsing the worlds—both inner and outer—I am honored to join with others to hail loudly and deeply this your 80th year. Your profound and complex "grokking" of all that we don't know, can know and will know, my friend, have served the cause of *ahimsa* so well and so gently.

Another word I learned from you, Michael, is catholic: small c. My God, Murphy, how broadly you lived it all! Muksha, Sidhi, Gospel, Drums, Music of the Spheres, Community, community, Commune, Going In, Going Up, Letting Go, Holding On, Letting Be, Chaos (theory or no), this life, that life, afterlife, Russia, China, Brazil, America, Europe, Muslim, Christian, Jew, Abrahamic, Holistic, Humanistic, Bibliographies, archives, supernormal, paranormal, body, mind, spirit, mind/body, body/mind, body/mind/spirit.... How could one piece of property hold it all? But you do and it does.

*Om Tat Sat* indeed.

As I age along with you, almost everywhere I go I see you and I see Esalen. I see it when a myriad of body theories and therapies are considered as part of contemporary health and even medical care. I see it when teachers in an emerging country wonder if there is another way to teach than by rote memorization and there are many answers to their question. I see it when business leaders consider lessons from disciplines not their own. And I see you when the mention of Esalen brings wide-eyed curiosity and wonder.

Thank you, dear friend.

Happy birthday.
Don't stop now.

tackle

# An Experiment

*A bit of background: Though a generation apart in age, like mother and daughter, Mary Catherine and Nora are actually sisters—both daughters of Gregory Bateson. Mary Catherine's mother was the anthropologist, Margaret Mead. Nora's mother was Lois Bateson, a family therapist. Gregory, Lois and Nora spent the last several years of Gregory's life at Esalen. When I asked Mary Catherine for a contribution to this volume, she suggested that Nora, who had actually spent more time at Esalen, might be a better contributor. I suggested that the two of them engage in a dialogue, for two reasons: First, Mary Catherine had done such a marvelous job of honoring her elders in such books as* Willing to Learn: Passages of Personal Discovery (2004), Angels Fear: Towards an Epistemology of the Sacred (1987) *written with Gregory Bateson, and,* With a Daughter's Eye: A Memoir of Margaret Mead and Gregory Bateson (1984); *now Nora could carry on that tradition. Second, Gregory had done such a marvelous job of honoring the beginner's mind of youth in the "metalogs" with young Mary Catherine that brighten the pages of his dizzying book of essays,* Steps to an Ecology of Mind. *Mary Catherine replied: "You realize you've upped the ante. In those metalogs, the form reflected the content." In this lightly edited transcript of their conversation, Nora and Mary Catherine rise to the challenge.*

**Catherine:** Okay, Michael Murphy, Gregory, Esalen.

**Nora:** Yeah. And a happy birthday to Michael Murphy.

**Catherine:** Happy birthday to Michael Murphy. Definitely.

**Nora:** Yeah. Well, I wanted to start by first of all saying that when I got this note from you initiated by Jay Ogilvy—I was immediately impressed that he refers to Esalen as an experiment. As time has progressed, this 'experiment' has become more lodged in its own kind of rhetoric. I hope that it doesn't forget that it's an experiment as Omega Institute and various spin-offs of the same concept have emerged all over the place. I love that it's an experiment, and I give Michael and Dick a lot of credit for that experimental spirit.

**Catherine:** I think there were many experiments within the larger experiment, because I guess in the beginning it was referred to as a 'growth center,' and then increasingly as a 'healing center.' So there were changes in emphasis and changes in policy, and various people living in the house in which you lived.

**Nora:** Yeah, absolutely. People have often asked me the question, "What was it like growing up with such an unusual childhood?" While for you that included the unusualness of your mother's life and all the conversations that took place around that dinner table, for me, a great deal of my childhood took place at Esalen—several years. The thing about being a child and growing up somewhere unusual is that you absolutely cannot answer that question, because you don't have anything to contrast it with.

**Catherine:** That's right. What you experienced is what's "normal."

**Nora:** That's right. So, what was it like growing up at Esalen? It was like growing up at Esalen.

[*both laugh*]

**Nora:** Exactly like that! I mean, it wasn't until much later that I was able to see the cultural contrast around how that experience was actually different, and why that difference was significant or might be of interest. I have often felt that the most important thing I learned at Esalen or that I took from that experience was that it was a place where the grownups—the adult world—had not plateau'd. The adult world was in a state of constant learning—

**Catherine:** Mm.

**Nora:** —and reflection, very painful sometimes, often very humorous, minings of their own mistakes. For me, I see that time at Esalen now as a kind of cultural imaginarium. Like a fun-house of warped mirrors and mazes and various exercises for looking at the confines of things that we have taken for granted, based on our cultural limits. It has been very useful—to base a life on that, to learn so young that there is no plateau; that you don't grow up and know everything you're going to know. The grownups aren't always right, and the mistakes that you don't work toward making peace with will eat a hole through you later if you're not careful. Those have been very important themes for my life and, I think…I think terrific things for kids to learn.

**Catherine:** I think kids could learn them in a different way from the grown-ups who were exploring those issues themselves. Because the grownups were breaking with a cultural past and exploring new territory, whereas for the children, all of this was presented as normal—as the way the world is.

**Nora:** I think Gregory's time there was important because he was one of the old folks, an elder.

**Catherine:** When you were there, the majority of the people there were people who had moved towards the counter-culture fairly early in adulthood. They hadn't spent years and years living by the old models. The elders who were there were people like Gregory, who had spent their lives trying to, you know, function in the world as it is and to communicate alternative ways of looking and thinking. There were a lot of people at Esalen who as 18, 20, 25-years-olds were hippies. Right?

**Nora:** Absolutely.

**Catherine:** So that's a very different experience. And even more different from growing up in an academic community in Cambridge, England, and immigrating to the United States and trying to function in American culture, and then seeing a whole style of thinking changing.

**Nora:** If rigor marked the first part of his education, then the imagination at Esalen was a nice bracket for the end. I think it's important to remember that during the end of the time he was at Esalen he was working with death. He was dying there, and that was an education for everybody.

**Catherine:** He never knew, as far as I know, that when he first went into the hospital with the lung cancer and they did the exploratory operation, the doctors told your mom that he wouldn't survive another month.

**Nora:** Yeah, it was borrowed time.

**Catherine:** And it was a pure gift of time.

**Nora:** With the underlying ethos of Esalen centered around the kind of question of how we can be more whole, how we can be more healthy and free from the toxicity of our cultural framework or our habits, it was important to note that death is an integral part of what a healthy system is.

**Catherine:** Mm hm. Death is essential. Couldn't do without it.

**Nora:** Couldn't do without it. So…let's see, where does that leave us here?

**Catherine:** Well, you know, sometimes he joked about some of the beliefs and fashions of people at Esalen. But what he valued most, in many ways, was Esalen as a warm and caring human community.

**Nora:** I think that it was valuable to him, and certainly to Michael and Dick, to have an experiment. It was the perfect storm, if you will, this remarkable place that needed to be completely isolated from the rest of our cultural reminders, right? Way out on the edge of the world on the rugged Pacific Coast is the perfect place to separate everybody from the grocery stores, the office buildings, the traffic lights, the education systems, and all the things that would reaffirm the limitations the people at Esalen in the beginning were trying to at least experiment with, if not break away from totally. Michael's and Dick's interests converging on that kind of a project, in the midst of the sort of explosive renaissance that had begun in the '50s and that was taking shape on a more public level in the '60s—I think that must have been really exciting. If nothing else, just on the level of…to see what will happen. All sorts of questions came up that explored the relationship between things that are very basic and things that are profound—from the food that we eat to the way that we communicate our version of the self to, my goodness, everything—the body, the mind and the spirit. That's what it was about. Pretty soon the basics became profound and the profound became basic and in this making of an un-rhetoric, a new rhetoric, of course, emerged. A whole new framework came out of the process of getting rid of the framework. [*laughs*]

**Catherine:** Yes, well [*laughs*]. Well, I think one of the interesting features about Esalen—I don't know if this was true from the very beginning—was the community of people who lived there for longer and shorter periods of time. I mean, people who were there for several years, people who were there for maybe a year, as an intern, or something like that. And then there was this continual flow in and out of people coming to take workshops. Now, my impression is that daddy's main interaction—I mean, all those recorded tapes were talks that he gave for—were they called interns? people who were spending how long? A year? Was that the right term?

**Nora:** Work scholars. There from a month to a year—yeah.

**Catherine:** So they weren't the people coming for weekends.

**Nora:** Nothing in the process of Esalen can be measured with exactitude—

[*both laugh*]—I don't think. But yeah, they were basically talks given to a group of people who were engaged in an ongoing conversation or experience of looking at things from a different direction. I don't think they knew which direction they were going to look at it from, just a new one. And that was part of the risk. The experiment carried a huge risk that some large percentage of its product was going to turn out to be gobbledy-gook. But if you don't take that risk, you don't get the small percentage that is so precious and insightful. I think that's something that I would really like to give Michael and Dick credit for—their wisdom in letting the process of the experiment unfold. Of course, one can't control a genesis like that, and they didn't try to. The b.s. was given space to form and pass through, and in doing that the seeds of a cultural renaissance were also free to emerge.

**Catherine:** Mm hm.

**Nora:** Of course we, the kids of Esalen, just like any children, had terrific bullshit detectors, you know—

[*big laughs from both*]

**Nora:** I have always held that they should have put us at the gate. Think of it—a team of kids that could have culled right away the ego-maniacs from those of pure-spirited integrity. We could have told them right away which were which [*both laugh*]. But really, there were beautiful things that came out of Esalen that could never have come about, had there been a greater level of control. I'll never forget when this psychic came, who channeled Monet and Picasso and could paint blind-folded marker-drawn replications of the Impressionists' paintings. Do you know this story?

**Catherine:** Yes I do. And I've always wondered whether you were the child that added details to the pictures.

**Nora:** I wasn't the child. It was a little girl I used to baby-sit. I was older. I was, you know, a seasoned veteran at that point. I think I was 11. But little Jessica was maybe 6. And she got marched into the lodge at lunchtime by a manager who had a black marker in his hand. She was in big trouble for defacing the paintings. This was serious business. That psychic was the darling of the month. After her crime had been explained, Gregory asked the managers and other witnesses, "How can you be so sure that it wasn't Jessica that was channeling the artists?" [*laughs*]

**Catherine:** Yeah.

**Nora:** But, you know, I think that was really wonderful—that moment of being loose enough with the epistemology that you can ask questions like that. It must have been, at the very least, entertaining for Gregory.

**Catherine:** So one of the real contrasts is the contrast between Esalen and some of the communes that were set up during that period, where people pulled out of the mainstream culture, but they pulled out to form their own little orthodoxies, within which everybody agreed.

**Nora:** Yeah, that's a tricky one, isn't it?

**Catherine:** I mean, I think the diversity that existed at Esalen is a tremendously important characteristic. It was not so much "a counterculture," in the language of the time, but a counter-process of culturation—an experimental and open-ended way of looking at epistemology and looking at human relationships and so on.

**Nora:** To that end it had its own sort of governors. When things would get too rigid, it could break out of its own rigidity with the emergence of a medium who could channel some wise entity in the sky or some new realm of psychological research, or a new kind of body movement, or food group or nutritional path—anything could come along and impact that system in such a way that it would keep moving.

**Catherine:** Well, I think your mom's an example of that, isn't she?

**Nora:** Yes.

**Catherine:** Because she brought in a lot of the stuff from the Hypocrites clinic and so on. And people started experimenting, and some of it continues, I guess.

**Nora:** It's an improvisation, really.

**Catherine:** [*laughs*] It is a lovely place. You know, I was there fairly recently—last fall. I gave a workshop with Jean Houston and Ralph Abraham—would you believe?

**Nora:** I think it's a great combination.

**Catherine:** Well, it was lovely to be there. It really was very beautiful. And it felt like a long time ago. I mean, the last time I was there was at the memorial for Gregory. But to go back, the other thing, I think, that's important to say, and is very relevant to Michael, was that there was always a kind of global thinking going on at Esalen—thinking, first of all, about environmental issues, the kind of stuff that Daddy was involved in—ecology, and the kind of work that Michael was interested in—dialogues with the Russians and getting beyond the cold war. The frame of reference of Esalen was really planetary, and still is.

**Nora:** There's always been this pull, and I think that it's a kind of tension that is very healthy, between a kind of deep introspection, the process of looking at the self—

**Catherine:** Mm hm.

**Nora:** —and a more global and planetary context through which to apply that self. You know, it's hard to get those two dances in step with each other, and to figure out when one should be featured and the other should not and vice versa. I think there have been only a few people who have been contributors to both of those processes. Michael is certainly one of them. The business of being able to zoom in on the self and micromanage the hurts, the experiences, the learning and the expansiveness that can take place there, while simultaneously being able to apply it to the level of global activism.

**Catherine:** Mm hm.

**Nora:** What I saw was that a lot of people got into the business of the "self" and got stuck there. Alternatively, it's also dangerously easy to not deal with the "self" at all, while externalizing and being a do-gooder on a global front. Both have enormous blind spots without the other. And yet, it's very difficult to bring them together. It requires a creative process.

**Catherine:** We are our own central metaphor. There's a metaphorical relationship between the individual organism and the entire planet.

**Nora:** There better be.

**Catherine:** [*laughs*]

**Nora:** I have wondered if in part it was intentional to bring people to the Esalen tubs and have them take their clothes off. It was sort of the first step in saying, "We're taking off our masks, we're taking off our cultural packaging, this is me, this is you and here we are, and we're just raw and real." In contrast, there was that other aspect that took place, where it was a crazy externalized ego-game. But, you know what? You couldn't have one without the other. And so getting to that metaphor of us all existing together in the natural world also requires, you know, looking at some of the shadow sides of that. And Esalen provided a playground for the light and the shadow.

**Catherine:** I think it's worth mentioning that Esalen took a great deal of courage. I mean, it takes courage to step outside everybody's familiar assumptions. It takes courage to have a lot of people together in the same place that are [*with a laugh*] stepping outside the familiar assumptions.

**Nora:** [*laughs*] Anything could happen.

**Catherine:** Anything can happen.

**Nora:** [*laughs*] And did—all of it.

**Catherine:** I expect it did. But, I mean, there are considerable risks involved, and very important discoveries to be made.

**Nora:** And a lot of garbage.

**Catherine:** There's a lot of garbage everywhere. It's just maybe less obvious.

**Nora:** Exactly. But it took a lot of courage. It was a huge risk. And that's why I love that it's being referred to as an experiment. Because—I'm not sure that when I was there that I thought of it as an experiment. We referred to it as the "institution", and that was, you know, kind of cheeky and sort of recognizing that we were all a little bonkers. But there was also a sense that Esalen was a template for the new world. And for some reason, that didn't register with me as being an experiment. Maybe it did for other people.

**Catherine:** It'd be a possible template—a partial template.

**Nora:** Yeah. A partial template—a work in progress. I guess that is an experiment. But it's nice that it's being identified in that way, because that leaves it open. There's more to be learned from the learning itself, and that's great.

**Catherine:** Yeah, I was making the same point when I made up that obnoxious word, culturation—

**Nora:** [*laughs*]

**Catherine:** —because…my sense is that Esalen was not modeling a product; it was modeling a process—a process of exploration and improvisation and openness, rather than saying, "We're there. Look at us."

**Nora:** Yes, I think that's right. I don't think it was possible to say, "We're there, we've arrived." Because every weekend a new bunch of people came, who were in the process of getting "there." The people who did say "we're there" were the ones to really watch out for. [*laughs*] That was the red flag. I remember as a kid thinking, "whoops, watch out for the ones who think they've got it down."

**Catherine:** What a good thing to learn as a kid.

**Nora:** You know, it was a very interesting place to be a child and hear people screaming and crying and hitting pillows and talking about how they had not fulfilled their relationship with their parents. Now, I'm sure there's someone out there who would say that that is not healthy, or it's too much information or something. But you know what? I have to say that in fact I think it was really important. It gave us—the children at Esalen—a reference point and a demonstration of the fact that what we did as children and the relationships that we cultivated throughout our lives would have an effect on how we would feel about ourselves, and that that was going to be an ongoing process of learning and internal housecleaning. That's amazing.

**Catherine:** Mm. Are you in touch with many kids from there?

**Nora:** You know, I am in touch with them. And we're a funny bunch, because [*laughs*]—you know, in some ways, this gift of a different kind of communication that we were exposed to was a great favor. When talking about the communication that happened at Esalen, it's easy to think about that communication as being form oriented, like "I" statements and whatnot. But the actual substance of the communication was a process of looking inside to find ways of understanding what we were "really" feeling. I mean, it's one thing to use words to *describe* what you're feeling, but it's another thing altogether to *know* what you're feeling.

**Catherine:** Mm.

**Nora:** It was what we were imbibing, like any children imbibe their surroundings. We were sponges. By nature, that's what kids are. So, we were absorbing this sort of two-fold way of being and communicating that on the one hand included tools for honing in on what was being felt and maybe why. And then on the other hand, we were soaking up language on how to put those feelings into words and communicate them. The only hitch was that then when we got out in the world, all the other people that we were interacting with hadn't had the same programming. [*laughs*]

**Catherine:** Mm hm.

**Nora:** It was a bit intense. What we were able to describe and discuss was just not of the same genre as the things that other kids or other adults or teachers—later, employers or spouses—were going to have. I've always felt that we were a sort of one-off tribe of people who had been given that set of skills and tools that we had been given. And, for better or for worse, we came out a bunch of turbo-communicators. It can be very off-putting. I can say it's gotten me into as much trouble as it's gotten me out of.

**Catherine:** [*laughs*] Well, you know, there's a whole tribe of kids who are referred to as 3rd country kids, who grow up as the children of parents working in other countries—children of diplomats or children of business people. They belong neither to the country their parents originally came from, nor to the country in which they were stationed. The people that those kids associate with have parents from 20 different countries, so they have 20 different home cultures. They have a whole different set of styles of how to make friends, how to deal with the transience of many of these relationships. And they seek each other out for the sake of mutual intelligibility.

**Nora:** Right. They're members of the same lost tribe.

**Catherine:** Right.

**Nora:** Members of the lost tribe. Yeah, I mean, I guess it would be interesting to see if you could see who the people were who were coming to Esalen. Because, on some level, my guess is they were similar. The people who came there were looking for something. And I think they were looking not only for a sense of healing and well-being and seeking for what the human potential might be, which was definitely there, but in that process, they were looking for other people who were also seeking.

**Catherine:** And who felt already before they came, to some degree displaced.

**Nora:** That's right. Isolated and alone.

**Catherine:** Right.

**Nora:** Misunderstood.

**Catherine:** Alienated. Except alienated is more political. And I think the issue is not so much political as what you see when you look out at the world. People with different eyes. Well, I think being at Esalen was very good for Daddy.

**Nora:** I think it was, too. I know there's a certain subset of scientists out there who think that when Gregory got to Esalen he didn't have anyone to talk to. For the record, I'd like to say that that's a mistake. He experienced frustration with anyone that he talked to, whether from a scientific or academic community, or from a non-scientific and non-academic community. At Esalen there existed a kind of community that offered him a different sort of wiggle-room to move around with his ideas—and other ideas too—of where we're going as a culture, as a future, of the ideas that help govern what changes we make. I think that was really important to him. Esalen was a good place to play with those ideas. Better maybe than the inside of an academic community with the confines of that tradition.

**Catherine:** *Much* better.

**Nora:** So it offered a kind of freedom that he wasn't going to get anywhere else at that moment. Lindisfarne was another place where he got that. It was important. It was very important. Esalen was an interesting experiment on how change works, and on the properties of change, which I think was fascinating to Gregory.

**Catherine:** Well, you know, we know a lot about new ideas developing at points where different cultures encounter each other—on the margins. There's a whole rhetoric at the moment about outliers, people who are at a certain distance from the mainstream culture. I think that's where the creativity is to be found.

**Nora:** Yeah, and what happens when you put a whole bunch of outliers in a hot tub and you parboil them? [*laughs*]

**Catherine:** What happens when you take a whole group of outliers and turn them into the staff of a short-term teaching institution, where people come, not because they're going to get a diploma and have a career, but because they want their thinking shaken up?

**Nora:** They want their thinking shaken up, they want to have a profound experience. They want to find new levels of themselves in the world they live in. They want to see something new. Thank goodness Esalen didn't offer a degree.

**Catherine:** Yes, right. Absolutely. I mean, I think one of the points about Gregory's thinking is that it frightened people. He asked people to stretch their minds in ways that made them seasick, queasy. They didn't have the familiar hand-holds.

**Nora:** Yes, it gave them vertigo.

**Catherine:** Vertigo—yeah.

**Nora:** Which he wanted. That was a good sign.

**Catherine:** Absolutely.

**Nora:** If you got vertigo, you were getting it.

**Catherine:** But, you see, that's not an acceptable characteristic of a higher education. [*laughs*]

**Nora:** [*laughs*] Why is that funny, really?

[*both laugh*]

**Nora:** You think that was more welcomed in the hot tub full of outliers?

**Catherine:** Yeah, I do.

**Nora:** I do too. I absolutely do. In fact, I think there was almost a... not a competition, but certainly a certain game afoot about tipping the status quo in various directions.

**Catherine:** Yeah. And I'm sure that in the people who came for a week or a weekend, you know, it was a form of daredeviltry sometimes. A vertiginous form of tourism.

# From *Education and Ecstasy*

## George Leonard

*No one would have been more eager to contribute to this volume than the late George Leonard, long-time editor at Look Magazine, highly respected expert on education, and sometimes regarded as Esalen's third cofounder (along with Dick Price). George was among Michael's very closest friends. Sadly, he died before this volume was initiated. But the following pages, drawn from his 1968 book,* Education and Ecstasy, *offer some hint of the high regard in which he held Esalen and its cofounder.*

Education's new domain is not bound in by the conceptual, the factual, the symbolic. It includes every aspect of human existence that is relevant to the new age. To move into it, we don't have to wait for the twenty-first century. Experimenters all around the U.S. and in some other nations as well already have established beachheads in the new domain. Some of these experimenters work within the academies, some without. Powerful and respected institutions have begun to show strong interest in helping education break out of the old subject-matter entrapment. A Ford Foundation official has become an authority on what he calls "affective education" (as opposed to "cognitive education"). The prestigious Twentieth Century Fund held a series of "Human Potential Luncheons" during 1966 and 1967 in New York City. Speakers at these luncheons ranged far beyond the conventional boundaries of education and psychology, even as far as speculation on extrasensory perception...

The one place you would go to find most of the new domain drawn together in some sort of coherent whole is an unlikely institute that psychologist Abraham Maslow has called "probably the most important educational institute in the world." To get there, you would drive south from Monterey, California, forty-five miles along the edge of the Pacific on one of the more spectacular roads in this hemisphere. Of this Coast Road, that at some places soars over a thousand feet above the sea, poet Robinson Jeffers wrote:

> Beautiful beyond belief
> The heights glimmer in the sliding cloud, the great bronze
>     gorge-cut sides of the mountain tower up invincibly
> Not the least hurt by this ribbon of road carved on their sea-foot.

The road would lead you to a cluster of cabins, a small dome, a rustic lodge, some meeting rooms, a swimming pool and hot mineral baths—all thrusting seaward on a point of land above the Pacific. This site was the home, up into the nineteenth century, of a tribe of Indians who called themselves the "Esalen." They fished in the ocean and the cold stream that cascades down an adjoining redwood canyon, hunted small game in the canyon, foraged for acorns and roots in fertile soil and worshiped the medicinal powers of the hot springs that gush from the hills all around. It is from this Indian tribe, not an acronym, that Esalen Institute takes its name.

Just as Synanon reflects the crusty personality of its founder, Chuck Dederich, Esalen reflects Michael Murphy, its youthful president and co-founder (with fellow-seeker Richard Price). In a thirties-type movie, Murphy would be type-cast as the student-body president (which he was, at Salinas, California, High). In a Western, he would be the Good Guy, too good-looking, too gentle and thoughtful for his own good, but capable of that final, necessary resolve.

Esalen's open-mindedness and inspired eclecticism (reflecting Murphy) are probably what accounts for its having become, since its modest beginnings in 1961, the freest marketplace for new ideas in the behavioral sciences of our time. I cannot claim objectivity (if such exists) on this subject. It is only fair to say that Michael Murphy is a close friend and that I have served as vice-president of the institute since 1966. Objective or not, I am unable to imagine an institute other than Esalen where people have enjoyed free-swinging weekends with such experts as Arnold Toynbee, Linus Pauling, the late Paul Tillich, Carl Rogers, B. F. Skinner, Frederick Perls, Joseph Campbell, Abraham Maslow, Alan Watts, Buckminster Fuller and others of their caliber—interspersed with seminars or workshops presided over by lesser-known but perhaps even more innovative leaders, meetings with such titles as "Sensory Awakening for Couples," "The Self and Physical Movement," "Meditation," and "A Workshop in Bio-Energetic Analysis." It is certainly the only place in the world where you would find arch-behaviorist Skinner delightedly giving a weekend "On Programming Nonverbal Behavior," or where a supercerebral seminar by British critic Colin Wilson would be immediately followed by a weeklong workshop on "Meditative Techniques and Depth Imagery."

When, in 1961, Aldous Huxley called for a great new effort in what he termed "the nonverbal humanities," he was able to cite only a handful of examples of what he was talking about. More than 650 Esalen seminars and workshops since then have revealed that the new domain is teeming with activity. In fact, every new area of education imagined for Kennedy School (with one exception) has been explored to some extent at Esalen Institute. A residential program was initiated in September 1966, in which graduate-level fellows spend nine months as full-time free learners in the new domain. They practice meditation, intensified inner imagery, basic encounter, sensory awareness, expressive physical movement and creative symbolic behavior. They learn to control their brain-wave patterns, using the simple brain-wave feedback device developed by Dr. Joe Kamiya of University of California Medical Center. They do extensive dream work, with the Senoi methods described in our school of the future. They also practice the all-action, antianalytical Gestalt Therapy developed by the venerable Frederick Perls, in residence at the Institute.

Even the Faraday project at Kennedy School was inspired by the work of a man I met at an Esalen Seminar, Dr. J. Richard Suchman. Suchman, then an official in the U.S. Office of Education, founded Inquiry Development, an educational approach that helps children work out their own concepts of the way the world is. Inquiring for themselves, fifth and sixth graders, for example, have come up with explanations of Archimedes' Principle that Dr. Suchman considers in some ways more elegant and precise than Archimedes'. Suchman is now developing Inquiry materials for large-scale distribution. In my view, the only weakness in the approach is that it was developed for the now existing classroom-and-teacher situation. The Kennedy Faraday project simply takes the Inquiry approach to its inevitable, child-and-environment, free-learning conclusion.

Like Synanon, Esalen resists description at less than book length. Any single episode, out of context, may make it *harder* to understand. Two visitors may report quite accurately on their particular experiences and discover little in common. Since so much of Esalen is truly experimental, nothing can be guaranteed to "work." Yet, most people who participate come away with the conviction that they have somehow been changed. And many of the Esalen experiments resonate with a characteristic sense of hope and an assumption that even the most intractable human problems contain within them the seeds of their own solution.

# The Russia Connection

# Michael Murphy:
# Quintessential American

VLADIMIR POZNER

This is about Michael Murphy.

But before I attempt to put my thoughts into words—an exercise that is always and in all cases bound to fail—I must share with you an explanation.

I am an American—no, not by birth, but brought to America by my mother when I was 3 months old. That is where I stayed, in New York's Greenwich Village, until the age of 5, when my father, having, as the adage goes, sown his wild oats, came to take us back to France. But I was back in the Village a year and a half later—France had fallen, my father's Jewish origins and pro-Soviet/communist views were hardly the kind of attributes appreciated by the Nazis, so he had to get out fast—which he did by bribing the Gestapo for an "aussweiss." He was offered the money by a wealthy Jewish family on condition that their 19-year-old daughter leave with us as my nanny. So here I was, back in my home town, going to a great private school on 7th Avenue and 12th street, and after that on to Stuyvesant High School, one of the best in the entire country. I was the all-American kid from the Big Apple, I was a Yankee fan, Joltin' Joe DiMaggio was my idol, I had a paper route, I saw F.D.R. brave the elements as he addressed a roaring crowd at Ebbets Field in Brooklyn as the rain pelted down. I was in love with folk music thanks to my school music teacher Pete Seeger; I was crazy about jazz because our cleaning lady, Mrs. Julia Collins, would take me to Harlem every Sunday—first to church and then to jam sessions. And then...

And then we left America. We left because of the beginning of the McCarthy witch hunts, the red scare that forced my father to leave. That was in December, 1948. I was 14, going on 15. And by the first time I returned, I was 52—thirty-eight long years after.

I am not going to bore you with stories about how I missed America. Suffice it to say, there was not a day when I did not dream the dream of returning: I had America on my mind, I followed her literature, her music, her movies, studied her history. In a certain sense, not being there made America even more important to me than if I had been living in my beloved New York, it somehow made me more American. I'll stop there, although I should perhaps add that in 1993 I became a U.S. citizen. So I am an American, as I said, but one with a heightened sense of what it is to be American.

So with the above proviso in mind, allow me to proceed with the matter at hand, i.e., Michael Murphy.

What is it to be American?

Well, it is many things, many grains of many matters. But if one were to sift through them much like the panhandler sifts for nuggets of pure gold, here is what one would find in the bottom of the basket:

"We hold these truths to be self-evident, that all men are created equal, that they are endowed by the Creator with certain inalienable Rights, that among these are Life, Liberty and the pursuit of Happiness." This, at least to me, is the very essence of the American character, something accepted as an axiom needing no proof.

All men are created equal. Be that your absolute bottom line, then your relationship to your fellow human beings is one of equanimity, respect, even brotherhood: you are above no one, nor are you below. Mike Murphy lives that truth.

All men are endowed by their Creator with certain inalienable rights. It really is of no consequence how you write that word—with a higher or lower case "C." What is of capital importance is that all of us are born with rights that cannot be taken from us. They are ours to no less an extent than the very blood that courses through our veins. And this is what not only gives us pride and self-respect and the natural ability to walk tall, but also to take pride in all others and to share the view, so powerfully expressed by John Donne that "No man is an island, entire of itself...therefor never send to know for whom the bell tolls; it tolls for thee." Mike Murphy lives that truth.

Life, Liberty and the pursuit of Happiness. In today's world there are not a few people who would condescendingly smile and say, "Oh, that's all very well, but it is naive, childish even to actually believe these are inalienable rights." That's a hard proposition to argue with. However, it is precisely that element of naiveness, that element of the child that makes Americans what they are: always curious, always asking "why?" and demanding a response, never doubting that anything and everything is possible, not taking "no" for an answer and respecting no authority except that of what is true and just. And that, too, describes Mike Murphy to a "T."

I could say much more—that he is a Renaissance man, that he is fun to be with, finally, and most importantly—at least for me—that he is my friend. The Russians say that to call someone a friend, you must have shared with that person one pood of salt—one pood being the old Russian equivalent of 16 kilos or about 35 lbs. Figure out how many years that's going to take.

Happy birthday, Michael!

# Moon Shots Are Us

JOSEPH MONTVILLE

How to do a brief memoir on a thirty year relationship with a person so central and critical to one's life? This could not be a routine birthday greeting. I struggled with writer's block for several months. Then in May, at the Kennedy Center Concert Hall, I found a hook to Esalen and Mike Murphy. Bay Area-based composer John Adams was in residence as a guest conductor of the National Symphony Orchestra. He was presenting his *Dharma at Big Sur*, inspired by Jack Kerouac, and his *Doctor Atomic Symphony*, on the centrality of Robert Oppenheimer's agonies as father of The Bomb. The program notes drew me in.

Adams was raised on the East Coast, went to Harvard, and responding to some call, moved to California in 1971. The Notes say, "His first experience of the Pacific coast—its dramatic cliff heights and thundering surf so unlike what he recalls as the 'generically picturesque coves and harbors' of his New England childhood proved to be an epiphany, imprinting the composer with a sense of new beginnings."

I was raised in New Jersey without memory of picturesque coves and harbors. After graduate work on the Middle East at Harvard, I went well further east to Cairo and cemented a life-long commitment to the politics and seemingly endless frustrations of traditional, official peace diplomacy. After diplomatic postings in the Middle East and North Africa, I fell in with a bunch of activist psychiatrists in the American Psychiatric Association who were fascinated by Egyptian President Anwar Sadat's claim that 70% of the Arab-Israeli conflict was psychological. I was in the Near East bureau at the State Department and then became chief of the Near East division in the bureau of intelligence and research (INR).

One day, in 1980, Jim Hickman came to see me in my INR office. He had heard about the psychiatrists and their dialogue work with Egyptians and Israelis and wondered if I would like to come to Esalen to talk about how psychology and peace making might be helpful to Mike and Dulce Murphy. They wanted help as they thought about the meaning and direction of their instinctive attraction to the Soviet Union which they had visited, and how they might help detoxify the U.S.-Soviet relationship. Naturally, my intellectual passion for healing wounded political relationships, and my carnal enthusiasm about soaking dreamlike in hot sulfur springs with California nymphs, helped me say yes immediately.

Thus began a relationship with Mike, Dulce and their many friends that opened up previously unimaginable opportunities to define and explore the uses of "track two," unofficial diplomacy to support and supplement, official, "track one," which is what I did. The "track two" term came to me at the first workshop in the Big House in September, 1980. It has since then taken on a widely recognized legitimacy in governments, universities and NGO's around the world. But in the beginning Mike invited me to do workshops at Esalen on the psychology of the U.S.-Soviet relationship. (In 1978, I had become a founding member of the International Society of Political Psychology.) At a minimum he might have thought it would be at least kinky to have an active duty State Department official with Top Secret and compartmented intelligence clearances working with him as he applied the insights he had discovered on human potential and the capacity for higher levels of learning and achievement.

Unlike the instant epiphany John Adams experienced on seeing the ocean at Big Sur, my epiphany under Mike's influence emerged more slowly. Adams was a genius. I was just a government worker. But Mike's charm, appearance of innocence, constant smile, taste for mischief, and grasp of the absurd in human relationships made the chance to work with him and Dulce every year at Esalen irresistible. I must have had a deep need to laugh hysterically because that's what I did with Mike whenever we were together.

A lot of it was gallows humor nourished in part by the memory of a mob-attack on the American consulate in Basra, Iraq, on June 5, 1967, where my wife, nine months pregnant, was alone at our home as the mob swirled around the compound. Luckily, our apartment was not entered, and she made it home to Paterson, NJ, where she delivered our daughter, Clea Aimee, thirty-six hours after landing at JFK. Iraq broke diplomatic relations with us, and I went on to Beirut for previously scheduled intensive Arabic language training at the U.S. embassy there. Lebanon was always tense, and I imagined the murmurs of mobs coming down the road that turned out to be the hum of air conditioners. I was there when Qadhafi and his revolution took over Libya in 1969, and in Morocco I witnessed two bloody—but unsuccessful—coup attempts against King Hassan II. Back in Washington, I saw Foreign Service colleagues killed in the Middle East and North Africa.

As I look back at the '80s, I realize that I had a real hunger for the release of laughter at the absurd that Mike was always ready to prompt. He also early on embraced the hope, some thought delusional, that track two and other forms of citizen diplomacy could head off nuclear war with the Soviets. And he gave me that chance to recruit Erik Erikson, my psychoanalytic hero, and his wife Joan who became the centerpiece of our annual workshops at Esalen on the psychology of the U.S.-Soviet relationship.

After the Murphys had brought Boris Yeltsin to the U.S. in 1989, for his first visit, which inspired him to go back to Moscow, take over the government, cripple the Communist Party and ultimately dissolve the Soviet Union—how's that for a trip report!—Dulce and I led a small team to Moscow for the first international conference at the new Gorbachev Foundation in 1992. I couldn't resist the chance to ask Gorbachev if he had a wire in the Big House during our Erikson workshops. One of our hottest subjects was "the psychology of enmity," and the phrase started popping up in the speeches of Gorbachev and other high officials. ("We know about this psychology and we will not play the role of your enemy.") Gorbachev just smiled and gestured with his finger toward the ceiling, the classic signal, "Can't talk now. Someone is listening."

Well before the 9/11 attacks on New York and Washington, Mike and I started talking about the challenges of religious fundamentalism and what we could do about it.

In 2004, we started with a workshop on Hindu fundamentalism that Jeff Kripal organized and I facilitated. After that Mike asked me to do Muslim, Christian and Jewish fundamentalism workshops at Esalen starting in 2005. In 2007, we did a strategic planning workshop on Muslim-Christian-Jewish fundamentalism that resulted in a grant from the Fetzer Institute to establish the Abrahamic Family Reunion (AFR) project that worked with seminaries and religious studies programs and interfaith NGO's in the Bay Area, LA, Washington, New York and Boston. There are detailed, edited proceedings from these workshops on the Esalen Center for Theory and Research web site—esalenctr.org—that I think are the deepest, and most enlightening texts that exist in print, virtual and otherwise. We have had follow-up AFR workshops with activists from the Bay Area and LA through 2010, and we will continue through 2011. We have a biweekly AFR Newsletter and a rich Web site, *abrahamicfamilyreunion.org* that is consulted internationally.

Mike Murphy thinks in terms of "moon shots." No small gestures for him. He wanted one for the work with the Soviet Union, and got it. He wanted one for the Muslim-Christian-Jewish fundamentalism problem. And he got one. Now he is going after the U.S.-China relationship. It's early, but the team of mainland and U.S.-based Chinese is inspired. They are preparing their own moon shot. They are solidifying the human connections between us and them. They are exploring all the nooks and crannies of our relationship.

And they stop to laugh, sometimes hysterically—as they go about their work.

Mike Murphy opened a whole new world of action and creativity for me to explore the deep dimensions of human relationships and the potential for healing history. I can't imagine any one else who could have done that. No subject has been beyond the pale. No passion or aspiration has been a bridge too far. As long as it was fun—and fundable—we could do it.

*Moon shots are us.*

We are planning for the next ten to fifteen years.

Happy birthday, brother.

My affection for and gratitude to you are infinite—and beyond.

# Putting It to Use

*Lessons from Michael Murphy and Friends*

LIZBETH HASSE

Davlat Khoudonozarov, whose friendship Michael and Dulce Murphy and I share, called on his way from Toronto to Detroit, "Liz, I think my life is now to be a grandfather." He had spent the week before playing with his 3-year old grandson in Berkeley, California and now he was off to his sister's grandchildren in Detroit. Davlat lives in Moscow, with his wife Gavhar, in exile from his homeland Tajikistan. It is no accident that Davlat described his life in terms of a relationship.

"One life at a time," Davlat was saying, "This is how mine is now." He spoke with an unembarrassed consciousness of his own peculiar history. He didn't sound unhappy. "Please be sure we are all at Esalen in October. Let Dulce and Michael know I will be there." The physical presence, being together in the same place, especially in that inspirational place, was important to him.

In many ways, Davlat is an exemplar of those who come to feel connected with Michael at and through his Esalen homestead. The two men and the unique place in Big Sur share the qualities of "charisma" and "connectivity," a combination that gives form and promise to human potential. Davlat was anticipating Big Sur days and nights at the Russian-American Partnerships Conference, a time to reconnect, reflect, recharge and expand, an intimate moment bringing together the thoughts and far-flung experiences of those who would dine and talk in the same room, soak in steaming outdoor tubs and walk under the same piece of open starry sky. There would definitely be an experience. The kinds of connections that Michael and Davlat have with each other and have developed through Esalen are essential to the creation and on-going creativity of that experience.

The life Davlat brings with him to Esalen has bittersweet historical significance. Having first met him in 1989, I know some of that history personally. Davlat was then in Moscow, a People's Deputy from Tajikistan to the USSR Congress, one of a group of its progressive members whose concerns focused on health, ecology and democratic processes. At the time, each of these humanistic concerns was a delicate flower needing attention, sensitivity and devotion to survive the rumble of changes in the vast shifting geopolitik of the Soviet Union. *Perestroika* (restructuring) was a positive and hopeful word for Davlat and he was clearly among its builders and optimists; but for him, *perestroika* could only be change within a balance, change that preserved a connection with the ground one walks on, a reverence for the small things in daily life. For him, it should preserve the music one's parents danced to in the Pamir mountain village of his youth, the sequence in which they cooked the rice, mutton and vegetables in their *plov* and the precise way in which they offered and spooned it out for visitors. Davlat was only one among many of the architects and pioneers of *Perestroika*, its pre-history and aftermath, invited by Michael and Dulce to the Esalen experience.

Davlat's first career was as a filmmaker of small stories in vast places, of mothers and daughters, sons and fathers, strong on their horses, vulnerable on their feet, independent in spirit and more human than any government that might endeavor to reorder their ways. His *Murmur of a Brook in Melting Snow* is one of a trilogy of tender and brave films, shot in the Roof of the World, the mountainous area in the Gorno-Badakhshan of Tajikistan's western Pamir range where he was born.

Artists were recognized as some of the freer minds of the USSR. With *glasnost* (openness), of which ultimately there seemed to be more than its companion *perestroika*, people looked to their artists and writers for independent guidance as they gave up on politics as usual and sought leaders untainted by power positions in the old state structures. And they also looked outside of the Moscow establishment. Soon this man of Badakhshan would have to give up the richly visual film medium he loved as he was pressed into larger and larger roles for his communities, first as a People's deputy, then in 1989 as the first non-Muscovite head of the USSR filmmaker's Union. Raised in the smallest of the Soviet republics and the furthest from the Soviet capital, he became a symbol for all those artists from outside the center of the state, from the many cultural regions of the USSR, that they were becoming recognized and could have some influence in this changing empire.

Davlat's Badakhshan is the high remote region that contains both southern Tajikistan and the mountainous north of Afghanistan, its immediate neighbor to the south. 1989 was also the year the Soviets ended their debilitating and aimless ten-year war with its Afghan neighbor. At this very time, Michael Murphy and Esalen's Soviet-American Exchange center were launching a Post-traumatic Stress Disorder project engaging American and Soviet specialists, an example of Esalen's experiential, humanist activism. They were bringing a group of Soviet Afghanistan War veterans to participate in an exchange of healing practices, trying to close gaps between traditional psychiatry and spirituality, seeking through expanding states of consciousness and shared experience to transcend resistant and disconnecting memories of physical and emotional pain and fear. Of those Afghan War veterans, some of Davlat's countrymen who served in the army of Soviet occupiers were especially affected. They shared surnames with those they'd fought and killed on the other side of the Panj river that ran along Tajikistan's southern border and right through Davlat's family village of Khorog, 3800 meters above sea level, a border of recent history and of someone else's making.

1989 was also the year that I first met Davlat. An optimistic lawyer from Berkeley, California, I was helping Davlat's predecessor at the Union of Filmmakers in his complicated efforts to find a reliable model for distributing Russian films into the channels of American entertainment commerce. Davlat and I sat over lunch in the Moscow filmmakers Union building, my 100 words of Russian matched by his equivalent English vocabulary, and we talked for hours, about the small things and the universal, about music and stories, about hope and freedoms, about dance and food, about films and beauty, about friendship and healing, about travel and borders. When we didn't have the words, we made them up. Something deeper than logos connected us and others in this exciting place. Excitement and tension were breathing in Moscow, invigorating the city; but also breathing down the necks of some at high and at low levels. Davlat expressed a humane sensitivity that embraced them all. Political change held out promises and unknowns. We wondered aloud, as did many, whether the new politics and the offices that progressives were assuming would lead to a new and better human condition. Many had high hopes. *Perestroika* presented an opportunity for what Michael Murphy might call "a new revolutionary adventure," for new kinds of relationships within and across borders and for creative syntheses in human and community interactions. People like Michael, Dulce, Davlat, and others (from Gennady Alferenko to Bill Walsh, from Glen Albaugh, Harriet Crosby and Jim Hickman to Abel Aganbegyan, Sergei Kapitsa and Joseph Goldin) who would come to engage in a Soviet-American encounter, through Esalen, were acting in accord with high aspirations they held for the human capacity. The making of friendships from previously forbidden relationships and the potential for new thoughts and insight that came with them was becoming Esalen's form of diplomatic strategy.

That day in Moscow, Davlat talked about "civil society." The two words together were full of meaning and promise to him; life breathed into them. A different politics could be a way of revitalizing public life and engaging the disenfranchised. In "civil society" and "society civil," the human element would be unlocked and re-enter the public realm. Relationships would be experienced, acknowledged, strengthened. The human components in them celebrated and nurtured. With genuine participation, something vital would find itself and would grow. The intimate within the vast would survive and create the human stories that define the larger meaning of living and responsive society.

Soviet politics in practice had come over years to demonstrate quite a different process and was now disintegrating. The political structure had certainly valued connections and relationships—but as the twentieth century marched on they looked more and more like values that required large statist manifestations of power and cohesion. Other kinds of connections and relationships had been stunted. There was an admission writ large that a political theory had failed. *Logos* and *mythos* had become unhinged. The *com*munity in *com*munism had suffered. The trade-offs to the state had not worked. But now in the disintegration of an old and failing monolith, the gasping body politic, there was a palpable feeling in Moscow that something healthy was emerging, something repressed was being restored, oxygen was refilling the lungs. Living human connections could replace the abstractions of the old politics.

Michael Murphy was very busy replacing disembodied abstractions with humanistic connections. 1989 was also the year that Michael and Dulce organized a celebration of the fiftieth anniversary of the publication of *The Grapes of Wrath* at both the USSR Union of Writers in Moscow and in Salinas, California with Soviet writers they brought to the native land shared by Steinbeck, Dulce and Michael. Like Michael, the Steinbeck celebrated by these Russian readers and writers, was truly a citizen diplomat. Steinbeck traveled to Russia after World War II with the aim of discovering the private lives of the Russian people. His *Russian Journal*, published in 1948 is a work of "honest reporting," his effort to set down what he and his travel companion photographer Robert Capa saw and heard, without editorial comment, without drawing conclusions, "about things we didn't know sufficiently." The *Russian Journal* is a work of empathy and humanity. Steinbeck's 1947 post-war trip became forty days of "witnessing reality." Capa and Steinbeck found themselves at the beginning of "a newly invented war" named the Cold War. No one knew where the battlefields were. As Capa said, "The Cold war gave him the same shivers it gave me.... We became a cold war team." Capa goes on with what could be the words of Michael Murphy, "It seemed to us that behind phrases like 'Iron curtain,' 'Cold war' and 'preventative war,' people and thought and humour fully disappeared. We decided to make an old-fashioned Don Quixote and Sancho Panza quest—to ride behind the 'iron curtain' and pit our lances and pens against the windmills of today."

Some people said Steinbeck must have been manipulated, that the Soviets surely showed him and Capa their Potemkin villages. He countered, "If someone came to your country, for the first time, wouldn't you receive them with the best you could offer?" He told a story of several men arguing over which one of them would invite the pair to dinner, the farmer with the largest table, the one whose wife had baked bread that morning, the one whose new house was just completed. Everyone brought what food they had to share with their American guests to the new house for the dinner.

Steinbeck was trying to re-open his own eyes at a time when he was unhappy in marriage, struggling with an unfinished play, admitting to feeling too much like a "gray and grizzled animal" and too far from experiencing through writing that "glory that shadows everything else." On this post war trip to the USSR, it was anthropological detail that invigorated Steinbeck. He wrote of the ugly detail of finding "an expanse of ruin" in Stalingrad: "Our windows looked out over acres of rubble, broken brick and concrete and pulverized plaster, and in the wreckage, the dark weeds that always seem to grow in destroyed places." There, fitting in with the terrain was "a little hummock like the entrance to a gopher hole. And every morning, early, out of the hole, a young girl crawled." Wherever he looked he marveled at what human beings could do, what they could endure and rise above.

The two men avoid abstraction, generalization and analysis in their Russian trip. There is no ideological obsessiveness in the writing or the photos. Their truth comes in the details, the small jokes, the gestures of a child, in the *experience* of those details. This is the same mixture of empathetic and documentary anthropological detail Steinbeck gives his stories of California, his homeland (that of Dulce and Michael, too), that attracted his avid Russian readers: "Listen to the motor. Listen to the wheels. Listen with your ears and with your hands on the steering wheel; listen with the palm of your hand on the gear-shift lever; listen with your feet on the floor boards. Listen to the pounding old jalopy with all your senses, for a change of tone, a variation of rhythm may mean—a week here?" There is a heightened reality in the movement of the sound of the words, the rhythmic repetition; the reader is there in hopes and anxiety with the Joads and others who spent their savings and dreams on a broken used car.

Fifty years after *Grapes of Wrath*, Dulce and Michael bring the experience of California to the Russian lovers of Steinbeck's works. Just as artists and writers were sought out as independent leaders within the opening Soviet society, Esalen found them to be valuable partners in an experiential co-evolution. The visiting Russians come to see and feel again, differently and the same, the California some had "fused" with when they first engaged in a private transformative experience of reading John Steinbeck:

"A few miles south of the Soledad, the Salinas River drops in close to the hillside bank and runs deep and green. The water is warm too: For it has slipped twinkling in the yellow sands before reaching the narrow pool...."

1989 is also the year that Michael and Dulce, through Esalen, host Boris Yeltsin (then, like Davlat, a People's Deputy to the Supreme Soviet) on his first trip to the United States. The trip is Yeltsin's introduction to an everyday experience of living with capitalism and, according to many, the seed of his political transformation. This time the transformation is described as taking place in a Texas supermarket where, in the company of Dulce Murphy, Yeltsin is astonished to see that ordinary US citizens have a choice of tens of thousands of food items readily available for purchase. "Are there many stores like this?" he asks, also wondering whether he's getting a Potemkin-like display. The press reports Yeltsin's anger that many of the facts of American life had been previously concealed from him by the "Iron Curtain," facts which would soon contribute to his break with the Soviet Communist party.

Not long after becoming chair of the filmmakers union, Davlat Khoudonozarov had his first encounter with Michael Murphy. He remembers their initial meeting as follows. "It was September 1990 and I came to San Francisco after a glorious time of cultural celebration at the Telluride Film Festival." He had been invited by Tom Luddy to bring his *First Spring Of Youth*, one of Davlat's 46 films, to the Festival in Colorado where he glowed with pleasure in identifying the rugged altitudes of the American western terrain with those of his Tajik homeland. "I was at a party at a home [this writer's] where many people excited about *perestroika* were talking about their experiences with the new and old Soviet Union. Michael and Dulce had a unique history of going there initially to work with Soviet psychologists and to open their eyes to a humanistic aspect of psychological thought and experience. Michael knew little of Tajikistan but he was very happy to hear I was from the Pamirs which he understood to be the north-north part of India, the country which gave real and imagined location to Michael's early transformation. The Pamirs lie in the land of Badahkshan, the territory influenced one thousand years ago by the philosopher and poet Nasir Khusraw, a teacher familiar to Michael as well as myself. We found a quiet place to meditate for about an hour and after that drank glasses of red wine together for the first time."

Davlat remembers experiencing a special connection with Michael, something opening up and something shared. The circumstance of that connection could be described in the words of the Badahkstan poet:

> *Whatever kind of knowledge I heard of*
> *I sat adjacent to its door (to acquire it).*
> *Not any kind of knowledge was left*
> *Of which I did not benefit more or less.*

—Nasir Khusraw, *Divan*, 25:24-25

Those words describe a situation, a way in which opportunities, ideas present themselves to a thoughtful, open traveler or engaged, inquiring reader. Michael and Davlat knew to make use of that situation, to exploit its potential, bringing their humanity and expectations to it, to expand themselves and, consequently (potentially), the experience and intelligence of those around them.

"Greater Badahkshan": it is the high and wide region where the mountains of the Pamir and the Hindu Kush face each other. This territory, taking in parts of India, Pakistan, Tajikistan, and Afghanistan, encompassed geographic and internal space for Davlat and Michael, a place of exploration, homeland, inspiration and spiritual growth. Nasir Khusraw, the poet of that place, gave them their connection. Someone who knew something about Nasir Khusraw, his travels and his intellectual and spiritual search, could say that in the moment of their encounter, each of them, Michael and Davlat, was an embodiment of Nasir Khusraw.

A thousand years ago, a Persian poet challenged the dominant religious conventions of his time. His name was Nasir Khusraw, and Ismaili Muslims celebrate him as their poet and founder. His literary work is different from that of many writers and poets of his time. Instead of heaping praises on a prince-benefactor, on the grandeur of the sultan's household or his horse, Nasir Khusraw wrote of the relation of learning, transformation and excellence or advancement.

> *The world is a deep ocean*
> *Its water is time.*
> *Your body is like a shell,*
> *Your soul the pearl.*
> *If you wish to have the value of a pearl,*
> *Raise up the pearl of your soul with learning.*
>
> *— Divan, 145: 47-49*

Nasir Khusraw was born in Balkh, one of the oldest recorded cities in the world, and not far from Davlat's birthplace. Balkh lies in the southern foothills of the Pamir mountains just south of the Oxus

River where present-day Afghanistan, Tajikistan and Uzbekistan come together. Traditionally the center of Zoroastrianism, Balkh is known as the place where Zoroaster first preached and where he died. Balkh's beautiful Zoroastrian temple, a shrine to Anahita, was considered an extravagant attraction for both truth-seekers and plunderers. Balkh was a site of Persian cultural renaissance and a point on the Old Silk Route where communities of various religions and ethnicities mixed. In the 10th century, Buddhist monasteries were active here; Sanskrit pharmaceutical texts were being revised and translated into Arabic and Persian; this was a lively educational center and a number of poets who developed Persian language and literature originated here. Born at the turn of the 10th and 11th centuries, Nasir Khusraw would have witnessed Buddhist, Sunni, Shi'a, Christian and Jewish people living in shared territory, sometimes relatively calmly, other times surviving by converting to the dominant religion, which at Nasir's time was becoming Islam. Two hundred years after Nasir, Genghis Khan would sack his birthplace and then another century later, Timur would do the same.

Like Davlat and Michael, Nasir Khusraw was a great traveler; he is famous for writing a travelogue, *Safarnama*, during the seven years that he visited ten great cities and many places in between: Akhlet (Armenia), Aleppo, Tripoli, Beirut, Tyre, Jerusalem, Cairo, Medina, Mecca, Basra and Isfahan. He is also famous for having sought out a variety of religions, comparing them and appreciating their differences and, at deeper levels, their essential similarities. Khusraw keeps accounts in his two important texts—the *Safarnama* and the *Divan*—that record the strange, beautiful and wondrous things he sees and learns about human achievement as he meets different people in different places. His writing is remarkable for its reflection of a scholar's open-mind, at once spiritual and intellectual. Some say it was in the multi-cultural percolations of his birthplace, enriched by the experiences of his travels, that he developed his ideas about engaging the intellect at once in spiritual and material life and about resisting dogma to achieve a potential that makes the most of the gifts humans have received:

*What did God give us alone of all the other creatures?*
*The intellect, by which we lord o'er all the beasts.*
*But note, that virtue and intellect which make us lords of*
*donkeys,*
*Are the very same traits which bind us as slaves of the Lord.*
*With intellect, we can seek out all the hows and whys,*

*Without it, we are but trees without fruit.*

*— Divan, 7:179-180*

Seek with that intellect, strive to know more and to be more, trees *with* fruit. Yes, we are above the donkeys, but if we don't make the most of what we've been given we can also fall into dogma and abstraction that make us slaves to a religion. There are those who fail to make use of their intellectual and sensory capacities:

*...They have hearts, but understand not with them; They have*
*eyes, but perceive not with them; They have ears, but they hear not*
*with them. They are like*

*Cattle; nay rather they are further astray.*

*Those, they are the heedless.*

*— Divan, 7:179-180*

Nasir Khusraw was always disappointed with the example of those who did not make the most of their gifts on earth, of the potential that was their special endowment as human beings. Physical knowledge and engagement with the world through the *external* senses could enable spiritual growth and perfection of the internal senses, described by Nasir as conjecture, thought, imagination, memory and recollection. The attainment of knowledge comes from the mediation of the internal capacities with the external, through activation of the senses in the world. Use the things of this world; don't waste opportunities to do so:

*This world is your bazaar; search for all your needs; Do not return
from the bazaar empty-handed. For if you fall ill and cannot leave
your bed,*

*You shall never find your way to the bazaar again.*

— *Divan, 180:51-52*

In Badakhshan, as in Moscow and California, at the time of Michael and Davlat's Khusraw-inspired encounter, *perestroika* and *glasnost* were lively words. They spoke of a new kind of engagement, a potential for different relationships within Russia and between Russians and others. How could the most be made of that potential, and what might it lead to?

The old-guard power in Tajikistan was at the time jealously held by the Communist Party in control in the flatlands of the northern Leninabad district. Promises of *perestroika* and *glasnost* that encouraged people from other regions of Tajikistan to demand participation were a threat to the established politique. In early 1989, tensions in the capital city of Dushambe between those who expected something different and those protecting the status quo led to hunger strikes and street fights. Davlat is known for his solo intervention, for walking between the warring sides, securing concessions from all and negotiating an end to violent confrontation on the spot. Soon a new "Democratic Party" was merging in an alliance, based primarily in the intellectually and culturally rich area of Badakhshan, between the "Popular Front" (Rastokhez) and the "Islamic Renaissance Party", a moderate group that had not as yet advocated Sharia law. Months later, these "Democrats" decided to challenge the monopolistic hold of the northern communists with their opposition presidential candidate. He was Davlat Khudonazarov, popular film-maker, People's deputy, and son of the former mayor of Dushambe, born in Gorno-Badakhshan's roof of the world.

Thus, a year after that first meeting with Michael, Davlat was traveling the Tajikistan countryside campaigning for president. His was an educational and grass-roots campaign with roadside visits in villages and collective farms, factory yard speeches at textile plants and stone quarries. Traveling with his group of supporters was the head of the democracy movement "party," a Tajik philosophy professor Shodman Yusuf. People ask why they are voting; why the candidates are not choosing the president from among them. Davlat explains that each candidate represents a different political party; they are not members of a politburo. One older cotton farmer asks: "Is it easier to solve people's economic problems or to make films?" Davlat responds that the economic problems are harder and demand more creativity, but that he has always thought of his films as tackling human problems, the ones on the surface, and the deeper ones.

Knowledge and action. Davlat is seeking a balance. His campaign is truly a think tank in civil society. Each step of the campaign through the Tajik countryside is like a step in a pilgrimage, as Khusraw describes it; it must be taken with knowledge of the significance of the journey. Performing acts without *batin*, without the knowledge of their internal meaning is "the lot of the animals." On the other hand, "knowledge without action," Khusraw writes, "is the lot of angels." Knowledge and action are the lot of humans, for they correspond to animals by virtue of their bodies; but by virtue of their knowledge, they are in that aspect the equivalent of angels. (*Wahji-din*, 75). The human animal as a transitional being, as Michael would describe it, always with the capacity to transcend its current level of existence. Khusraw says that the human task is a middle road between the animals and the angels, but the one that has the task and the potential to attain the most in its combination of knowledge and action, *batin* and *zahir*. The combination allows for enlightenment, best defined in Khusraw as wise improvement:

> If you would light a lamp within your heart, make knowledge and action your wick and oil.
>
> — *Divan*, 78:16

Davlat lost the presidential election that year, beaten by the incumbent CP candidate in what observers described as a corrupted election, ballots in gutters and ballot boxes stuffed or missing. Still Davlat Khoudonozarov's score of 35% of the counted votes would put pressure on the government to open the country to a multi-party system. Initially, however, the aftermath of the election was civil war among a dissatisfied population, not the "civil society" Davlat had dreamed about. Was Davlat discouraged or angry? "The first lesson of democracy," he responded, "is to *know how* to lose and to prepare for a long evolution. We are only trying to calm the people now, to calm their souls." Khusraw might have provided some guidance: "Peace of mind from the torment of ignorance comes from knowledge." (*Divan, 25:26*).

The civil war was linked in no small way to the residue of the Soviet effort to craft national identity out of the regional differences, to the disconnect created by the imposition of ideology on the daily life diversities endemic in this mountainous territory. Traditional ways had been violently repressed by Stalin. Islam was outlawed; the Arabic, Latin and other regional alphabets and languages were replaced by Cyrillic characters and a bureaucratically-styled Russian; nomads were forced into collective farms; collective farms were given industrial plans to produce single crops; unremitting cultivation of single crops, cotton especially, left the soil worthless; eroded industrial farming areas could no longer sustain plant growth; children manifested congenital conditions from over-exposure to agro-chemicals; dams which changed the direction of rivers destroyed homes and communities. All this sounds bad and brutal, but at the same time, under the Soviet system, access to health care had improved geometrically, illiteracy had been eliminated, transportation and electrical infrastructure were developed. Now, in the post-Soviet period, as the imposed structure collapsed, all was becoming unstable. The bad remained bad, and the good crumbled. The center didn't hold.

Nasir Khusraw would have said that first effort should be to apply reason to action, to be calm, try as Davlat was doing to calm their souls, the inner, *batin*. But the effort didn't work for Davlat at the time. Like Khusraw among the Sunnis and Shi'i, Davlat had no choice but to flee from his homeland. Many who had supported him in Tajikistan were attacked or assassinated; his life and the lives of his relatives were threatened. Ultimately, he was exiled, first granted asylum in the US as a "distinguished artist;" later in Moscow where he and Gawahr continue today to attend to the needs of other Tajiks in exile from their homeland, the migrant workers alienated or lost in urban Russia.

Exile takes shape in the words of Nasir Khusraw who, for all his attempts to engage actively with the world, ultimately flees from dogmatists who saw his Ismaili teaching as heretical. Khusraw sought refuge in mountainous Badakhshan (ironically the home that Davlat is forced to leave) where a learned prince who appreciates his art and spirituality takes him in. Sometimes Khusraw felt angry that he had been forced from his life of travel and engagement:

> *The scorpion of exile has stung my heart so, that you would say heaven invented suffering just for me.*
>
> *— Divan 6:1*

He blames those with closed minds and false religions; those who attack him are dogmatic leaders of simplistic vision who are intolerant of other sects: *By day you fast and moan and finger your rosary...You've memorized the texts of deception quite smoothly, so now you're grand Mufti of Balkh, Nishapur and Herat.... By your words, you are full of knowledge and wisdom, but by your actions, fiercely hypocritical....when you do not do as you say* [when your spirituality does not connect knowledge and action; when spirituality is not stabilized in practice], *everything you say comes out as lies and fraud. (Divan, 11, 1-6)* Khusraw found refuge, not only with the wise prince of Yumgam in Badakhshan, but also in his intellect. He had taken things from the bazaar of the world throughout his life and has a store to draw on. His intellect, engaging the worldly and spiritual is his primary tool for raising questions and reaching new thoughts and truths.

> *Why is the vicious wolf not condemned before god for his acts while we are held responsible for ours? Why with its mean cawing and crowing is the crane not held in contempt, but we are?*

He is always asking: what is it to be human? By challenging dogma (a precursor to the Religion of No-Religion) and insisting on the high value of combining intellect with action in the world, of mastering action with knowledge, Khusraw confirms an elevated place for purposeful human action:

> *If you wish to dwell in a meadow of mercy and blessing, Graze on knowledge and action today. Moisten the seed of action with knowledge, For the seed will not grow without moisture.*

> — Divan 130, 20-1

The next time Davlat and Michael meet is ten years after Davlat's exile began. They are in Michael's homeland, the remarkable place of his youth, now Esalen, with its gorgeous coastline, its butterflies and eucalyptus, its fecund gardens and, like Davlat's home village of Khorog (also at the edge of a world), its natural hot mineral baths. There is something alive in the energy of the baths on the cliffs. They bring a deep heat to the surface connecting an unseen world to that exposed to the elements, as Khusraw would say, the *batin* with the *zahir*. They are also something shared, the geothermal energy of the earth—renewable and available.

It is mid-September 2001 and Davlat's little homeland of Tajikistan is suddenly at the center of the world. The southern border of Tajikistan is the northern part of what the world outside of Afghanistan is learning to call the *Northern Alliance* (or UIF), a group of Tajiks, Uzbeks, Hazara and Turkmen united in their fight against the Taliban. Americans are learning the names of Ahmed Shah Massoud, Abdul Rashid Dostum, Mohammed Fahim, Ismail Khan, and Karim Khalily. The Northern Alliance is the group friendly to Europeans and the USA. A large proportion of those in the Northern Alliance are Tajiks from Badhakshan. A day after the 9/11 attacks, US investigators have found out that Ahmed Shah Massoud had died on September 9, the victim of an attack by Al-Qaeda posing as Saudis. The Tajik general Mohammed Fahim, Massoud's second in command, would succeed Massoud almost immediately and begin to cooperate with the US in its initial attacks on Taliban strongholds in Afghanistan and in its hunt for Osama Bin Ladin.

Michael and Dulce responded to the tragedy of September 11, 2001 by doing what they do best; they invited their Russian friends and others in Track 2, including Jay Ogilvy, Victor Erofeyev, Sergei Kapitsa, Davlat and Gavhar to Esalen to talk and think, to expand the vocabulary and their minds. The meeting was given a name: The World As We Know It has Changed. On the first evening, Davlat told those who had just assembled about how it had not changed. He talked of tribes— the Tajiks, Hazara, Uzbeks, Kulyabis, Shughnis, Wakhis, Mangal, Durrani, Ghilzai and Pashtuns—of their movements, relationships, dynamics. This is a region of unrelenting upheavals, invasions, conquests, civil war, migration, absorption, conflict. Davlat pointed out that some scholars say the Pashtuns are the descendants of one of the twelve tribes of Israel, the tribe of Joseph, *Yusuf Zai*. Davlat also talked about the origins of Ismaili.

While the religion of the vast majority of Tajikistan's population today is Sunni Islam, the majority of those in the Badakhshan Pamirs, home of the Northern Alliance, profess the Ismaili faith, with the openness that their connection with Nasir Khusraw suggests. Davlat tells the group a story about the Pamiris who were converted to Ismailism in the 11th century by this educated Persian philosopher who had first looked at lots of different religions and had visited different philosophy schools all over Central Asia and the Middle East. Khusraw had a spiritual awakening that is sometimes described as a moment of exquisite clarity in a dream. He sees someone who tells him to seek out that which increases his potential as a human being. The teacher's instruction in the dream is three-fold: attend to the clarity of your senses; seek to increase your wisdom and reason; and guide others to that reason. The dream leads Khusraw to the Ismaili because that faith always requires a living person to help interpret the teachings. An interpreter with knowledge in the world, a hermeneuticist who connects the internal with the external, one who helps to coax out internal meaning in purposeful action.

Davlat is speaking to a jet-lagged group; they are nodding off to slides of old maps with shifting borders and to the sounds of tribal names and ancient places. Some are in a semi-dreamlike state, connecting the mysterious words through a grainy haze to an interior space between imagination and experience. At this hour, talk is too dry. Moisture is needed:

> *Moisten the seed of action with knowledge,*
> *For the seed will not grow without moisture...*

Michael and Davlat's next move is prefigured by Nasir Khusraw in his travels through Tiberias. Always looking for the wondrous in human ingenuity, Nasir saw that the people in Tiberias built a bathhouse over a spring with "water so hot that until it is mixed with cold water you cannot stand it....I went inside to try it out." Nasir was impressed with the creativity of the human mind that harnesses the energy of the earth, so hot it is dangerous, and makes of it a cleansing, social environment. Davlat and Michael and the rest of the sleepy group retreat to the Esalen baths, another triumph of nature and culture, where they are able to partake in a moist experience of human ingenuity and to feel individually, and together, an expansion of the connected body and mind into the open starry sky above.

The next gathering, the one Davlat insisted he would not miss, is scheduled for October 2010. It will follow upon a harsh season of financial discomfort, militant posturing and the very visible catastrophe of the Gulf of Mexico oil spill: species dying; large swathes of the earth suffocating under oil; a spreading slick depriving the ocean and its marine life of oxygen. Some efforts to contain it have limited effect, some fail. A thousand years ago, Nasir Khusraw told a relevant story about a different emergency: in Basra, a whirlpool had developed at the mouth of one of the river channels making it impossible for boats to navigate. A solution was proposed by a wealthy woman who ordered that 400 of her boats be filled with date pits. They were then sealed shut and sunk into the whirlpool which calmed, restoring free passage for the boats on the surface above.

By October 2010, will the *Deepwater Horizon* well have been stuffed with date pits and other garbage? Or will some other solution have been borne of the human mind in action, under pressure of catastrophe, with its special potential, between that of the angels and the animals, to combine knowledge and action, to imagine a solution and to implement it. Disasters like *Deepwater Horizon* remind us just how stressed the globe has become, shrinking with the increase in populations and the detritus so many people can produce. Sometimes boat loads of date pits work. Other times we try military intervention, social sanctions, threats of isolation or financial boycotts to solve large scale problems. The proposed solutions are a lot like the problems and don't often work. They tend to replicate the catastrophes. And as the world shrinks it will become more and more apparent that these old mechanisms don't work. It is hard to imagine that the problems of poverty, disease, racism, starvation and ecological degradation will be addressed without transformative thinking and newly inspired action. Is such a thing possible in a world that values consumption, power, the growth of GNP? The old paradigms are particularly unhelpful in a shrinking world with its over-burdened ecology. We must instead be able to see the value of cooperation, of connection and of peaceful coexistence to survival in this world.

Vaclav Havel, who truly sees the value of transformative practice in the world at large, has spoken with urgency: "Without a global revolution in the sphere of human consciousness, nothing will change for the better in the sphere of our being as humans, and the catastrophe toward which this world is headed—be it ecological, social, demographic, or a general breakdown of civilization—will be unavoidable." He is very serious about the need to put away constricting ideologies and find spiritual intelligence through reverence and appreciation for what different people have to offer. He sees the critical importance of a paradigm change: "The meaningful task of the next [this] century is to be the best it can possibly be—that is, to revivify its best spiritual and intellectual traditions and thus help to create a new global pattern of coexistence."

Michael Murphy knows such improvement and new patterns are humanly available, that the human being is a transitional animal, that we are capable of developing our many human abilities to a far greater extent than we have. In the small world of ours, this will require an emphasis on empathy, synergy, being with the other and expanding through that connection. It will also require engaging the human capacity for improvement in new integral practices that will implement the emphases on empathy, synergy, sharing, and being with the other in real public social life.

> *Whatever kind of knowledge I heard of*
> *I sat adjacent to its door (to acquire it).*
> *Not any kind of knowledge was left*
> *Of which I did not benefit more or less.*

Nasir's situation really only captures the first two parts of the three-fold process his dream-teacher instructed. "Attend to the clarity of your senses; seek to increase your wisdom and reason; and guide others to that reason" implies more. Michael knows we can go a lot further with the opening up of our imaginations, that we have the capacity to "improve our lives, the lives of those around us, and the whole wide world by exploring our hidden potentials" and embodying them, by applying what we learn in that exploration to social action.

He provides thought, tools, encouragement, people, a place for co-existence, moisture and a persistent appreciation of the critical importance of not letting the human potential go unused. And that's important. At the opening of the 21st century, it's planetary survival.

[Quotations from the *Divan* are from the translation by Alice C. Hunsberger available in her comprehensive book on the poetry and philosophy of Nasir Khusraw: *Nasir Khrsaw, the Ruby of Badakhshan* (I. B. Tauris & Company 2000); those from the *Safarnama* are from Wheeler Thackston's *Naser-e Khosraw's Book of Travels* (Albany, NY 1986) as quoted by Hunsberger.]

# Adventures in
# the Paranormal

# Michael Murphy and the Extraordinary in Human Life and Experience

ELABORATED WITH FONDNESS BY HIS FRIEND:
STU KAUFFMAN (AT 70!)

It's his smile, you see. Radiant, penetrating each of us, the room, out to beyond the reaches of Esalen. Maybe it's because he is Irish. Maybe it's because he fits his skin with ease and grace, but the smile just captivates us all.

Then there is all that this Murphy fellow knows. About so many things, and always willing to share, eager to learn. I know. Thanks to the man with the smile, I have had the fun and joy and learning and exploring of 7 (Seven) meetings at Esalen among philosophers, biologists, business people, psychologists, exploring different aspects of biological and human evolution, emergence in the face of the long history of pure reductionism, trans-expected human experiences, the extraordinary in our human lives.

Michael was at every meeting and his questions, talks and issues were on target virtually all the time. I think this is unexpected given the golf book, his obvious passion and expertise.

More, I have personally, myself, experienced the human extraordinary at Esalen, whence invited by Der Murphy. Seated, I was, right alongside Richard Bakerroshi. "I bend spoons," he offered. "Oh yeah," say I. "Easy," from my Buddhist friend. "Don't concentrate on it, hang the spoon at your side where you can feel it and rub lightly on the top of the spoon where it starts to bend down. It gets all soft and bends." "Yeah," say I.

"How much," I add, a bit obviously. "360," silence.

OK. I get a spoon, sit next to Richard, don't look, hang it at my side, rub gently, (doctor's touch you see), the spoon gets a bit soft and rubbery and....bends. It bends 70 degrees. No more, no less. I'm not a Buddhist, I guess. Extraordinary? I think maybe? Unexpected? Yes. Ever repeated with other spoons, Esalen or elsewhere? Never.

Michael has spent years hosting Americans and Russians in the depth of the Cold War, where who knows how much his smile has historical significance, but maybe more than we think, I'd think.

Michael has also spent years exploring with a real, if gentle, passion, the possibility that there really are extraordinary human capacities and experiences.

I thought, smile or no, he was a bit...

Now I suspect he is right and I'm about to dilate on why, in a sort of serious way. I've been thinking for 15 years about the mind-brain system, the philosophy of mind, and the relation of quantum mechanics and classical mechanics to the mind-brain. Briefly, Descartes told us of his dualism: Res Extensa and Res Cogitans, i.e. Actual stuff and mental stuff. Now one of the problems, of many, with this dualism is this: How can mind act on matter? Suppose the brain is a classical physical system like a table of billiard balls. Then it is a deterministic dynamical system, it goes deterministically from one Actual state to the next, given by initial and boundary conditions and integrating equations of "neural motion" for the brain. Then there is nothing for Mind to do. Each state of the brain is sufficient for the next state of the brain. Worse, there is no *way* for the mind, mental stuff (consciousness actually) to ACT on the brain.

This is a conundrum that has stopped us for 350 years.

But what if the mind-brain system is both *quantum* and classical, passing back and forth from quantum to classical and classical to quantum. There is increasing evidence that this two way passage in what I call the "Poised Realm" can happen. Then we can overcome Descartes and 350 years of struggle about how the mind can act, *classically*, on the brain. Well the answer is simple, the mind does not act classically— causally on the brain at all. It goes from quantum Possibles to classical

Actuals by a process called decoherence, the loss of phase information from a quantum system to its quantum environment. So the mind can *acausally* have consequences for classical brain "stuff." By going back and forth, quantum to classical to quantum to classical, the mind brain system can interweave as a mind-brain quantum coherent-decoherent-recoherent system.

Mike, the mind-brain system may really be partially quantum. So what about your extraordinary human experiences? Well it is established in quantum mechanics that "entangled quantum particles" can be far apart, causally separated, too far for light to propagate between them in the time available, yet if one is measured, the other is *instantaneously* correlated with the first. It's called EPR, Einstein Podolsky and Rosen, and its true.

It also requires either that physics can be non-local in space, or that we give up "counterfactual definiteness." Give up what? Roughly, we can choose to give up the law of the Excluded Middle. Aristotle said, "Either A is true, or A is not true. There is nothing in the middle." But 19th Century philosopher C.S. Pierce said, A is true, A is Possible, A is false. Possible is in the middle between A is True and A is False.

So we can avoid all the problems with a new dualism, gasp, drinks, lights, drums: The ontologically real Actual and the ontologically real Possible. I call them Res Extensa and Res Potentia. Descartes would have hated it. Whitehead proposed it in 1927 or so. And if the Possible is real, then what consciousness IS may be a participation, a prehension, of the Possible.

Michael Murphy, I no longer think you are a bit.........

Not only do I begin to seriously think you were right all along, you helped inspire me and enable me to do my own searching.

You are one wonderful man, you have done so much, so many love you. Me too.

This little note is my happy birthday present to you, friend Mike.

*Stu Kauffman*

# Michael Murphy and the
# True Home Field Advantage

### DAVID HARRIS

Nothing since has approached the madness we reached that season thirty years ago when Michael Murphy breached the envelope of football reality and revealed both the unfathomed dimensions of Mind and the dark powers of The True Home Field Advantage which I now feel compelled to recount for the first time.

I am—given Murphy's dotage—the only remaining unimpaired witness to those 1981 developments, and the responsibility for keeping their secret has weighed more and more heavily as the years have passed. I now fear that either Murphy's remarkable manipulation of Newtonian reality will be lost to memory and a definitive episode in the history of consciousness will disappear without trace or that, dotage or not, Murphy will escape accountability for what was, quite possibly, an unconscionable breach of both sporting ethics and conventional morality and which, frankly, haunts me to this day. Either way, the need for transparency has become overwhelming.

At the time, of course, we each knew that the other's primal, even mystic relationship with the Forty Niners far transcended the shallow boosterism commonly attached to pursuit of the ball with a point on both ends. Murphy's profound attachment had been nurtured as a teenager at Kezar Stadium from the Niners' Day One; I, born the same year as the team, gave myself to them in Fresno, during a black and white television experience at age 10. Both manias, however, were of a kind. And by late September, 1981, both of us were under a cloud. The team, then in Bill Walsh's third year at the helm, was expected to end a long run of mediocrity but that expectation was looking extraordinarily misplaced. The Niners were barely 2-2 and lucky to be that.

Murphy finally raised the issue with me in a solemn voice. He could feel it in his bones, he said. We had won ten games and lost thirty four over the last three years and our mutual obsession's slide into football doom seemed about to begin once again.

"Unless," he added with a lift of his eyebrows, "you're willing to do something about it?"

That, I now know, was a fateful moment. I often wonder what would have happened had I just ignored his come on, sloughing it off with a shrug, perhaps, or a chuckle. But I didn't.

"What do you mean?" I asked instead.

Murphy motioned me to sit down, it was a long story.

What he was about to tell me had grown out of the intersection of his Niner self with his then considerable meditation practice. He had been spending as much as six hours a day cross-legged on a cushion, eyes blank, chasing the transcendental, for months now. That search of his inner ether had been amplified with a series of techniques for remote viewing and telepathic communication taught to him by a trio of Kazaks from the Central Soviet Bureau for the Study of Mind-bending, as well as the Hindu yogic trance inductions he had dabbled with as a young virgin on the ashram and his sports psychology research into performance enhancement and out of body visualization.

I nodded as though I had some grasp of what he was talking about.

Michael, now speaking with such urgency that flecks of spit flew off his lower lip, explained that it had come to him in a jolt, deep into one of his six hour sessions exploring the void: The connection to the Niners we experienced as separate individuals was merely the surface ripple marking our linkage to a vast shared grid of psychic energy and elemental consciousness, obscured only by the shortcomings of our own understanding and the divergence of the grid's inherent physics from "normality." He called this grid "The Web." It was generated by the shared obsession of the Niner Faithful and occupied a dimension beyond the one with which we were familiar, yet was available for parapsychological exploitation—a force with enormous potential for influencing and even rearranging physical reality. This, he proclaimed, was "The True Home Field Advantage," especially for the Niners, whose fans were just loopy enough to make the necessary steps to access other dimensions and wield this seemingly limitless tool. One had simply to connect to the Web and develop a transmission system to channel its energies to our team's purposes. And, he announced, he was now prepared to take that step into the unknown. He felt he had no choice.

He also needed an accomplice.

In his few experimental episodes out in the ether since stumbling over the Web, postulating ways to connect and manipulate it, he had found that channeling was impossible with only his efforts. He'd called the Kazaks in Moscow and they, though horribly drunk at the time, had told him before passing out that the key to mobilizing that Web energy was Triangulation. Adding a third pole to the interaction of Web and game would change all the psychic angles and supply the necessary leverage.

That's where you come in, Murphy declared.

Me? "I have no idea what all this goo goo shit is about," I told Michael—much less any faith in the drunken Kazaks—but he would hear nothing of it.

"You won't have to navigate the void or make the Web connection," he explained. That was the hard part and he would do that. "All you have to do is connect to me so we can channel energy from two different poles." That secondary connection would require only a little training in harmonic convergence, a meditation technique reportedly pioneered by the great Buddhist sage Milarepa himself and taught to Michael by an exiled Mongolian Ph.D who had been experimenting with levitation down in Tierra del Fuego. Murphy could no longer remember the Mongolian's name—though he did remember the man had shown up at Esalen driving a purple school bus—but his techniques were sound, he assured me with a cherubic smile. I could acquire sufficient skills for our purposes with a fifteen minute introductory lesson.

Fifteen minutes later, I had managed to generate a little buzz in my extremities by staring as hard as I could at a point on the wall. Michael said that was great. He insisted we were now ready to get after it. "We don't know much about what we're about to do," he admitted in a further attempt to reassure me, "but we'll figure it out as we go along."

I found that small consolation at the time.

Nonetheless, I was ready for our experiment the following Sunday, when the Niners were playing on the road against the Redskins in D.C. Michael was stationed in front of his television in Mill Valley and I in front of mine in Menlo Park. The Niners jumped out to a 7-0 lead but the Skins answered with a drive down to the Niners' 22 yard line and looked like they were about to punch it in. At that point, my phone rang. It was Murphy.

"Let's take this baby out for a test drive," he said.

Lacking any other calibration, he told me he was just going to take as strong a hold onto the Web as he could. The rest was just a matter of transmission. Once he ascertained we were on the same wave length, he instructed me to engage my harmonic convergence, lock onto the screen, and stay that way. He'd take care of the rest. Then he hung up.

I did as instructed.

And so, apparently, did he.

When the Redskins lined up for the next play, with me in a half-assed trance state staring at the television, a sudden onslaught of heat rushed out of my cortex and down to the soles of my feet. The air in the room instantly took on a purple haze, like after dropping Owsley acid in the old days, then, to my considerable amazement, I rose about an inch off the couch and hovered there with a ferocious wind rushing through my ear drums. The Skins ran a sweep to their left and, through the haze, I saw Ronnie Lott come up from his cornerback spot like a heat seeking missile. Just as Lott collided with the runner, the Niner cornerback dipped his helmet so it hit squarely on the ball, popping it out of the runner's grasp, straight up in the air, where Niner safety Dwight Hicks grabbed it and ran 80 yards the other way for another Niner touchdown.

I dropped back on the couch, feeling suddenly spent. The haze evaporated and the clamor in my ears receded. I called Murphy before the Niners lined up for the extra point.

"What the fuck was that?" I demanded.

"I think we're onto something," Murphy answered.

Although grateful for the Niners' victory over the Redskins, I was seriously spooked by the display of power we seemed to have induced and cautionary when we spoke the next day, but not Michael Murphy. He had no doubts about pursuing this further. He apologized for the "side effects" I had experienced and allowed that he had failed to adjust for the karmic winds that swirl over the surface of the Web. These winds were a significant element that had to be manipulated if we expected to direct the Web with any precision and, of course, he had a plan for that. The point was to generate positive karmic tail winds for our team, adding to the force of their momentum, and that was best done in the lead up to the game rather than on game day itself. Again Triangulation was key, but in this case we had to find a way to anchor our channeling to the team's preparations.

At three the following morning I thus found myself with Murphy in front of the Forty Niners' old headquarters in a residential Redwood City neighborhood next to a Senior Center about fifteen minutes from my house. Clouds covered the moon as we made our way over a chain link fence to a corner of the practice field. Our mission was to bury a small plastic bag containing a toy football signed by legendary Niner Frankie Albert during Murphy's adolescence and a Forty Niner ornament that had been hanging on my Christmas trees since the early days in Fresno. These lifelong keepsakes would provide psychic ground to which we could automatically connect and through which we could generate the necessary karmic tailwinds as our team prepared. I'd brought a shovel but soon discovered that Murphy's relationship to such a tool was only abstract. When I'd finished the burying, he led us both in a short tune in session for our harmonic convergence and then we fled. On the way home, Murphy ruminated at length about how the Dallas game this weekend would give us a good yardstick. The Cowboys were an NFL power and had beaten us the year before, 59-14.

This year, however, was no contest. Niners 45, Cowboys 14.

After that, Murphy had the bit in his teeth and, I must confess, I increasingly submitted to being a lab rat in his experiment. When we deflected a field goal during the first game with the Rams, I ended up levitating halfway across the very purple room. The next time we played them, Murphy amped the Web up so high it shattered my aquarium, leaving a puddle of seaweed and dying tropicals all over my family room rug. But the team kept winning. After holding off the Giants, I was left with scorch marks all over my television's plastic case. Against Pittsburgh, Murphy directed our psychic beam at Joe Montana to buck him up but it was a gigantic failure and Montana had his worst big game of the season. Finally with the Niners clinging to a three point lead with under a minute to go and the Steelers facing a fourth down in our territory, Murphy made a frantic phone call. "Peewee," he screamed—meaning Dwayne "Peewee" Board, one of our defensive ends—"lock on to Pee Wee." I instantly switched my convergence to number 76, the ball was snapped, and Board sacked the Steeler quarterback to end the game. Our only outright failure was when Cleveland came to town, and, overconfident, we abandoned our triangle and went to the game together. Cleveland 15, San Francisco 12, during a rainstorm that flooded the Candlestick parking lot and required us to use a public bus shuttle to get from the City to the stadium. Afterwards, a line of buses was waiting and the attendant at the door of the one I got on stopped Murphy from boarding after me, saying it was too full and to take the next one. My last view of Michael that day was of him standing in the torrent addressing my departing bus.

"Triangulation," he shouted. "The Kazaks were right! You have to triangulate."

Otherwise the results were plain to see. The Niners finished the regular season 13-3 and sailed through the first round of the playoffs with a victory over the New York Giants in ankle deep mud at Candlestick.

By then I was feeling pretty much as though we had nothing left to prove, but not Michael. The Dallas Cowboys were coming to town to decide who would go to the Super Bowl and Murphy was about to trump everything we had done with The True Home Field Advantage thus far.

Dallas in the playoffs would be a game unlike any other, Michael explained that Tuesday as we got in my car for a five minute drive from Menlo Park to East Palo Alto. Look at the early Seventies, he insisted. Three times in a row the Niners had played the Cowboys on the verge of the Super Bowl and three times in a row the Cowboys had come from behind to deny us. Clearly the karmic winds this week would be treacherous. Unwilling to risk disappointment, he felt the need for a secret weapon. And the Kazaks had helped him find one, whom we were now about to visit.

After crossing the freeway overpass, we turned onto the frontage road and parked in front of an abandoned rib joint, with a peeling sign declaring "Uncle Pig's Memphis Style" that tottered on the roof. Four foot high weeds were growing around the rib shack's foundation.

Michael finished briefing me before we got out of the car. The man we were about to see, Swami Loobootoolooboot, also went by the alias, "Meatball Rinpoche." The Kazaks had once used him to good effect in a staredown along the Chinese border. The swami, a.k.a. Meatball Rinpoche, had remarkable meditative powers. And this week, the karmic winds would require the Web to generate far more energy than Michael's connection could muster on its own. The answer was to complement our reach into the Web with a push from the other side. The Swami would lock onto the game and follow the signal back through his television across the airwaves and into the consciousnesses of all the Web's unknowing participants, amping up each of their energetic contributions and throwing the Web into Hyper Drive.

That ramping up, however, would have a very finite limit, perhaps a minute at most, and could only be invoked in the highest of emergencies. It also required me to play a special role. The Swami had given up speaking forty-seven years ago and refused to even be near a telephone. He communicated by writing in Hindi on a notepad. To invoke his intervention, I would have to rush over the freeway to where he would be seated in front of a television and signal him by writing the word "Swaraj" on his pad.

I, true to my lab rat role, promised to carry out my task.

We then entered Uncle Pig's Memphis Style through the back door, to which Murphy had a key. The rib joint was a hollow shell inside except for the defunct counter. In the empty space where the ovens once stood, a man—perhaps four and half feet tall and dressed in a flowing white dhoti with hair that had not been cut in more than four decades piled up behind him on the floor—was seated on a cushion in front of a television. Nothing was playing at the moment we entered and Michael whispered that the game would be on the next time I saw the Swami. Murphy exchanged Hindi notes with a.k.a. Meatball Rinpoche, the tiny man looked me over, and then we left. Outside, Michael handed me the keys to Uncle Pig's and repeated how critical my role was. The season was riding on it.

I was nervous on Sunday and secretly hoping my dash over the freeway wouldn't be needed, but it was obvious by the end of the third quarter that wouldn't be the case. Before the game was over, the Niners would have turned the ball over five times. We began the fourth quarter clinging to a one point lead but the longer the quarter lasted, the more the Cowboys seemed to be prevailing. Then we gave them the ball with a fumble at the 50 yard line and they converted it into a touchdown. With 4:54 left in the game, we got the ball back on our own eleven yard line, down 27-21.

As Montana walked the offense up to the line of scrimmage, my telephone rang. It was Murphy on a pay phone at Candlestick. "Go to Meatball," he shouted.

I rushed out to my car and headed across the freeway only to find the frontage road blocked by an overturned big rig. I frantically detoured through the back streets of East Palo Alto, all the while following the game on the radio. The Niners were moving down the field running the ball then dinking passes, six yards here, nine yards there. At the 2:00 minute warning, they had reached midfield. Under a minute, they were on Dallas' 6, third down with play stopped for a time out, and I burst in the back door at Uncle Pig's. The Swami was in front of the television. The camera was focused on Montana consulting with Walsh along the sideline. I snatched the pad at the Swami's side and wrote the code word.

The Swami's eyes bulged a little at the message and then all hell broke loose. The room got purple instantly and the hurricane roar I'd previously heard in my ears seemed to shake Uncle Pig's like a pit bull with a rat. I, of course, was locked onto the Swami's television and could only guess at what was happening around me.

By the time Montana lined the team up for play, wisps of smoke were coming out of the back of the tv and the Swami was levitating over the floor with his face just inches from the screen. As the ball was snapped and Montana rolled to his right, the Swami's enormous pile of hair broke into flames and the room was suffused with acrid smoke. The Cowboys chased the Niner quarterback towards the sidelines as he looked and looked for someone to throw to. Then he spied Dwight Clark along the back of the end zone and cut loose. It would later be a subject of much debate between Michael and me whether the Web had altered the trajectory of Montana's pass to make it catchable or had lifted Clark high enough to reach it, but either way it was a Niner touchdown. As Clark took two steps after the reception and held the ball up in triumph, however, the Swami's tv exploded in a cloud of electronic debris.

The blowback sent a.k.a. Meatball Rinpoche flying across the room and knocked me on my butt. I started to scramble to the Swami's assistance but he needed none. The explosion had doused his hair and he picked himself up before I could get to him, brushed off his singed eyebrows, and returned to sitting on his cushion in front of the demolished television. Convinced everything was all right at Uncle Pig's, I ran for my car, turned on the radio, and headed back over the freeway.

I would later return to Uncle Pig's to check on the Swami but when I did, I found the back door open and no Swami. The place had been cleaned out, television and all, and the only signs of what had happened were a few scorch marks and the vague odor of burnt hair. After that, whenever I would ask Murphy what had happened to Swami Loobootoolooboot a.k.a. Meatball Rinpoche and Uncle Pig's Memphis Style, he would always cryptically shrug that "the Kazaks had taken care of everything."

In the meantime, I drove home on Super Bowl Sunday with the blazing vision of Meatball Rinpoche fresh in my mind, listening to the Niner defense throttle Dallas' last ditch attempt to drive for a field goal. Game over, Niners 28, Cowboys 27. The crowd at Candlestick was going berserk when I got back to the television waiting for me next to the counter where my fish tank had once sat. The phone was ringing.

It was Murphy on another stadium pay phone. The crescendo of the primal wail around him made his voice barely audible, but he was obviously drunk on the moment. The wicked witch of Dallas was dead.

"Fuck the karmic winds," he screamed into the receiver. "Fuck the fucking karmic winds."

The Super Bowl was an anti-climax. We only had to invoke the Web at relatively low levels on two occasions in the third quarter when the team went mysteriously dead in the water. It ended 26-21, and we had gone from on the verge of collapse in October to World Champions in January.

I saw Michael several days later. Both of us were still in transports of ecstasy, glowing visibly, and understandably full of ourselves for what we had pulled off. Murphy could not stop smiling.

At my mention of The True Home Field Advantage, he blushed sheepishly and arched his eyebrows like Michael Murphy does when he has something even more off the wall brewing in his inner ether.

"You know," he said, "we'll have to do this again sometime."

# The Myth of Michael Murphy

SAM KEEN

Overwhelming evidence suggests that Michael Murphy is a fictitious character created by the collective unconscious to fulfill its need for a new kind of hero.

To begin with, "Michael Murphy" is one of those common names shared by a million anonymous Irish men and often, like John Doe, is an alias used to obscure questionable dealings and heavy drinking. For instance, Wikipedia reports: Michael Murphy may refer to: Michael Murphy actor, author, diver, politician, priest, rugby footballer, former lead singer of REO Speedwagon. If you make a list of the high jinks and supposed accomplishments attributed to MM you will find they are too numerous and fantastic to be the work of any one person.

It is a fact that MM along with Dick Price founded the Esalen Institute, but beyond that the picture gets hazy. MM seems to have enabled every possible legal experiment designed to promote greater awareness. Early on, the likes of Abraham Maslow, Fritz Perls, Bill Schutz, Bernie Gunther, George Leonard, Virginia Satir, Alan Watts, Stan Grof, John Lilly, et all were members of the madcap community dedicated to expanding consciousness, with a little help from medicinal herbs, hot tubs, massage and encounter groups. In the early days everyone, except MM, was wandering around the property "processing" big experiences, and obsessively trying to lose their egos.

Strangely, suspiciously, MM was seldom if ever seen and never photographed in the hot tubs or having an Esalen massage. He never allowed Fritz to gestalt his psyche or Ida Rolf to deconstruct his body. On the few occasions when he took part (?) in encounter groups, he was known to fall asleep just when the going got rough. In short, MM was not the type of person who went to Esalen.

In spite of the great game of Capture the Flag (i.e MM) he remained unconverted to any of the constantly changing neo-orthodox gospels of total enlightenment. He had a well developed bullshit detector that could spot spiritual tyranny a mile away. On occasions when the natives rebelled and tried to take over the farm, MM showed his management talent for making clear the limits of absolute democracy—i.e. if you own the playground you are more equal than others and must be more responsible. To this day, the flag remains safely in his care.

While others were lolling around the baths and developing their full potential, MM was meditating on the likes of Sri Aurobindo and Hegel, who were concerned with the future evolution of everything— the descent of Big Mind into Matter, Spirit into History. From them MM got the ludicrous idea that the best place to observe the ongoing incarnation of the Oversoul was in sports. Yes, sports.

Soon, he was playing mystical golf with a bunch of imaginary companions such as Shivas Irons during which time everyone had so many out–of–body experiences they frequently forgot to hit the actual golf ball.

One thing led to another and before you knew it MM was attending 49er games, placing hexes on enemy players and using psychokinesis to control the trajectory of passes. Whether his mystical technology had any positive effect on the 49ers standing in the NFL is open to question. He did cooperate with the famous quarterback John Brodie to write a book about the psychic aspects of football, but all concerned— Management? Other players? Publishers, John Brodie himself—saw to it that the book was never published for the consideration of more literal minded fans. Not to be deterred, Michael collected thousands of accounts of miraculous happenings from all kinds of athletes and introduced a new way of viewing the psychic and spiritual side of sports

MM may have failed to transform an entire football team, but he did transform his own body. His incarnation as an athlete is a study in paradox and irony. In the early 1970s when we were both living on

Telegraph Hill, I frequently caught sight of him and can testify that he was rolly polly—not an athlete. In fact, in those days he referred to himself as a "lofty softy" because he did his meditation seated in a large, over stuffed easy chair. Not exactly Zen rigor. But within a couple of short years, he progressed from taking slow walks around Washington Park (after espresso at the Trieste) to a slow jog along the Embarcadero, to becoming one of the top rated master class runners in the United States.

MM's personal transformation was so dramatic that he nearly fell off the deep end—went too far in the right direction. His own athletic progress plus his taste for evolutionary spirituality led him to the notion that the future of the body was limitless. His logic seems to have been this: If I, at 40 can break the 4.5 minute mile, why can't the human body evolve endlessly and develop all kinds of unusual powers? By way of researching this preposterous notion, he began to collect yet more thousands of accounts of people who had had strange experiences of transcending the normal limits of the body—teleportation, remote viewing, bi-location. In a unique book, *The Future of the Body*, he gives endless empirical evidence of the existence of these extraordinary powers the Hindu called siddhis.

Not satisfied with the project of creating a glorious new body, MM decided to transform the body politic. It all came about because reports were leaking out from behind the Iron Curtain of experiments with psychic powers that could transform the face of war. MM was intrigued by what he heard and took off for enemy territory. Miraculously, the old shaman infiltrated the labs where the experiments were being conducted. When he returned to the US with wild tales, the FBI and the CIA got their panties in a bundle and demanded that he tell them about psychic warfare. MM informed them that they could find similar experiments going on in psychology departments in the US—as in Stanford. For a decade MM, Dulce, Jim Hickman and a host of characters traveled to the USSR and made friends with dissidents, scientists, writers, artists and liberal politicians. Some Sovietologists have suggested that The Esalen Soviet project and the citizen diplomacy it inspired had as much to do with Glasnost as did the official diplomacy of the State Department. It was widely rumored that the parting of the Iron Curtain was in some measure due to MM's ability to beat the Ruskies at the Vodka game and by the desire of many Soviet diplomats to visit the hot tubs in Big Sur.

There are more equally improbable achievements that might be listed—endless conferences on the latest advancements in physics and biology and efforts to bring the great Abrahamic faiths together. All the while, by a combination of charisma, vision and ninja management skills, MM kept Esalen at the cutting edge of the exploration into the further reaches of the human spirit and oversaw the transformation of a piece of rocky coastline into a Garden of Eden.

I could go on and on listing his achievements but that would only gild the lily. Honesty does demand that, before ending, I reveal one item that runs counter to the evidence I have presented that MM is a mythic phenomenon.

For 40 years he has been my unwavering friend, a constant source of wild ideas and ready laughter—a joy. If the future of the body includes reincarnation, next time round I would like to come back as Michael Murphy.

# From Luke Skywalker to the Corps of Discovery: The Sursem CTR Series

EMILY AND ED KELLY, ON BEHALF OF THE SURSEM GROUP

A t the end of the 19th century—specifically, January 6, 1882—an unusual group of scholars, scientists, philosophers, theologians, businessmen, and others met in London. What brought this diverse group together was their shared belief that the question of survival of human personality after death, up until then considered a matter of faith, is instead a basic question about nature that can be approached the same way other questions about nature were increasingly being approached: scientifically, that is, using the tools of empirical observation and rational thought. The immediate result was the formation of the Society for Psychical Research.

As with most groups, there quickly arose dissent and disagreement, and some of the early members eventually departed. But this group held together, primarily thanks to the SPR's first and longtime President, the philosopher Henry Sidgwick: "Few people could have exercised such [firm] control better than Sidgwick…and there was no one under whose sway all shades of opinion would have been more likely to receive a patient and a fair hearing" (Gauld, 1968, p. 139). His leadership and direction helped foster in the SPR a strong sense of camaraderie and, most importantly, a shared sense that they were forging a revolutionary new direction by which to address the most important question a human being can ask: Am I just a momentary thing, extinguished at death by an impersonal universe? Or am I in some fashion a continuous, continually changing participant in an infinite and personal universe? With this strong sense of mission and momentous purpose, the early members of the SPR produced in less than 20 years an astonishingly immense body of empirical evidence showing that human beings have latent capacities that go far beyond ordinary mental and physical functioning. Additionally, one of the members in particular—Frederic Myers—laid out an ambitious theoretical framework suggesting that these capacities collectively point toward the continuation of human personality in a wider, postmortem environment. The scope and strength of the empirical and theoretical efforts of the SPR attracted wide attention, and the work quickly spread to Europe and America.

Myers had described the years just prior to the SPR's founding as "the very flood-tide of materialism, agnosticism,—the mechanical theory of the Universe, the reduction of all spiritual facts to physiological phenomena" (Myers, 1893/1961, p. 15). The excitement and optimism of the group derived in part from their belief that they had already seen the "flood-tide" and that their efforts would help hasten the ebbing of the waters. But many of the core members of the group had died by the early years of the 20th century, before they could have had any inkling that the crest of the flood had not yet even been glimpsed. Instead, in the 20th century that flood-tide became a raging tsunami. Although the early work of the SPR (and that of their few successors who soldiered on virtually in isolation) was by no means destroyed, it was certainly deeply submerged by the flood.

At the end of the 20th century—specifically, December 6-11, 1998—another diverse group of scholars, scientists, philosophers, and others gathered at Esalen, convened by Mike Murphy to begin mending the "broken lineage" between what he called the "Golden Age of survival research" a century ago and a new generation dissatisfied with contemporary physicalism. Mike's primary purpose was to bring together representatives of as many empirical and theoretical perspectives as possible to focus on breaking down "the ever-present (and for me ever-amazing) chasm between the immense magnitude of the survival issue and the failure of mainstream academia and science to address it, a chasm that gives our work immeasurable consequence" (Murphy, personal communication, March 31, 2009). For all members of Sursem (SURvival SEMinar), as the group was quickly christened, the issue of survival after death represents the ultimate challenge to the mainstream view in modern science and philosophy that consciousness is reducible to brain processes and hence necessarily snuffed out when the brain dies.

At the first meeting participants discussed some of the kinds of evidence for survival provided by the early psychical researchers and their few successors, evidence that ranges from the indirect kind such as psi (telepathy, clairvoyance, precognition, and psychokinesis) to the more direct kinds, such as near-death experiences, cases of the reincarnation type, veridical apparitions, and trance mediumship. At the second meeting, in February 2000, participants also began canvassing existing models of consciousness that offer a wider perspective than contemporary physicalism. By the end of that year's conference, a concrete plan of action for the group had been proposed.

Mike and nearly all the other Sursem members had long been impressed, and even strongly influenced, by the theoretical model of mind developed by Frederic Myers and elaborated in various respects by contemporary figures such as William James and Henri Bergson. Recognizing that 2003 would mark the 100th anniversary of the publication of Myers's monumental work, *Human Personality and Its Survival of Bodily Death*, the group decided that a major step toward mending the "broken lineage" could be taken by producing a book that would re-evaluate Myers's empirical and theoretical contributions in light of the ensuing century of psychological and neurophysiological research.

On the surface, this plan may have seemed a diversion from the original intent to focus on the survival question, but in fact Sursem was following directly in the footsteps of Myers himself, for whom the survival issue was unquestionably always the focus. Myers had recognized that no amount of survival-related evidence, however good, will be convincing, or even taken seriously, unless it can be fit into a larger understanding of the human psyche in which it makes sense to suggest that consciousness might survive the destruction of the body. Like Myers, Sursem members therefore identified two long-term goals: first, to show empirically that contemporary physicalism in its various forms is inadequate to account for vast areas of important human experience; and second, to find a better theoretical framework. Our book would focus primarily on the first goal, but would also point the way toward the second as subsequent Sursem conferences identified and evaluated possible candidates for a comprehensive theory.

The group's interest in Myers, however, reflects more generally important parallels between Myers's thinking and Mike's. (We have sometimes even joked that Mike might be the reincarnation of Myers!) First, Myers's methodological approach exemplifies the natural-history approach that lies behind so much of Mike's work, from his exhaustive bibliographical review of studies of meditation (Murphy & Donovan, 1997), to his ongoing collection of the testimony of sports figures about their exceptional experiences (Murphy & White, 1978/1995), to his own monumental work *The Future of the Body* (1992). Both men have critically canvassed the literature of unusual human experiences to an unparalleled degree. Like Myers's, Mike's work has exemplified his commitment to William James's radical empiricism, which (in Mike's words) is "a willingness to investigate any and all phenomena on their own terms" (unpublished 2000 Sursem Conference Summary, p. 15). For Mike, a major flaw in academic psychology—reflected in the neglect of Myers and his colleagues—has been its lack of a sufficiently comprehensive natural-history phase, particularly in virtually ignoring extraordinary human abilities.

Second, Myers's model of human personality—like that of another of Mike's great intellectual inspirations, Sri Aurobindo—is thoroughly evolutionary. For Myers, as for Mike, the rare and unusual human abilities ignored by most psychologists are indications of latent higher capacities that are emerging, as all other levels of matter, life, and mind have emerged, through an evolutionary process—not only on earth but at other, normally hidden, levels of existence. Mike has referred to this as Myers's idea of "pre-adaptive evolution," in which latent capacities are already present, ready to emerge and develop. Moreover, they are already apparent in psi experiences, uprushes of genius, and all the kinds of phenomena catalogued by Mike in *Future of the Body*, which he calls "metanormal" and has emphasized because they suggest that such capacities can be deliberately cultivated by transformative practices such as meditation in its various forms. In sum, for both Myers and Mike, what is implicit is gradually made explicit through evolution.

Mike also shares with Myers and Aurobindo a view of human personality that involves both a Self (upper-case) and a self (lower-case), or an "I" and a "me":

We are part of a supreme evolutionary adventure in which part of our individualized personality is manifesting higher and higher potentials. The I witnesses, while the self evolves. The dichotomy between the witnessing ground and the evolving self was portrayed in the Rig Veda in the following way: There are two birds on the World Tree, one eats the sweet fruit, while the other watches and eats not. This is the dichotomy between the changeless, primordial Self and the self engaged in the dance of life.... Survival research dwells on the second self, which is equally important. (Murphy, unpublished 1998 Sursem Conference Summary, pp. 25-26)

For the next 6 years, from 2001-2006, Sursem's conference participants focused on fleshing out and evaluating the empirical content for the book (eventually given the title *Irreducible Mind: Toward a Psychology for the 21st Century*), while also continuing to take stock of various theoretical perspectives and models of mind. As with many ambitious undertakings, the evolution and emergence of *Irreducible Mind* took longer than the group had anticipated. We missed our goal of the 2003 centennial of *Human Personality* by a wide margin, but it finally appeared, over 3 years later. We did achieve one of our goals, however, which was to have the book reflect the fact that Sursem, like Esalen itself, has under Mike's leadership become a community. We did not want an edited volume of individual, isolated contributions. We wanted a book that was a seamless whole, reflecting the thinking and goals of the group.

One of the people to whom *Irreducible Mind* was dedicated was Mike, and this was not just because Mike launched and directed the Sursem conferences in which the book was conceived and developed. The premise of the volume—that reductive materialism is not only incomplete but false—has been the premise of much of Mike's work, and many of the topics addressed in the book were ones Mike had been thinking and writing about for years, such as phenomena of extreme psychophysical influence, genius-level creativity, and altered and mystical states of consciousness.

Included with the hardcover version of *Irreducible Mind* is a CD of the entire text of Myers's *Human Personality*, as well as its most significant contemporary reviews. Putting this book into digital form launched another project of Sursem, which is to make other historically important books on survival and psychical research available online at Esalen's Center for Theory and Research website. In addition to *Human Personality*, thus far *Phantasms of the Living* by Edmund Gurney, Frederic Myers, and Frank Podmore (1886) and *Animal Magnetism, Early Hypnotism, and Psychical Research 1766-1925: An Annotated Bibliography* by Adam Crabtree (1988) have been digitalized for the CTR website (www.esalenctr.org), with additional volumes in process.

In one of our early conferences, Mike had characteristically pictured Sursem's first goal—to demonstrate the inadequacy of contemporary physicalism—in dramatically combative terms. He likened our role to that of Luke Skywalker: Our mission was to aim a missile skillfully into that tiny exhaust port on the Death Star, contemporary reductive materialism, and blow it up. *Irreducible Mind* was our missile, and we launched it in December 2006 (www.esalen.org/place/bookstore/kelly.html).

We turned next to our second goal—to develop a more comprehensive theory to replace the Death Star—and again Mike gave us our new role. No longer Luke Skywalker, we are now Lewis and Clark's Corps of Discovery. Like Jefferson, Mike gave us our mission: to explore the uncharted Territory, catalog its natural history, and provide a comprehensive map. Unlike Jefferson, he is coming with us, leading the expedition.

Membership in Sursem has varied over its history, both in number and in the kinds of backgrounds represented, and so far over 50 people have come to one or more of our conferences. Unlike the SPR, membership in Sursem is by invitation only, and as the goals and needs of Sursem have changed and evolved, new members with needed knowledge and skills have been recruited, sometimes at the suggestion of other members, but usually from among Mike's vast circle of colleagues and friends, and always with Mike's ultimate direction and approval. At the first conference, there were eight invitees, two Esalen staff members, and of course Mike. By 2010 the number of members has grown to nearly 2 dozen. At the first conference all the invitees were people who for years had been involved, in one way or another, with survival research, and the authors of *Irreducible Mind* (with one exception) were people who attended this first conference. As that book progressed, however, the group's second goal of a new theoretical model moved to the forefront of our thinking, and as a result the group began to expand to include people from other disciplines and perspectives to provide the wider, synoptic approach that has always been the hallmark of Mike's approach to any issue. New members added during the early years who have become a permanent part of Sursem included a theoretical physicist, an historian of science, and a Whiteheadian philosopher. As our discussions evolved, directed by Mike's vision of the range of data to be accommodated by a new theoretical model, commonalities across a wide range of approaches—ranging from those of Myers and William James at the empirical center, to quantum theory and Whiteheadian metaphysics on one side and the wisdom traditions on the other—began to appear: Mike described this as a partly hidden but common figure emerging from the fog and mist. To reinforce this process, in recent years we have added not only more people from the scientific side, including two more physicists and a basic neuroscientist, but also several people representing various branches of the wisdom traditions, including Neo-Platonism, Buddhism, and Tantric outgrowths of Hinduism such as Aurobindo and Kashmiri Shaivism.

In short, Sursem is bringing a three-pronged perspective to bear on the problem of survival after death and the other "rogue" phenomena catalogued in *Irreducible Mind*: that of empirical science, that of theoretical metaphysics, and that of the great wisdom traditions with their generally similar although far-from-identical views. Not surprisingly, such a broad approach has brought with it occasional tensions and disagreements about how best to balance the three areas. Like Henry Sidgwick before him, however, Mike—our not-so-still center!—has kept the group intact, its camaraderie ever-growing, and its focus now converging on a new concrete plan of action, a second book. In effect, by virtue of his deep roots in all of the relevant areas of inquiry, Mike has enabled the formation of a community of inquirers capable of overcoming the centrifugal forces that would quickly tear apart most groups so intellectually diverse.

Although our group has thus held together in the sort of creative tension that Mike appreciates and fosters, we are nowhere close as yet to reaching consensus on a new theory. At this point we are still uncertain even as to whether what we are looking for is a scientific theory, a metaphysical theory, or some combination of the two! A realistic next step, therefore, is essentially a progress report. In Sursem's next book, we will first outline empirical data and issues that candidate theories must address in a satisfactory fashion if they are to be of long-standing value. Second, we will discuss criteria for a useful theory and for adjudicating among competing theories. Finally, we will provide a sampling of the theoretical outlooks that currently seem promising to us, including a description of how each candidate theory deals with the relevant empirical phenomena, as well as a critical discussion of each showing what problems or gaps remain.

Tackling the question of life after death: What could possibly be more important—or more ambitious—an undertaking than that? And who but Mike could have been less intimidated by the enormity of the issue? Many people have approached it from their various perspectives—scientific, religious, experiential, philosophical. Who but Mike would have had the vision—and the audacity—to bring together all those divergent and sometimes warring perspectives to focus on the ultimate common goal of answering that question? All of us who are members of Sursem have come into the group with our individual perspectives, biases, and personal aims. Who but Mike could have provided us all with a better model of how to combine our skills and transcend our limitations and work together in a common purpose? We also all share something else—pride and gratitude at being part of Mike Murphy's Corps of Discovery. What could be a greater honor than that?

## References

Gauld, A. (1968). *The Founders of Psychical Research*. London: Routledge and Kegan Paul.

Murphy, M. (1992). *The Future of the Body: Explorations into the Further Evolution of Human Nature*. New York: Jeremy P. Tarcher.

Murphy, M., & Donovan, S. (1997). *The Physical and Psychological Effects of Meditation* (2nd ed.). Sausalito, CA: Institute for Noetic Sciences.

Murphy, M., & White. R. A. (1995). *In the Zone: Transcendent Experience in Sports*. New York: Penguin. (Original work published 1978)

Myers, F. W. H. (1961). *Fragments of Inner Life*. London: The Society for Psychical Research. (Original work published 1893)

# The Innkeeper's Work

DAVID E. PRESTI

*Both David Presti and Charley Tart are members of the Sursem group.*

things aren't what they seem

some questions are too big
for universities
    for governments
requiring deep re-visioning
that only a mystic innkeeper
might facilitate

what is consciousness, really
    can this rift in humanity be healed
does mind extend beyond the body
    can these people talk with one another
addressing colossal issues
in a thoroughly scientific manner
    in an inspired and pragmatic manner
with a radically empirical approach

the image of the ball in sight
a turquoise ball down the middle of the fairway
guided by streamers of heart power
toward a physics of the spirit
with the certainty

as much as anything might be certain
that it will also be a key
to logarithms of the just

as with so much of the work
of this innkeeper
the world depends on it
and most importantly
there is still time

God bless Michael Murphy.

*David E. Presti*
*University of California, Berkeley*

# Protecting Me from the Dreaded Murphy

## CHARLES T. TART

There are so many good things I could say about Michael! Like my friend, though, my life is overfull of projects and deadlines loom, so I shall limit myself to the amusing story of how we met—in spite of the efforts of my Betters....

As late summer of 1963 approached, excitement grew. I had my newly minted PhD, a lovely wife, a 2-year old daughter, a newly-born son, and all sorts of psychological and spiritual knowledge that, I believed, ordinary folks on the East Coast, where I lived, didn't have. I had already studied hypnosis, sleep, dreams, esotericism, occultism, and ESP, e.g.

For a long while it looked like we would be moving to Topeka, Kansas, where I had been offered a two-year postdoctoral fellowship with one of the greats of American Psychology, Gardner Murphy, at the prestigious Menninger Foundation. My graduate advisors at Chapel Hill, though, were horrified! Murphy had once been very mainstream and respectable, a former President of the American Psychological Association (APA), but he had not only developed interests in parapsychology (a big plus to me!), he had recently published a book called *Asian Psychology*. My advisors would never have admitted to any cultural biases and limitations, of course, but what could we scientific psychologists possibly learn from Asians? I had already shown way too much interest in unorthodox ideas—they didn't want an impressionable young man like me exposed to someone like Murphy.... Their intentions were good, I'm sure.

Ironic that it was a Murphy they had to worry about, they just hadn't gotten the first name right...

So they got on the phones, worked the old-boy network, and presto! I was offered an even better postdoctoral fellowship with Ernest R. Hilgard at Stanford University. Hilgard was also a former APA President, but he had made his reputation on learning studies, very establishment, and was now doing hypnosis research the proper way, with lots of psychological tests and free of mystical overtones.

So I, the too impressionable young man, was saved from those wild influences in Kansas and sent to California at the peak of the Psychedelic Revolution...a close call! And after growing up on the stodgy East Coast, I was in California! As Lama Sogyal Rinpoche (many years in my future back then) was to describe it, in the East people believe in the importance of accumulating lots of good karma—so you can be reborn in one of the god realms—like California!

My less orthodox connections kept working, though, and I was referred to a wonderful humanities professor at Stanford, Jeffrey Smith. After we had talked a while he decided I really should meet another young friend of his with great ideas...and so Michael Murphy showed up on my doorstep one afternoon.

I had never known anyone like Michael! He knew all the wild spiritual stuff, the Eastern ideas that I knew, and much more! And it wasn't just words, he had actually spent time in an Ashram in India! Michael and I exchanged ideas in so many ways that we literally gave each other headaches and would have to take time to recover from our visits with each other!

And not only was he an incredible intellectual, he was one of a very strange breed to me, a jock! There was a whole physical, body connection that was really novel to me. As an intellectual I could talk about the body and the physical world, but I thought people who were jocks didn't really know anything...a stupidly snobby idea, a defense against my own inadequacies I can see in retrospect, but it took a long time, helped greatly by visits to Esalen courtesy of Michael, and years of

Aikido training, to really start to put body and mind into a harmonious relationship for me.

And I have made "progress" in talking with Michael: I usually don't get a headache from it any more! But that probably means I'm getting old and not being aware of just how exciting his ideas still are.... Well actually I have headaches all the time as I get older, so maybe that excitement Michael stirred up has really never settled.

What I find quite amusing as I finish this brief tribute to my friend Michael Murphy, is that my advisors were right, so much so that I'm tempted to joke they may have been being "psychic" in the attempts to protect me from the psychic and other wild stuff that was coming down the road. They knew they had to keep me away from a Murphy, they just protected me from the wrong one.... And it's only taken me 47 years to notice the connection...

# The Next Great Work:
# The Enneads at Esalen

ROBERT MCDERMOTT

For their concluding session, the Enneads, nine wise elders, so-called both for their number and as a way of recollecting the nine sections of the six books of Plotinus, traveled again to Esalen Institute in Big Sur on the rugged California coast, the furthest reach of western civilization. They were meeting at Esalen because it is known to be the vessel for visions and for the unexpected. The Enneads made their way from the lodge, where they had enjoyed a hearty Esalen breakfast and lively conversation, to the Big House where many wise men and women had gathered in recent decades to share ideas, agree and disagree, and in the process attain to wider and deeper insights. During their previous day together the Enneads enjoyed informal conversation while fully occupying the famous places for conversation at Esalen—the lodge, the baths, and the famous Big House living room. As each of the nine entered the large white house they felt themselves surrounded by the rhythmic sound of the Pacific Ocean below. Michael Murphy and I greeted them at the start of an urgent and unprecedented one-day symposium.

These nine brought to this conference a lifetime of research and more theories than they would be able to express in the one day available to them. They also brought a commitment to meet the goal of this rare opportunity—the theme or message of the next "great work" worthy to serve as the defining worldview for the 21st century. In anticipation of this event, the Enneads had unanimously agreed that none of the prominent worldviews—theism, atheism, pantheism, pragmatism, existentialism, materialistic secularism, or various religious orthodoxies—would be adequate to meet the challenges of the 21st century. They agreed that their meeting on August 15th, 2009 would have to articulate a shared vision of an evolving Earth community and a method by which such a vision could be extended and implemented.

Because Plato's *Symposium* is a dialogue, and because it climaxes with a revelation concerning Eros—i.e., it is about mutual participation of the human and divine, the very essence of panentheism—and because it is inspired by a goddess, most of the Enneads considered it to be a perfect model for their own symposium. The Enneads had a shared source and starting point but they did not yet have a vision that would fire the imaginations of the next seven generations. They clearly hoped that before they would conclude their dialogue they too would be graced by a divine revelation.

The Enneads, gathered from around the world—from Europe, Tibet, and India, as well as from the United States, the host country, the youngest culture as well as the most powerful and influential. It was unanimously understood, though unspoken, that because of its dominant position in the world, and because it is the battleground between an anachronistic Christian theism and a strident scientistic atheism, America is desperately in need of a worldview these nine were striving to establish. They also understood that as they were all males, this might be the last opportunity to make positive use of the privileges their gender had assumed in previous centuries.

As they had at previous meetings, the Enneads began by speaking their names in chronological order. They included their defining works as a way of reminding themselves and each other of their place in cultures that helped to form them and to which they owed a special responsibility. This particularity of culture was perfectly complemented by their shared realization that they were each called upon to contribute a 21st century worldview in service to the whole of humanity and the imperiled Earth.

- J. W. von Goethe (1749-1832), *Metamorphosis of Plants* and *Faust*
- G. W. F. Hegel (1770-1831), *Phenomenology of Mind*
- William James (1842-1910), *Varieties of Religious Experience* and *Essays in Radical Empiricism*
- Alfred North Whitehead (1859-1947), *Process and Reality* and *Adventures of Ideas*
- Rudolf Steiner (1861-1925), *An Outline of Esoteric Science*
- Sri Aurobindo (1872-1950), *The Life Divine* and *Savitri: A Legend and a Symbol*
- Carl Gustav Jung (1875-1961), *Memories, Dreams, and Reflections* and *Symbols of Transformation*
- Pierre Teilhard de Chardin, S.J. (1881-1955), *The Human Phenomenon*
- His Holiness the Dalai Lama (1935- ), *Kalachakra Tantra: Rite of Initiation* and *The Universe in a Single Atom: The Convergence of Science and Spirituality*

Before their arrival, it was known to New Age bloggers that an important conference of wise elders would be held at Esalen, known worldwide as the source of significant new ideas. The internet showed evidence of intense opinions concerning those in attendance as well as recommendations for alternatives. Some called the symposium a guaranteed failure because it included not a single woman. (Not including women—e.g., Helena Blavatsky, Alice Bailey, or the Mother of the Sri Aurobindo Ashram, of course, was the point: could the males make positive use of this last effort by their gender to produce a worthwhile world view?) Others considered it ridiculous that neither China nor Japan was represented. Some would have preferred one or more of the following: Einstein, the greatest scientist since Newton and an advocate for global peace; one of the great figures in the raising of ecological consciousness—Thoreau, Aldo Leopold, Rachel Carson, or Thomas Berry. Some wanted Vaclav Havel, Nelson Mandela, or Archbishop Desmond Tutu, all leaders of national transitions from oppression to reconciliation and freedom.

Various groups of bloggers accused one or more of the Enneads of various limitations:

- Goethe of being anti-philosophical
- Hegel of being dated and Eurocentric
- James of being indecisive
- Whitehead of using too many neologisms
- Aurobindo of being vague and Victorian
- Steiner of being too esoteric
- C. G. Jung of emphasizing the symbolic at the expense of the historical
- Teilhard of being too orthodox Roman Catholic
- and Dalai Lama of being insufficiently evolutionary

However aware the Enneads themselves might have been of these and other weaknesses, as they set out to formulate the essential message of the first great work in more than half a century (since Teilhard's *Human Phenomenon* in 1955), they clearly were focused on the positive contributions of each. They regarded positivity as a defining characteristic of their work together and of the vision of the future they sought to bring into focus and to bequeath.

Some of the Enneads proved especially effective in representing various sources of human wisdom:

- Goethe brought a "gentle empiricism" in service of Nature
- Hegel brought the entire history of western philosophy from the Greeks to the early 19th century
- James brought a rich synthesis of psychology, philosophy, and religion
- Whitehead introduced insights based on the scientific revolution initiated by Einstein
- Sri Aurobindo presented a vast evolutionary Neo-Hegelian, Neo-Hindu integral vision culminating in the transformation of the physical world
- Rudolf Steiner presented esoteric traditions and the conception of Christ forming the subtle body of the Earth

- C. G. Jung brought the whole of western psychology as well as religion, art and culture psychologically considered
- Pierre Teilhard de Chardin espoused a seamless synthesis of science and Roman Catholic spirituality
- The Dalai Lama brought the entire Buddhist tradition complemented by Gandhian non-violence

Informed observers generally agreed that these nine individuals, despite their limitations individually and collectively considered, probably comprised the best possible source of the next great work to be created by the males of the modern and contemporary era.

As they began to chat with each other informally in the living room that had served as a site for so many seminars of wise elders during the previous forty years, the Enneads knew that the world urgently needed the kind of vision that they had resolved to bring forth and to make available. They also knew that all nine diverse perspectives would need to find expression in the next great work, and that there would need to emerge one perspective, one vision, one big Idea—as well as a compelling method for its implementation. Each of the nine had attained an authority well past the level of opinions; they all spoke confidently on the level of Ideas, and were recognized by the others to be speaking on this level, from a non-ordinary or inspired source. It remained for them to harmonize these deep (or transcendent) Ideas into a single vision. As anyone who has been to a seminar at Esalen can attest, such meetings often involve a breakdown of the ordinary states of consciousness, a dissolution of the usual separation of material and spiritual realms, of the temporal and eternal. At Esalen, one expects a startling mix of intense temporality and eternal Ideas, very specific situations mixed with fundamental archetypes.

Because eight of the nine Enneads who met at Esalen in August 2009 were no longer living on the Earth, many who had heard about this symposium assumed that it had not really taken place in time and space. The eight discarnate Enneads being who they are (not merely who they had been), the radical separation of matter and spirit, and of living and deceased, forcefully maintained by the dominant worldview, simply did not prevail. The Dalai Lama was the one Ennead who was still breathing earthly air. As is well known, His Holiness is well used to communicating with the so-called dead. It is not

Immediately known but it was assumed that he was alone in Daramsala, his home since his emigration from Tibet in 1959, and able to concentrate exclusively on the discussion taking place with the other nine Enneads at Esalen.

All of the Enneads agreed that dichotomous thinking has drained life, intelligence, and meaning from the cosmos, and has created a chasm between humanity and the rest of the Universe. For several centuries, humanity as a whole, and individual human beings, have experienced themselves to be increasingly distant from the wonders of the sky, from plants and animals, and the Earth as a living organism. When they entered into conversation, the Enneads immediately agreed that this materialist, secularist, flatland view had led the Earth to a state of extreme peril, and humanity to despair. The Enneads disagreed on many important topics but they certainly all agreed that reality is more complex, more integral, and more mysterious than the Cartesian-Newtonian paradigm that has dominated western thought and culture for the past three centuries.

It has been difficult for Michael and myself to describe and explain just what we saw and heard on August 15th. Michael and I do agree absolutely that it was the Enneads themselves who had listened to each other and had expressed their individual opinions—or rather, their Ideas. The Enneads left us no room for doubt that the words spoken issued from the individual minds of the Enneads themselves. Exactly how that happened remained something of a mystery.

To varying degrees, the Enneads were conscious of the date: August 15th. No one mentioned whether the conference had been scheduled to end on this date because it was the birthday of Sri Aurobindo. (As Sri Aurobindo and his disciples noted quite emphatically in 1947, India's independence was occurring on Sri Aurobindo's 75th birthday). Similarly, most of the Enneads familiar with the thought of C. G. Jung noticed that this date was the feast of the Assumption of the Virgin Mary. In *Answer to Job* Jung claims that the Roman Catholic declaration in 1950 of the bodily assumption of the mother of Christ as an article of faith is the most important religious event in the past five hundred years. But, of course, the significance of Sri Aurobindo's birthday and of the *Assumptio Mariae* seemed not particularly important to Alfred North Whitehead, the Dalai Lama, and some others. It was like that with many perspectives and recommendations: what was significant or illuminating to some tended to be unnoticed by others.

The Enneads were grateful that they had come to know each other and each other's ideas during the previous day but they were also distressed by their shared realization that they seemed to be far from a single vision, a compelling Idea held to be foundational by all of them. Despite, or perhaps because of, their wide and deep wisdom, the nine had the habit of relying on nine root metaphors, nine different lexicons of special terms, nine specific intellectual and imaginal commitments. Yet, as diverse as the Enneads had shown themselves to be during informal conversation on the previous day, several threads emerged, and reemerged with regularity. The most prominent of these threads was the affirmation of the eternal feminine:

- Sri Aurobindo was ever conscious of his consort, the Mother
- Teilhard was devoted to the Virgin Mother
- Jung emphasized the Divine Mother archetype
- Steiner argued for the identity of Isis, Mary, and Sophia

The prominent role of the eternal feminine seemed unmistakable from the beginning of the seminar and perhaps more intensely so as the Enneads aspired to the wisdom of Sophia in the course of this, their one day together.

As they took their usual seats, each could clearly see at the end of the room two well-worn flip charts, one of several departures from the original symposium on the Acropolis. On one was written the words of the Hebrew book of Proverbs (29:18):

"Where there is no vision the people perish."

This text was considered by all to be an accurate warning at a time when all terrestrial and species life, including the future of human civilization, and planet Earth itself, appear to be in peril. All of the Enneads specialize in vision but thus far their visions remained unique and discrete, still too different from each other's to serve as a foundation for the next great panentheistic work. Just a few feet away stood another flip chart with the warning words of Sri Aurobindo from his one-page prophecy, "The Hour of God":

"It is the hour of the unexpected"

The Enneads accepted the truth of Sri Aurobindo's words—it could not be more evident that the clock was ticking, the light fading, the time for saving humanity and the Earth disappearing rapidly, but they had not come to an agreement on whether "the hour of the unexpected" referred to this particular morning, or the current year, this decade during which humanity is gradually awakening to forthcoming ecological devastation, or more generally to the loss of spirit (the "Death of God") in the West over the previous several centuries. Perhaps "hour" referred to all of these time frames, all of these existential contexts.

Toward the end of the morning, when optimism for a single vision or Idea that would serve the world in its most desperate "hour" was obviously wearing down, there emerged a sense that there had been too much talk and not enough silence. When Sri Aurobindo quoted the epigram of Mira Richard, the Mother of the Sri Aurobindo Ashram, "No more words," the group entered into meditation, no doubt in a variety of ways. What happened next is difficult to describe. They repeated phrases such as "inaudible, and yet amazingly audible," "words, and yet silence," "individual voices, and yet one voice."

The Enneads clearly had difficulty explaining to each other just what was happening but they recognized that it was something deeply mysterious, something of a gift, almost certainly from a deeper or higher level. All of the great spiritual teachers accept the concept of *adequatio*—that only those with a higher kind of hearing can hear higher Ideas, and only those with a higher kind of sight can see subtle events. Not everyone at the first symposium, the archetypal symposium on the Acropolis, was able to understand the Idea of Eros taught by Diotima. For many, Diotima seemed a literary device, whereas others saw her as a goddess. Similarly, with her supersensible sight, Mary of Magdala could see the resurrected Christ, but the Apostles did not, at least not without His help.

It would certainly seem that these nine Enneads, presumably above all others, would have the requisite eyes to see and ears to hear a higher revelation. Was there such? Did they hear and see something special, an Idea, that would help the world at the present time, and if so, what was communicated and how? The Enneads seemed eager to share their experience but unable to describe it or summarize what they heard for fear of not expressing what each of the others had heard. They each seemed aware that his experience was the same as the others, and that it was at the same time uniquely his own. In the end, they realized that both were true—their singular Idea, an invocation to Sophia (or inspiration by Sophia?) really was the Idea of the group, equally owned, equally expressive of the biographies and aspirations of each of the nine.

By mid-afternoon, it was clear that the message was the event itself, the divinely inspired unity of individuality and community, unity of interiority and conversation, unity of meditation and seminar dialogue, unity of one voice and nine, unity of human and divine. The experience of these unities, these dissolved dichotomies, had something of the experience of *kairos*, the touching of the human and divine in time and space. Like *glossolallia* at Pentecost, Sophia descended into this particular group because each member had prepared for such a revelation, for the divine presence.

Like the experience of Arjuna on the firing line of Kurukshetra in dialogue with the god Krishna, this avatar experience was time and place specific. Their experience was similar to Arjuna's in that it was both the arrival of a being from afar and the realization of the divine within—with the difference that this was the experience not of a lone warrior but of a group of nine individuals with extremely different biographies yet united in a single endeavor. The divine feminine, Sophia, that is omnipresent manifested in response to the call of the Enneads, and the call itself was made possible by the lifelong efforts of each of the nine joined in solemn purpose.

In that *kairos* moment of noon, August 15, 2009, the medium and the message joined so as to disclose the theme of the next great work: let those with eyes to see and ears to hear attend to this event, the next great work was heard and authored by nine great souls in relation to Sophia. In their agreement and in their particularity, in their universality equally as in their unique individual modes of consciousness—whether American, Austrian, English, French, German, Indian, Swiss, or Tibetan—they recognized and sought to announce that the next great work is the revelation of the divine feminine, particularly by the overarching concept of Sophia and her many manifestations. The Enneads had learned that participation is revelation. As James, Steiner, Jung, and the Dalai Lama in particular have explained so brilliantly, the divine is revealed in its pluralism; no one concept of the divine is adequate to the variety and complexity of human-divine relationships. Sophia is radically plural as well as singular.

This is what all of the Enneads had come to understand, and it is the theme of the next great work: unity issues from diversity in communion. Many are at the table, yet it is one feast; many are in the orchestra, yet it is one symphony; there are nine voices and yet one voice in this richly singular, temporal and eternal symposium. As the experience of the Enneads confirmed, the divine is neither exclusively eternal nor exclusively temporal; it is here and now and it is inexhaustible, eternally preserved.

Discarnate human beings make themselves known and heard to those with eyes to see them and ears to hear them, just what the Enneads did, or was done to them, but only because they had prepared, had followed talk with a silence filled with a new, Logos-Sophia revelation. In the beginning was the Word, and in the present moment is the Word;

in the beginning is Isis-Sophia, infinite and eternal Wisdom, and in the Esalen Big House living room is Isis-Sophia, speaking-showing Wisdom to those with ears to hear Her, with words to speak for Her—in several different languages. Perhaps it was Goethe, the oldest of the nine, who saw this first and had made it central to his life's work: he saw that all creative work, and apprehension of true knowledge, proceeds by the simultaneous evolution of the total work and the parts.

Goethe's idea of metamorphosis would be a key to the next great work: writing it would be like writing a drama that can only come to be by articulating the revelation. Logos helps to reveal Sophia. Though it was only retrospectively that the Enneads were able to understand this to be so, the Enneads in the hour of the unexpected had heard and spoken as one and many—a drama unfolding. The realization dawned slowly because the Enneads all experienced their hearing as peculiarly their own (as each character in a play tends to think that his or her part is what the play is really about). Eventually, all of the Enneads realized that their individual speaking was equally their own and the speaking of the entire revelation which began to emerge as an invocation to Sophia.

Slowly, Sophia revealed Herself as the core of the next great vision. The unexpected hour witnessed the manifestation of Sophia and the transformation of dichotomies—matter/spirit, external/internal, divine/human, divine/earthly, human/earthly—into creative polarities, the human-divine, the Earth-divine, the silent-double word, Logos-Sophia. Another Goethean ideal, polarity, had emerged as a key to a sustainable future.

By the inspiration and guidance of Sophia, stubborn dichotomies gave way to polarities in the last hours of this remarkable meeting:

- Goethe affirmed the Hegelian grand historical vision
- Hegel added a contemporary understanding of Asian thought and culture
- James affirmed Sri Aurobindo's conception of unity
- Steiner recognized the genius of William James and the profound karmic role of American thought and culture

- Whitehead granted the idea of personal immortality
- Teilhard embraced Steiner's and the Dalai Lama's account of the contribution of Buddha to the evolution of human consciousness
- the Dalai Lama committed to a more explicit account of earthly evolution
- and they all resolved to practice Goethe's "gentle empiricism" in service of the ailing Mother

Determined to attend to the fate of human and earthly life, the Enneads recognized the need to understand and explain their shared prescient moment at Esalen in the context of the unfolding future, and particularly in response to their two defining texts. They needed to assess whether their vision would prevent the people—and the Earth—from perishing, and they needed to understand what their unexpected hour might portend. In varying degrees, all of the Enneads were convinced that their vision of Sophia, and their invocation to Her, came to them at precisely the right 'hour,' could not have come sooner, and would continue to gain in significance in the future. The great *kairos* they experienced together enabled them to see their experience as a new beginning, truly a New Age, the lineaments of which they were able to see even before they departed from Esalen and from each other.

# For Our Friendly Neighborhood Innkeeper

## JOHN CLEESE

I well remember the first time I met Michael Murphy. I was visiting Esalen, having been invited to play in the annual table tennis tournament, sadly discontinued nowadays, due to the frightful injury suffered by Mother Teresa in the 1985 Ladies Final.

What happy days those were!

Anyway, I had just defeated Aldous Huxley in the first round, and he insisted on taking me over to meet Ken Wilber, whom I was seeded to play in the quarter finals, who was having tea with Bertrand Russell, and Mahatma Gandhi. Suddenly a friendly little fellow, with a disarming grin, arrived with a tray of tea, scones, and good red wine. "Hello," he said, "I'm Mike Murphy. I'm the inn keeper."

I sent him off for a caramel latte, and Aldous took the opportunity to point out that Mike owned the place. Michael's father, I learned, had won the Esalen estate, playing cards with William James. So, by the time Michael scurried back with my coffee, I was ready to fawn appropriately, and asked him about the time he had spent with Sri Aurobindo. However the conversation did not last long, as Michael was keen to catch the last few holes of the Augusta Masters.

As I watched him running into the distance, I was astonished to see Sir Isaac Newton approaching from the direction of the baths. Astonishing coincidence, because I was playing him in the second round of the table tennis that very evening. I introduced myself, told him I was a big fan of his "Opticks" and asked him whether he had come all the way from England just to display his famous pen-holder grip.

"Oh no," he said. "I come to Esalen because this is where the weird-est people on earth can talk about what's really on our minds. In my case, astrology." "Oh!" I said, "and what sign are you?" and to my sur-prise he hit me.

# And Seriously…

# Michael Murphy
# and the Two Realms

### ROBERT B. REICH

When we or someone we love has a significant birthday—usually ending in a zero—we are drawn to introspection about where we've been and where we are heading, along with new resolve about how we wish to use our remaining years. It is an occasion for renewal. Societies move through similar repeated occasions. For example, the start of every fourth year—when a new president is inaugurated or begins a second term—invites new resolve about how we will improve the nation. Both recurring urges—toward self-renewal and public renewal—require persistent enthusiasm and unending hope.

To help us in these efforts, we often seek two kinds of guidance. One tells us how we can improve ourselves—by losing weight, becoming healthier and fitter, making more money, better enjoying sex, getting in deeper contact with the cosmos or ourselves, becoming more influential, or otherwise fulfilling our potential. The other tells us how to improve society—by cleaning up the environment, reducing nuclear stockpiles, relieving poverty and inequality, and so on.

The two kinds of advice often begin from different premises. The path of self-renewal assumes that our private lives are unsatisfactory in some way and that by following some prescribed course of action we can achieve happiness and fulfillment. The path toward public renewal assumes that certain cherished ideals we hold in common are unfulfilled and that by mending our collective ways we can achieve a good society.

Most of us carry around both sets of aspirations—one for our-selves and our families, another for our society (or for mankind, future generations, the planet). The two are not always in perfect harmony. The public interest, after all, is different than the sum of our selfish wants—the musings of microeconomists and political power brokers to the contrary notwithstanding. The task of improving society involves more than satisfying the personal desires of some people without mak-ing others feel worse off.

Research into political attitudes reveals an important difference between the two realms. Although people sometimes vote on the basis of what's good for them personally, they also put aside personal inter-ests to a surprising degree. Years ago, it was found that people's views on busing to achieve racial integration have been shown to depend less on their own experience with busing (or the likelihood that their chil-dren would either be bused or go to school with children who were) than on their beliefs about the value of racial integration in general. People's ideas about the overall level of unemployment and about hard-ships it causes have more effect on their voting patterns than whether they themselves are unemployed or in danger of becoming so. Attitudes toward the wars in Iraq and Afghanistan turn much less on whether one (or one's family members or close friends) have experienced it first-hand than on one's general views of American foreign policy. Attitudes toward Government programs to provide universal health insurance or guarantee jobs are better correlated with one's general political views than with one's own health or employment status. And so on.

Indeed, the two realms of aspiration are sometimes at war with one another, just as are our selfish and social inclinations. America's passion for public improvement waxes and wanes over time, alternating with periods in which we are more preoccupied by personal aspiration. We have seen that periods of public consciousness—the Progressive era of the first decades of the last century, the Depression and war decades of the 1930s and 1940s, the reformist 1960s—eventually end in exhaustion and disillusionment when reforms fail to achieve the exaggerated hopes that fueled them, causing the public to turn inward. Eras of personal consciousness—the 1920s, 1950s, 1980s, the 2000s—ultimately end when people feel empty and unconnected from one another even when their personal ambitions are satisfied, causing a society to turn outward once again.

The true role of leadership is to bridge the two realms, but few leaders manage it. Great statesmen and prophets through the ages have decried the narcissism, greed, and self-indulgence that divert attention from social ideals. They admonish us, in effect, to stop being obsessed with our own self-renewal and focus instead on the needs of others. Great spiritual leaders and personal guides, by contrast, reassure us that we shouldn't feel guilty, bad or otherwise inadequate because of what "society" demands of us. We'd be far better off if we stopped listening to all the preaching imposed on us and responded instead to personal aspirations that arise from deep inside. By freeing ourselves from societies' "oughts" and "shoulds" we can become more spontaneous, energetic, and authentic.

Which brings me to Michael. For reasons that only he knows, he has been able to combine the two realms of aspiration into a single vision. Esalen is about self-actualization but also about social-actualization. Michael founded it on his deep conviction that society cannot be good and just if its citizens are not good and just; and that, likewise, individuals have no true chance of personal fulfillment if their society is wracked by social ills. The two aspirations are, in fact, completely interdependent. Michael is both a spiritual leader and a social leader—dedicating himself to achieving hugely ambitious and almost impossible public goals (consider, for example, the audacity of bringing Soviet leaders together with American leaders at the height of the Cold War), while at the same time leading generations toward deeper personal insight.

Although most of us hold both aspirations—self renewal and public renewal—in our heads simultaneously, we tend to be more responsive to one of them at one time in our lives than at another. When we first reach political consciousness—typically between the ages of 18 and 21, or whenever we first leave home—the self-absorption of our teen-age years gives way to a greater concern with the society around us, its aspirations and the inevitable gaps that lie between such aspirations and reality. Then, with the start of our own families, individual concerns tend to take precedence once again. After our children leave home, many of us return to the public realm—improving our communities, involving ourselves in social movements, seeking positive change. Our personal wants and public wants cycle back and forth in this way as we live out our lives.

Not Michael. He has consistently and unfailingly sought both. He founded Esalen when he was a young man, patiently nourished and grew it as he moved into the middle years of his life, and continues to give it and the ideas and ideals on which it is based ever greater and deeper scope. His zest, energy, humor, and insight have fired up generations of personal reformers and social reformers who understand the connections between the two. To those who know him by reputation he is merely remarkable; to those who have had the pleasure and privilege of knowing him personally, he is transcendent. His 80th gives us an opportunity to contemplate not only his own renewal but our own, and our world's.

# Applied Hope

## AMORY B. LOVINS

*This tribute is adapted from the opening essay for*
*Rocky Mountain Institute's 2007–08 Annual Report*

What I admire in Michael is his lifelong quest not only to see the best in humanity—call it *human potential*—but also to make that potential actual, in others as in himself. Call it *applied hope*.

The early bioneer Bill McLarney was stirring a vat of algae in his Costa Rica research center when a brassy North American lady strode in. What, she demanded, was he doing stirring a vat of green goo when what the world really needs is *love*? "There's theoretical love," Bill replied, "and then there's *applied* love"—and kept on stirring.

At Rocky Mountain Institute, we stir and strive in the spirit of applied hope. Our ninety people work hard to make the world better, not from some airy theoretical hope, but in the practical and grounded conviction that starting with hope and acting out of hope can cultivate a different kind of world worth being hopeful about, reinforcing itself in a virtuous spiral. Hope, after all, is (as Frances Moore Lappé notes) "a stance, not an assessment." Nor is applied hope the same as theoretical hope. Applied hope is not about some vague, far-off future but is expressed and created moment by moment through our choices.

So, likewise, at Esalen.

Michael is a thinker, a writer, a novelist, a mystic, and a philosopher. He could have settled down on the land his grandmother left him and lived the life of a gentleman scholar. He could have built a mansion and crowned himself Baron of Esalen. He could have contemplated sunsets across the Pacific and meditated on a better future. But no. He insisted on making it so. He gave away his inheritance and, together with Dick Price, created something new under the sun.

At the core of Michael's mission, Esalen's mission, is "the religion of no religion," in the words of one of his teachers at Stanford, philosopher Frederic Spiegelberg. After dropping out of graduate school in philosophy, after his journey to the East and his sojourn in an ashram founded by Sri Aurobindo, Michael created an institution dedicated to the incarnation of spirituality. Not a new church, God help us, but a place where people could explore their highest potential.

Perched on those awesome cliffs, Esalen offers its guests an opportunity to challenge themselves to become better human beings, even as its beauty inspires them to do so. Esalen's natural beauty is only part of its magic. Michael has nurtured a culture of incarnate spirituality where mind and body, heart and soul, mix in a community of amazing individuals. Managing an institution like Esalen is a tall order. Just try to exercise authority in a community of anti-authoritarians!

At RMI we think a lot about energy, then we go out and do something about it. So, likewise, Esalen's practitioners don't just think about "energy." They poke and prod and knead and massage, both literally and figuratively. They till the earth and feed their folks. Both RMI and Esalen are all about improving our metabolism. Realizing human potential, applying hope, is earthy stuff.

Applied hope is not mere glandular optimism. The optimist treats the future as fate, not choice, and thus fails to take responsibility for making the world we want. Applied hope is a deliberate choice of heart and head. The optimist, says David Orr, has his feet up on the desk and a satisfied smirk knowing the deck is stacked. The person living in hope has her sleeves rolled up and is fighting hard to change or beat the odds. Optimism can easily mask cowardice. Applied hope requires fearlessness.

Fear of specific and avoidable dangers has evolutionary value. Nobody has ancestors who weren't mindful of saber-toothed tigers. But pervasive dread, currently in fashion and sometimes purposely promoted, is numbing and demotivating. Sometimes after I give a talk, a questioner details the many bad things happening in the world and asks how dare I propose solutions: isn't resistance futile? The only response I've found is to ask, as gently as I can, "Does feeling that way make you more effective?"

Freud and Jung were spelunkers in the depths of human sorrow, pathology, and psychosis. Carl Rogers and Abraham Maslow showed the way toward the heights of self-actualization. We need maps of both geographies, and Esalen is a place where both extremes are honored.

To be sure, mood does matter. The last three decades of the 20th Century reportedly saw 46,000 new psychological papers on despair and grief, but only 400 on joy and happiness. If psychologists want to help people find joy and happiness, they're mostly looking in the wrong places. Empathy, compassion, humor, and reversing both inner and outer poverty are all vital. But the most solid foundation we know for feeling better about the future is to improve it—tangibly, durably, reproducibly, and scalably. Prior to 1962, there was nothing quite like Esalen. Today there are clones across the United States and around the world, from Germany to Brazil.

At RMI, we're practitioners, not theorists. We do solutions, not problems. We do transformation, not incrementalism. In a world short of both hope and time, we seek to practice Raymond Williams's injunction: "To be truly radical is to make hope possible, not despair convincing." Hope becomes possible, practical—even profitable—when advanced resource efficiency turns scarcity into abundance—creating abundance by design, not scarcity by inattention. Then the glass is neither half empty nor half full: rather, it has a 100 percent design margin, expandable by efficiency. Esalen does much the same for psyches.

RMI and Esalen and our myriad partners around the world, known and unknown, are all on a long journey of applied hope. As signs of effectiveness proliferate, our challenges are chiefly those of success—of needing ever more discriminating focus as the world moves our way, demanding that our limited resources be rapidly scaled to serve nearly infinite needs. We can't do everything; doing just anything may miss the mark; doing nothing is unacceptable; but doing the right things at the right time can make all the difference. We are intently engaged in discerning and reaching those goals.

We also know we're making half-century changes that many of us will not live to see. This requires relentless patience and unflappable equanimity. It works best in the spirit of applied hope encapsulated by Michael C. Muhammad: "Everything works out right in the end. If things are not working right, it's not the end yet. Don't let it bother you, relax and keep on going."

In a world so finely balanced between fear and hope, with the outcome in suspense and a whiff of imminent shift in the air, we choose to add the small stubborn ounces of our weight on the side of applied hope. And if ever our hope flags, if too many miles on too many flights bend our bodies into kinks of tension, we return to Esalen for nurturance and inspiration. Thank you, Michael!

# Michael Murphy and Embodied Practices

## Robert N. Bellah

Michael Murphy is a man of many gifts and many interests. What I want to comment on is an area of interest that I share with him: embodied practices as a central form of human activity, one that is the basis of many of our more specialized activities. My path has not crossed Michael's often over the years. I have read some of his published work and share his interest in sports, particularly our enthusiasm for the San Francisco 49ers in the era of their greatness. My wife and I had one memorable stay at Esalen. I don't remember the exact date except that it was during the period when Mikhail Gorbachev had opened the door to free discussion and all kinds of fascinating things were happening in Russia. A leading figure in Gorbachev's circle was visiting Esalen and I was among those invited for conversation with him. The discussions were indeed stimulating and it was most interesting to hear a leader of then still Communist Russia discussing Soloviev and Berdyaev. It seemed everything was on the table in a way that only a few years earlier would have seemed forever impossible.

Yet, interesting though the discussions were, it was the overall impression of Esalen and the many things going on there that had nothing to do with the discussions with the visiting Russian that made the biggest impression on my wife and me.

There was the sheer beauty of the place, only a few miles from the Zen monastery at Tassajara, though a long way by any means other than hiking, where I had been before. Esalen was just as beautiful as Tassajara with the added glory of the ocean so close at hand. Just being there created a powerful bodily reaction, and with the hot baths, massages, etc., it seemed a place for the fullest relationship between our bodily reality and the cosmos within which it exists.

At the time of my visit to Esalen, though I had been using the idea of religious evolution as the organizing theme of my most frequently taught course, on the sociology of religion, I had not yet begun the thirteen year project of writing a book on the subject that consumed my life from my retirement in 1997 to the completion of the manuscript in 2010.[1] One of the central organizing themes of that project derived from the work of the evolutionary psychologist Merlin Donald. Donald has traced the evolution of human culture through four stages, the first, episodic culture, being shared with other higher mammals. Distinctly human culture begins with mimetic culture in which meanings are expressed through bodily actions and gestures and language was absent or only incipient, and then goes on to mythical culture where full human language allows narratives to arise and myth to form the focus of cultural organization. The fourth cultural capacity arose with the emergence of theoretic culture in the axial age, giving the possibility of universalizable discourse, but not replacing any earlier cultural form. In Donald's scheme each form of culture is reorganized with the emergence of successive capacities, but not abandoned. It is worth quoting from a recent paper of Donald's as to the relation between the various capacities:

> This notion, that every stage of human cognitive evolution found a permanent home in the evolving collective system, is somewhat similar to the evolutionary principle of conservation of previous gains. Previous successful adaptations remained in the system where they proved themselves effective, and the system slowly became more robust, and capable of surviving almost any major blow. This occurred without changing the basic facts of human biology, or the existential dilemma facing every human being.

---

[1] Robert N. Bellah, *Religion in Human Evolution: From the Paleolithic to the Axial Age*, Cambridge, MA: Harvard University Press, 2011.

The modern mind reflects this fact. It is a complex mix of mimetic, mythic, and theoretic elements. Art, ritual, and music reflect the continuation of the mimetic dimension of culture in modern life. The narratives of the great religious books reflect the mythic dimension, as do the many secular myths of modern society. These two great domains—the mimetic and the mythic—are mandatory, hard-wired, and extremely subtle and powerful ways of thinking. They cannot be matched by analytic thought for intuitive speed, complexity, and shrewdness. They will continue to be crucially important in the future, because they reside in innate capacities without which human beings could not function.[2]

In our dominant rational/technological culture we have given "theory" a kind of iconic status, as the source of answers to all our problems. Donald's work is important for validating the common sense of many that science and reason, important though they are, are not the whole story of human culture. Theory can never replace embodied practices and narratives, even though theoretical reflection on these aspects of culture may be helpful.

Embodied practices are things that we share with other animals. Other animals can outrun us and, with claws and teeth and sheer muscle strength, outfight us if we face them without weapons. It has sometimes been said that humans specialize in being generalists, and, of course, in being intelligent. However, we need to note some remarkable human bodily capacities that developed along with our growing cognitive capacities. Other apes lack two skills that are important for humans: the ability to throw accurately, undoubtedly helpful for hunting with weapons, and the ability to keep together in time, without which skillful dancing would be impossible. As Kathleen Gibson puts it:

Humans are certainly surpassed by many other animals in strength and speed, and they fall short of most apes in arboreal locomotor

---

[2] Merlin Donald, "An evolutionary approach to culture: Implications for the study of the Axial Age," in Robert N. Bellah and Hans Joas, eds., *The Axial Age and Its Consequences*, Harvard University Press, forthcoming.

skills and in pedal manipulative capacity. It is doubtful, however, whether any animal exceeds humans in the ability to construct novel body postures and rapid, smoothly produced, sequences of novel postures, such as those that are used in dance, swimming, gymnastics, some complex tool-making-using endeavours, mime and gestural sign languages.[3]

Michael Murphy has been especially sensitive to these human bodily capacities, in the realm of sports, for example. He is particularly interested in states of consciousness that have their origin in bodily practice, For example, he writes that in sports,

> concentration can produce a state of mind graced by extraordinary clarity and focus. British golfer Tony Jacklin said, for example: 'When I'm in this state, this cocoon of concentration, I'm fully in the present, not moving out of it. I'm aware of every half inch of my swing.... I'm absolutely engaged, involved in what I'm doing at that particular moment. That's the important thing. That's the difficult state to arrive at. It comes and it goes, and the pure fact that you go out on the first tee of a tournament and say, 'I must concentrate today,' is no good. It won't work. It has to already be there.' Many sportspeople have described 'the zone,' a condition beyond their normal functioning. Describing such a condition to me, quarterback John Brodie said: 'Often in the heat and excitement of a game, a player's perception and coordination will improve dramatically. At times, and with increasing frequency now, I experience a kind of clarity that I've never seen adequately described in a football story.' As they try to describe such experience, athletes sometimes begin to use metaphors similar to those used in religious writing. Listening to such accounts, I have come to believe that athletic feats can mirror contemplative graces."[4]

---

[3] Kathleen R. Gibson, "Putting It All together: a Constructionist Approach to the Evolution of Human Mental Capacities," in Paul Mellars, et al., *Rethinking the Human Revolution*, Cambridge, UK: McDonald Institute for Archaeological Research, 2007, p. 70.

[4] Michael Murphy, *The Future of the Body*, Los Angeles: Tarcher/Perigree, 1993, p. 444.

This passage in Murphy's book is particularly interesting because, though the focus is on embodied practice, what Donald calls the mimetic, it shows the integration of several levels of culture/consciousness. It points back to episodic consciousness that we share with the higher mammals, that is, a state of open, total, awareness of the situation one is in, something like the Zen practice of mindfulness, being fully in the present moment. And it points ahead to when such moments of total presence can become the focus of reflection about reality, leading to philosophical and religious understanding.

In short, I would argue that Murphy is a cultural healer, helping us to bring together what has been for too long rent asunder. We are our minds, to be sure, but we are also our bodies and our bodies never lose the power to change our consciousness. He is not alone in that teaching but he has made a significant contribution to it.

# Synoptic Flag Burnings

## Don Hanlon Johnson

There is ample reason to celebrate Michael Murphy's 80th birthday just in gratitude for the personal contributions he has made to so many of our lives. However, these personal delights—his seductive charms, disarming smile, bawdy laughter, Irish tall tales, flowing sensuality, delight in high-flying conversation—combined with the glitter of Esalen can obscure the profound intellectual significance of Michael's heritage. To give Michael his due, I use this chance to reflect on his heritage, which lies in the connections between his personality and the visionary ideals he has strewn about many corners of the planet.

The opening words of his magnum opus, *The Future of the Body*, contain it all:

> We live only part of the life we are given. Growing acquaintance with once-foreign cultures, new discoveries about our subliminal depths, and the dawning recognition that each social group reinforces just some human attributes while neglecting or suppressing others have stimulated a worldwide understanding that all of us have great potentials for growth. Perhaps no culture has ever possessed as much publicly available knowledge as we do today regarding the transformative capacities of human nature.

This is not a disembodied Platonic Idea: it's Michael himself. His boisterous intelligence finding delight in new books and people; his generous warmth with new and old friends; his passion for finding ways to address the crises that face our common world; his devotion to running and meditating; his meticulous cleaning up of the messes we tend to make in the Big House kitchen during late night conversations.

Generous with us all, while letting no one of us capture the flag. That fully embodied realization that each of us lives only part of the life we are given, which makes him open to what is yet to be found in each of us, and the broken world.

## A Preamble on Walking Idealism

In *Being and Time*, Martin Heidegger dismantles Plato's theory of a world of Ideas as an illusory move to avoid facing the fact that because we are embodied, we die. The question then left is what to do in the absence of those magnificent ideals which carry us forward; how to avoid cynicism and despair when we realize that such ideals are not eternal nor given from a higher omniscient divinity, but creative products of others muddling through life like us. Heidegger answers this dilemma by a turn towards historical figures, people who do indeed inspire us by revealing the multitude of possibilities of being more fully human. Because they are caked with the muck of ordinary humanity, their pursuit does not leave us in the inevitable discouragement at comparisons with sanitized abstract ideals. These people present real possibilities, even if they require from us a stretch of our constricted notions of what seems reachable. The viability of this alternative to classical idealism is not so obvious; it can easily slide into the imitative life of the disciple who has relinquished his or her soul to the supposed ideal person. Heidegger argues that being situated in one's own vision is crucial to this encounter with the visionary other if one is to avoid falling into imitating heroes:

> The authentic repetition of a possibility of existence that has been— the possibility that Dasein may choose its hero—is grounded existentially in anticipatory resoluteness; for it is in resoluteness that one first chooses the choice which makes one free for the struggle of loyally following in the footsteps of that which can be repeated....the repetition makes a *reciprocative rejoinder* to the possibility of that existence which has-been-there. But when such a rejoinder is made to this possibility in a resolution, it is made *in a moment of vision; and as such* it is at the same time a *disavowal of that which in the 'today' is*

*working itself out as the 'past'*. Repetition does not abandon itself to that which is past, nor does it aim at progress. In the moment of vision, authentic existence is indifferent to both these alternatives.[1] [Italics in Heidegger's original text.]

The key notion is "the moment of vision." If I am actually involved in sweating out the details of embodying my own vision and I encounter another visionary, I can join that person, with respect, even devotion, without surrendering my soul. If I am bereft of vision in that encounter, I may easily lose myself to that person in visionless obedience.

Michael shows us how to do this. His life has been spent among visionaries, often those who delight in cultivating obedient disciples. But he has not permitted anyone to capture the flag over his soul. He has continually made the "reciprocative rejoinders" to those visionaries, incorporating their ingenious perspectives on reality into his ever-growing one. In his carrying forward of Aurobindo, Perls, Rogers, Ramana Maharshi, Thomas Merton, and the like, he does not "abandon himself to that which is past," nor does he construct yet another definition of progress, but reshapes this vision-to-vision encounter within his evolving vision. The familiar slogan—'At Esalen, no one is allowed to capture the flag'—is the being of Michael himself.

## Revolution or Transformation

'Flag-taking' is the recurrent virus infecting social revolutions. In light of the many failed experiments, there is a difficult question about whether it is possible in the modern era to have institutions grounded in a passionate mystical vision with a democratic rather than a hierarchical form. Is it possible to have a vision large enough to encompass "humanity" without falling into fascism or more subtle forms of authoritarianism? Norman O. Brown, Herbert Marcuse, Hannah Arendt, Theodore Roszak were among the many strong voices of the 1960s who raised the

---

[1] *Being and Time*, trans. J. Macquarrie & E. Robinson (New York: Harper and Row, 1962), p. 438.

question of whether there is an alternative to the long repetitive cycle of revolution as a revolving door in which the old oppressed became the new oppressors. Was it possible, many wondered, to have a genuinely new society that was more populist-based?

Michael and I were led into our friendship by the fact that we had shared an arcane research interest probably shared by no more than a very few quirky scholars. The data in question were voluminous accounts in mystical literature in many cultures of body transformation in the lives of supposedly holy people—elongation, levitation, teleporting, clairvoyance, emitting sweet odors long after death, even immortality. While Michael was in India with Sri Aurobindo, I was with the Catholic religious order of Jesuits. Despite the wide geographical and ideological gaps between those two worlds, my teachers and his shared a common notion that serious work with the body—intricate awareness of flows of bodily energy, postures, breathing, movements, diet, fasting, exercise, and painful physical austerities—were the foundation of spiritual transformation.

In *Love's Body*, Brown makes an argument that ran counter to everything I had assumed before I stumbled across it during the same year both of us first went to Esalen:

> Union and unification is of bodies, not souls. The erotic sense of reality unmasks the soul, the personality, the ego; because soul, personality, and ego are what distinguish and separate us; they make us individuals, arrived at by dividing till you can divide no more— atoms. But psychic individuals, separate, unfissionable on the inside, impenetrable on the outside, are, like physical atoms, an illusion; in the twentieth century, in this age of fission, we can split the individual even as we can split the atom. Souls, personalities, and egos are masks, spectres, concealing our unity as body. For it is as one biological species that mankind is one...; so that to become conscious of ourselves as body is to become conscious of mankind as one.[2]

---

[2] *Love's Body* (New York: Vintage, 1968), p. 82

Until I confronted this passage and actually worked through it over several crucial weeks in my journey, I thought it was obvious that unification could only be among souls. You are *there*, with your private inner world reading this text with your eyes and nervous system; I am *here* keyboarding my inner notions onto a screen. We cannot be unified in the flesh. And yet, everyday in our personal lives and in the great worlds of social bodies, we see that union in the realm of the disembodied is impossible. Even between two people, the congruence of ideas and values collapses in the face of dialogue. What is left are shared hunger, touch, comfort, grief, felt hostility, what Edmund Husserl called the intertwinings of our preverbal experiences.[3] "...to become conscious of ourselves as body," as beings who see each other, touching, feeling together, yearning, regretting, ...: here is where we might join, if at all, where ideas lose their overbearing tenacity, leaving room for intimacy and effective collaboration.

In *The Mass Psychology of Fascism*, Wilhelm Reich writes that all freedom-fighters until now have made this miscalculation: "The social incapacity for freedom is sexual-physiologically anchored in the human organism. It follows from this that the overcoming of the physiologic incapacity for freedom is one of the most important basic preconditions of every genuine fight for freedom."[4] He argues that the thriving progressive German community of the 1930s failed to grasp and resist the impact of Hitler because they believed that social change was a matter of debating ideas. They did not understand mass psychology—the power of embodied images, vocal cadences, uniforms, flags, symbols, music, marching, even haircuts and mustache trims.

In his analysis, "embodiment" refers not only to the primal strata of eros and sensibility but to everyday details of life in the world:

---

[3] *Analyses Concerning Passive and Active Synthesis: Lectures on Transcendental Logic*, trans. A. Steinbock (Dordrecht, Netherlands: Kluwer, 2001), p. 283.

[4] *The Mass Psychology of Fascism*, trans. V. Carfagno (New York: Farrar, Straus & Giroux, 1970), p. 347

At first it is only the idea of being like one's superior that stirs the mind of the employee or the official, but gradually, owing to his pressing material dependence, his whole person is refashioned in line with the ruling class....He lives in materially reduced circumstances, but assumes gentlemanly postures on the surface, often to a ridiculous degree. He eats poorly and insufficiently, but attaches great importance to a 'decent' suit of clothes. A silk hat and dress coat become the material symbol of this character structure.[5]

The revolutionary movement also failed to appreciate the importance of the seemingly irrelevant everyday habits, indeed, very often turned them to bad account. The lower middle-class bedroom suite, which the 'rabble' buys as soon as he has the means, even if he is otherwise revolutionary minded; the consequent suppression of the wife, even if he is a Communist; the 'decent' suit of clothes for Sunday; 'proper' dance steps and a thousand other 'banalities,' have an incomparably greater reactionary influence when repeated day after day than thousands of revolutionary rallies and leaflets can ever hope to counterbalance. Narrow conservative life exercises a continuous influence, penetrates every facet of everyday life...[6]

Michael and Richard Price, each in his own idiosyncratic mode, took bushwackers to those disembodied conventions, laying bare the fertile soil underneath, giving room for the primal to emerge. When a teacher would appear who edged towards raising a flag over this garden of earthly delights—an Ichazo, youthful 'Baba' Ram Dass, the Nine...—Michael and Richard would see to it they were melded into the loam of direct challenging conversation and quiet baths.

There is a curious parallel between the social analysis of the body in Reich and in that of Aurobindo and Gandhi. Despite many profound differences, they shared a radically similar notion that the body was the foundational battleground in the fight for freedom. Gandhi's notion

---

[5] Wilhelm Reich, *The Mass Psychology of Fascism*, trans. Vincent Carafagno (New York: Farrar, Straus & Giroux, 1970), p. 47.

[6] *Ibid.*, p. 47.

of *satyagraha* was an explicitly embodied strategy for revolutionaries rooted in hatha yoga, diet and fasting, celibacy, and hands-on therapy. In the context of a Christianized Europe, Reich emphasized the need for sexual liberation. In colonized India, as in the Rome of early Christianity, celibacy was a radical move against the dominant culture. Gandhi argued that celibacy, natural healing methods, and hatha yoga were practices of resistance to the ruling classes.

The work of Jeffrey Kripal has been helpful in his situating Michael's revolutionary moves within the older traditions of Indian tantra and the newer one of Wilhelm Reich in which liberation is grounded in the body. It is no accident that Charlotte Selver, teaching intricate sensory awareness, was the first official teacher at the launch of Esalen in 1964. Soon there followed a host of pioneers in developing strategies for liberating the wisdom and agency lurking in the flesh: Alexander Lowen, Fritz Perls, Ida Rolf, Moshe Feldenkrais, Ilana Rubenfeld, Judith Aston, Fritz Smith, and....to the very present. At the same time, what is perhaps the most longstanding subculture at Esalen began to form: the massage and bodywork crews with their ever-growing brilliant fleshy synthesis of the many teachers who came their way.

But this 'body' which lies at the core of Michael's life vision is not just any body—the animal body feared by spiritual teachers, the body of confusion distrusted by Plato and Descartes, or the thing-like body of empirical science and calisthenics. It is the luminous body of the mystics, the body of Christ, the flesh of the world—the expansion of our senses, movements, urges and pulsations into the network of relations extending ever-outward into the cosmos.

This new emphasis on the body launched by Michael contains a riposte to the ongoing critiques of Esalen and the Human Potential Movement as narcissistic. From the beginning, inspired by his time with Aurobindo and his early readings of the Christian mystics, Michael sensed that the cultivation of the little explored intricacies of direct bodily experience were the key to a different notion of self embedded in a communal world. His support of the many teachers who were exploring bodily practices has become a strong antidote to the self-enclosed narcissism of popular culture, because these practices are oriented towards what Maurice Merleau-Ponty called "intercorporeity" and the "flesh of the world."[7] In that move, he can be better understood as carrying forward the sociopolitical ideas of Reich rather than the individualism of Fritz Perls.

Eugene Gendlin, the founder of Focusing, penetrated to the heart of this popular misconception of Esalen in "A Philosophical Critique of Narcissism: The Significance of the Awareness Movement." In that seminal piece, he argues that the dilemma facing both leftist and rightist critics of this movement is that the predominant notion of the self was the ego-self, a creature of sociocultural norms already established. In that view, the only alternative was either to conform to those norms or to cast them aside in self-indulgent rebellion. Gendlin, following in the tradition of Edmund Husserl and Maurice Merleau-Ponty, argues that there is a newly emerging social possibility based on a community of people who are learning how to pay attention to the patterned intricacies within direct bodily experience.

> People are now living and working in the old forms, again. On the one hand, they do not rebel openly against the old forms. On the other hand, they do not fully identify themselves in them. They identify themselves with an inward complexity, even when there is no way to live from it.[8]

That is the problem facing us: how to create institutions within which we can live this intricacy. Here is where Michael's work is situated, not within the movements of self-indulgence.

> The critics of the Awareness Movement cannot imagine an inner emergence more ordered than external programming. The body has no order of its own. For Foucault the task of his "genealogy" was "to

---

[7] "The Intertwining—The Chiasm," in *The Visible and the Invisible*, trans. Alphonso Lingis (Evanston, IL: Northwestern, 1968), pp. 130-155.

[8] "A Philosophical Critique of Narcissism: The Significance of the Awareness Movement," in David Michael Levin, ed., *Pathologies of the Modern Self: Postmodern Studies on Narcissism, Schizophrenia, and Depression* (New York: New York Univ Press, 1987), p. 254.

expose a body totally imprinted by history and the process of history's destruction of the body." For Foucault there is not even a primitive 'narcissistic' body left over. Aside from external programming there is nothing at all. For others there is a primitive narcissism. But all these thinkers assume that any intricate and relational experience can only reflect unconscious programming.[9]

The current split (inward freedom/outward conformity) accepts intricate experience as cut off from the environment. That split comes largely from helplessness, the impossibility of affecting external arrangements so that one could live from intricate experience. The self's new intricacy seems only inner because the external controls prevent it from being lived out. Therefore it can be lived only in private *self*-responding. But if the intricacy is accepted as *inherently* only something inner, then the social controls are accepted without having been noticed. What prevents one's outward efficacy is masked and unseen.[10]

Intricate Esalen is Michael's response to the need that Gendlin articulates for social structures that mirror a new sense of self, communal embodiments of lived intricacy. Grounded in that unique piece of the planet and grounded also in his life-long practices, Esalen and Michael's other projects reach towards a communal, democratic vision.

## One Species, One Planet — Synoptic Empiricism

That vision stands out in relief against our dark histories rife with tribalism, cultism, and particularism. Periodically there have emerged movements towards building a *human* community. Biblical humanism reaches for it based on the belief that we are all children of one God; Marxist humanism, that we are all one biological species; Sufi humanism, that all are united in the heart and mind, or something like that. But these great humanistic visions keep butting up against

---

[9] *Ibid.*, 256.
[10] *Ibid.*, p. 257.

the alienating shift towards Popes, Chairmen, Ayatollahs, Mothers and Fathers of myriad cults, those who would see to it that we follow the vision as they envision it, by extreme force if need be. Michael's great contribution is to have consistently grounded his magnificent visions of 'the human' in attention to breathing, running, stretching, sexing, and the range of experiences that makes us ever aware that we are earthly just as much as heavenly. And as earthly, the foundational virtue is humility, from *humus*, the dirt from which Adam was formed, a humility which radiates from our beloved elder on his birthday.

# The Moral Arc of History

ROBERT W. FULLER

The arc of the moral universe is long but it bends towards justice.
— Martin Luther King, Jr.

## One Tribe Becomes Many

Fifty to one hundred thousand years ago, a small group of *homo sapiens* made its way out of Africa and established settlements in what we now call the Middle East. Over the millennia, we multiplied and spread across the whole earth. In response to variations in climate, one race became many.

As earlier hominids had done, we gathered and we hunted, preying on whatever and whomever we could. We also sought power and used our language and model-building[1] skills to turn nature's power to our purposes.

Our forebears domesticated plants and animals, steadily improved their tools and weapons, and honed their fighting skills. By the time different tribes ran into one another, they no longer recognized they were all of one family. Other humans looked strange, sounded stranger, and made us afraid.

When facing enslavement or death, we used our martial skills to defend ourselves. Or, if we had the advantage, we could prey on others. All it takes is one predatory tribe to drag others into the fight.[2]

---

[1] For a primer on modeling, see Chapter 3 of *All Rise: Somebodies, Nobodies, and the Politics of Dignity* (San Francisco: Berrett-Koehler, 2006)

[2] As Andrew Bard Schmookler points out in *The Parable of the Tribes: The Problem of Power in Social Evolution* (University of California Press, 1984), if any one group adopts an aggressive policy towards others, the targets of that aggression must either develop a commensurate martial capability or submit to domination.

Among the models we built, those pertaining to social organization and governance were especially important to the power we could mobilize. The nature of relationships within a group can either facilitate or undercut alignment around a common political purpose. Prosperity and solidarity, both so powerfully affected by institutions of governance, determine a group's capability to defend itself against other groups or to dominate them.

## Power Rules

The "olden days" often seem rosier in hindsight than they did to people at the time. So, it's not hard to understand why, in the thick of the struggle for survival, the authors of Genesis conjured an Edenic paradise. We've been comforting ourselves with stories of bountiful origins ever since.

Archeologists tell a different story. In place of noble savages living in abundance and harmony, they give us a picture of "constant battles" driven by scarcity of food and resources.[3] Humans multiply quickly; our numbers can soon outstrip the food supply. But, the precise causes of conflict are not relevant here. Very likely they ranged from competition to survive in the face of dwindling resources to dreams of empire. Life presented an endless series of choices that turned on kinship. Friend or foe? To embrace or exploit?

One choice sees strangers as lost relatives, the other as potential aggressors, or as prey. In the struggle for survival, "we" have just what "they" need—food, water, tools, territory, animals, child-bearers, manpower—and vice versa. If resources are scarce, appropriating those of other humans may be the only chance for survival, or it may simply recommend itself as a get-rich-quick scheme.

Once the choice is made to regard others as prey, the aim, if not to kill, is to subordinate and enslave. Far from being an aberration, slavery has been commonplace in history. Only in the nineteenth century

---

[3] *Constant Battles: The Myth of the Peaceful, Noble Savage*, by Steven LeBlanc and Katherine E. Register (New York: St. Martin's Press, 2003).

was its legitimacy seriously questioned. Slavery continues to this day in overt forms (child-slavery and human trafficking), and in the indirect form of subsistence wages. As Reverend Jim Wallis has put it, "Poverty is the new slavery."[4]

Of course, modern humans didn't invent the predatory option. We absorbed it imitatively from our hominid ancestors, and before that, from primates whose internecine battles have been well documented.

To limit injury to self, we, like other predators, opportunistically targeted the weak. None of us would be here if our own ancestors had not been either relatively successful predators (or relatively good evaders of others' predations).

Sari Nusseibeh, president of Al Quds University in Jerusalem and a descendant of an aristocratic Palestinian family, quotes his father as telling him, "All family dynasties can trace their histories back to some act of brigandage."[5] I have heard the same from the heirs of several American fortunes.

## Hierarchy and Rank

We tend to think of rank as sanctioning abuse and exploitation, but, in its conception, rank served as a device for *regulating* predation within the group. By concentrating power in a "top dog" or a "king" and a ruling class, rank served to replace anarchic predation with regulated predation. Despite the privileges taken for itself by the aristocracy, this represented progress at the time.

Every human society, of any size and complexity, has employed hierarchical control. Not to do so was to fall victim to groups that did avail themselves of the superior organization afforded by the tools of rank and hierarchy. Law and order trumps anarchy. In return for providing order, the ruler and the ruling class take a share of the fruits of the labor of those they protect from anarchy and foreign invaders. No

---

[4] *God's Politics* by Jim Wallis

[5] This quote appears in a New York Times book review by Ethan Bronner on March 29, 2007 of Sari Nusseibeh's book (with Anthony David) *Once Upon a Country: A Palestinian Life* (New York: Farrar, Straus and Giroux, 2007)

wonder we're suspicious of rank—it's the linchpin of the archetypal protection racket. With a few notable, game-changing exceptions, lordship degenerates into overlordship.

But, the existence of the occasional benevolent ruler makes the point that rank is not inherently evil: we admire, we even love, just, fair-minded authorities who serve the group and eschew personal gain.

When rulers violate the terms of the tacit contract they have with their subjects—by unduly exploiting them, self-aggrandizement, or by failing to protect them against external predators—indignities multiply, fester, and may lead to rebellion and revolution. Over the long-term, the result is to rein in the powers of the governing class. Reforms that hold rulers accountable diminish rank's prerogatives and represent progress for human dignity and human rights.

Think of the examples that follow as milestones towards a world in which the opportunity for abusing the power exercised by officials is reduced. In listing a few key figures and landmark events in the expansion of the circle of dignity, no attempt is made at inclusiveness. This is merely a "starter" list, the purpose of which is to provoke readers to make nominations to their own dignitarian hall of fame.

## Milestones on the Road to Universal Dignity

> I believe in Spinoza's God who reveals himself in the orderly harmony of what exists, not in a God who concerns himself with the fate and actions of human beings.[6]                              — Albert Einstein

### Monotheism

In contrast to polytheism, where the various gods may be at odds with one another, a single god is presumed to have a comprehensive, unitary consciousness.

Monotheism is the theological counterpart of the scientist's belief in the ultimate reconcilability of apparently contradictory observations

---

[6] *Albert Einstein—Creator and Rebel*, Banesh Hoffmann (Viking, New York, 1972), n. 1, p.254.

into one consistent framework. If God is of one mind, we cannot expect to know that mind until, at the very least, we have eliminated inconsistencies in our data and contradictions in our partial visions. This democratizes the search for truth by undercutting the notion that the imprimatur of authority (e.g., the Church) makes a proposition true.

Monotheism is therefore a powerful constraint on the models we build. They must be free of both internal and external contradictions; they must not depend on who it is that's doing the observing. This is a stringent condition for models to satisfy, and few do.

Theistic religions proclaim the existence of a personal, caring God. Given the supreme importance of dignity and human beings' spotty record when it comes to providing it to each other, it's the rare person who, when worldly options are exhausted, has not imagined acceptance from a supra-human source. As the "dignifier of last resort," a supreme being, whose judgment trumps that of our community, can validate our strivings when our fellow humans reject us.

If and when we discover life elsewhere in the universe, the question of monotheism will arise again: if extra-terrestrials worship a god, is their god our God, or are we back to polytheism?

The same laws of nature that obtain on Earth hold as far as we can peer into the Universe. If there is a Creator, it would appear that He doesn't reinvent the wheel. If the same physical laws hold throughout the universe, then it's plausible that aliens will honor dignity as we do. This will be a good thing for us, if, as is statistically likely, we are not the most advanced life-forms in the Cosmos, because then more advanced beings will watch over us, much as we protect endangered species.

### The Golden Rule

Just as good parents do not play favorites among their children, so God, conceived of as a single idealized father figure, would presumably accord equal dignity to *all* his "children." The Golden Rule is a symmetry condition—equal dignity for all, regardless of rank or role—that, with slight variations, is found in virtually every religion or ethical code.[7]

> Do not do to others what would cause pain if done to you.
> — Hinduism

> Treat not others in ways that you yourself would find hurtful.
> — Buddhism

> What you do not want done to yourself, do not do to others.
> — Confucianism

> What is hateful to you, do not do to your neighbor.
> — Judaism

> Do unto others as you would have them do unto you.
> — Christianity

> Not one of you truly believes until you wish for others what you wish for yourself.
> — Islam

> We should behave to our friends, as we would wish our friends to behave to us.
> — Aristotle

> Act only on that maxim through which you can at the same time will that it should become a universal law.
> — Immanuel Kant's Categorical Imperative

Contrariwise, a deviation from equal dignity is a broken symmetry and, as in physics, a deviation from symmetry signals the existence of a force that breaks it. Among humans, asymmetries take the form of inequitable or preferential treatment of persons or groups and, as in the physical world, these deviations from the symmetry implicit in the Golden Rule signal the existence of coercion. For example, slavery requires force or the threat of force.

---

[7] See www.loyno.edu/twomey/blueprint/GoldenRule.jpg and http://religioustolerance.org/reciproc.htm

## *Hammurabi's Legal Code[8] (18th century BCE)*

I had an ah-ha experience as a boy when I heard about King Hammurabi's practice of posting not only a list of crimes, but right along side each one, the specific punishments that would be meted out for committing them. By having the code carved in stone, the Babylonian ruler was signaling that the laws were immutable, universal, and not even subject to the whim of the king himself. Hammurabi's Code is one of the first to establish the presumption of innocence until proven guilty. I urged my parents to emulate Hammurabi.

## *The Ten Commandments of Moses[9] (15th-13th century B.C.E.)*

The notion of a commandment raises the issue of the authority of the command-giver. Although most of the Ten Commandments sounded reasonable in Sunday School, I wondered about their origin. How could anyone be sure they came from God? Moreover, not everyone believed in the existence of God in the first place. I thought it would be important to non-believers to demonstrate that these rules could be justified in terms of their contribution to social wellbeing. And, if they could not be so justified, to drop them. Among other things, the Commandments give expression to the idea of monotheism and its corollary of a single Fatherhood within which we are all brothers and sisters deserving of equal dignity.

## *Confucius[10] (551 B.C.E.–479 B.C.E.)*

Confucius emphasized personal and governmental morality and justice. Like the biblical prophets and their Kingdom of Heaven, Confucius imagined a Mandate of Heaven in which rulers chosen on the basis of merit, not birth, would bring peace and prosperity to the people through the power of exemplary moral behavior. Again, the

---

[8] Wikipedia: http://en.wikipedia.org/wiki/Hammurabi#Code_of_laws
[9] See Exodus 19:23 and Deuteronomy 5:2. Also, Wikipedia: http://en.wikipedia.org/wiki/Ten_commandments
[10] Wikipedia: http://en.wikipedia.org/wiki/Confucius#Teachings

idea is that the governing class is not above the law but rather is honor bound to serve others, not self.

## *Mo Tzu's Family of Man and Doctrine of Universal Love[11] (5th century B.C.E.)*

Mo Tzu is less well known in the West than other Eastern prophets, but no less significant. He may have been first to see the world as a village of kinsfolk, and from this insight he deduced that aggressive war is never justified. His doctrine of universal love and his argument that it is "supremely practical" were prescient and original. Mo Tzu's place in the Dignitarian Hall of Fame is unassailable, despite his diatribes against music and dance. Even in antiquity, futurists had their foibles.

## *Jesus (6 B.C.E.—30 C.E.)*

An advocate of universal love and teacher of dignitarian values, Jesus instructed: "You shall love your neighbor as yourself."[12] This goes beyond assurances of equal dignity, but a world in which no one fears for his or her dignity will likely be one in which brotherly love will feel much nearer at hand than it does to most today. Absent indignity, love might just possibly "bust out all over."

## *Magna Carta[13] (England, 1215)*

When King John yielded to the demands of the barons at Runnymede—that he spell out his powers and guarantee their privileges—he was starting down a road that would lead to constitutional democracy. The "Great Charter" he was forced to sign famously includes the writ of habeas corpus, enshrining the right to appeal against unlawful imprisonment. I suspect that there were voices at Runnymede who resisted taking those first baby steps towards democracy on the

---

[11] An introduction to Mo Tzu's thought is provided by Burton Watson, *Mo Tzu: Basic Writings* (New York: Columbia University Press, 1963). See also Wikipedia, which gives his name as Mozi: http://en.wikipedia.org/wiki/Mo_Tzu

[12] Matthew 22:39

[13] Wikipedia: http://en.wikipedia.org/wiki/Magna_carta

grounds that gorillas had not done so and therefore it was contrary to nature to devolve power. That kind of thinking, still heard today, fails to appreciate the extent to which human intelligence and communication skills make possible complex organizations that, by tapping the power of numbers, can trump brute force.

### Martin Luther and the Protestant Reformation[14] (Germany, 1517)

The Protestant Reformation began as a protest against systemic corruption within the church hierarchy, extending even to the Pope. In his magisterial account of political revolutions, Eugen Rosenstock-Heussy[15] argues that the least corrupt countries are heirs of the Protestant Revolution.

### Oliver Cromwell, Charles I, and the "Divine Right of Kings" (Britain, 1649)

Putting the king on trial and chopping off his head unambiguously made a point, (subsequently reiterated by the French in the headless person of King Louis XVI), that indeed there was no *right* to rule, divine or otherwise. Once the Divine Right of Kings has been nullified, people are free to ask, "Who *does* have the right to rule?" and to imagine that governing is not a right at all, and that our governors should serve us, not vice versa. The shift from monarchy to democracy prefigures the shift from faith-based to evidence-based truth: trust your own eyes over authority.

### The Glorious Revolution[16] (British, 1688–89)

The Glorious Revolution marked the end of absolute monarchial power and the beginning of modern English parliamentary democracy. The monarch could no longer suspend laws, levy taxes, make royal appointments, or maintain a standing army during peacetime without

---

[14] Wikipedia: http://en.wikipedia.org/wiki/Protestant_reformation

[15] Eugen Rosenstock-Heussy, *Out of Revolution: Autobiography of Western Man* (Norwich, VT: Argo Books, 1969)

[16] Wikipedia: http://en.wikipedia.org/wiki/Glorious_Revolution

Parliament's permission, a historic step towards civilian control of the military. The Bill of Rights it produced is a milestone in the history of liberty, justice, and human dignity.

### Frederick the Great[17] (King of Prussia, 1744–97)

Unlike many of his contemporaries, Frederick did not believe in the Divine Right of Kings. He saw himself as the "first servant of the state" and joked that the crown was "a hat that let the rain in." To attract a more skilled citizenry, he generally supported religious tolerance, proclaiming, "All religions are equal and good and as long as those practicing are an honest people and wish to populate our land…we will build them mosques and churches." Yes, mosques.

### The U.S. Constitution (1776–1787)

Its genius was to assume the worst of politicians and design an elaborate system of checks and balances to minimize corruption and maximize the accountability of office holders. Its most egregious flaw was the creation of two kinds of exclusions: women and people of color were held in abusive, exploitative second-class citizenships.[18] It took the Suffragette movement of the 19th century to win women the vote and the Civil War and the civil rights movement to win equal rights for racial minorities. Despite its shortcomings, the U.S. Constitution is a landmark in circumscribing the prerogatives of government and, as amended, upholding the rights of citizens.

### "Liberté, Égalité, Fraternité" (France, 1789)

France's tri-partite revolutionary slogan has inspired reformers for two centuries. A puzzling omission is **Dignité**, which trumps the slogan's three stated goals.

---

[17] Wikipedia: http://en.wikipedia.org/wiki/Frederick_The_Great
[18] See forthcoming book by Richard Baldwin, *Re-Birth of a Nation: American Identity and the Culture Wars.*

*The Abolition of Slavery (Britain, 1833; Russia, 1861; and the United States, 1863)*

Slavery was regarded as business as usual until the 18th century when Enlightenment thinkers criticized it for violating the Rights of Man and Quakers condemned it as a violation of Christian ethics.[19] Czar Alexander II freed the serfs in Russia in 1861 and Lincoln issued the Emancipation Proclamation freeing the slaves held in the Confederate States in 1863. Two years later, the 13th Amendment to the U.S. Constitution prohibited slavery throughout the country.

*Labor Unionization (19th—20th century)*

A landmark in the struggle between Nobodies and Somebodies (in the respective roles of Labor and Management) was the adoption of legislation guaranteeing the right of employees to unionize and bargain collectively.

*Gandhi and Decolonization (20th century)*

In the 20th century the imperial powers were forced to abandon colonialism as subjects learned to mount effective resistance to foreign occupation. Once the costs of enforcing exploitation exceeded the value of what could be expropriated, colonialism in its traditional form was finished.

*Universal Declaration of Human Rights of the United Nations[20] (1948)*

The United Nations Charter elevates dignity to the status of a human right and charges governments with protecting it.

---

[19] The story of William Wilberforce and the abolition of slavery is told in Adam Hochschild's gripping book, *Bury the Chains: Prophets and Rebels in the Fight to Free an Empire's Slaves* (Boston: Houghton Mifflin 2005) http://en.wikipedia.org/wiki/United_Nations_Declaration_of_Human_Rights

[20] http://en.wikipedia.org/wiki/United_Nations_Declaration_of_Human_Rights

## The Civil Rights, Women's, and Other Identity Movements (late 20th c.)

Exploited subgroups have learned how to organize so as to resist predation by their fellow citizens. Much as slavery lost its sanction in the 19th century, the residue of slavery and segregation—racism—lost legitimacy in the 20th. Other discriminatory "isms" (anti-Semitism, sexism, ageism, ableism, homophobia) have joined racism in disrepute.

But identity politics can take us only so far because it's predicated on an "us" versus "them" distinction. In contrast, dignitarian politics is all-inclusive. All of us are both victims and perpetrators of *rankism*.[21]

In every struggle to overcome an ism there are some non-victims who nevertheless ally themselves with the victims and attempt to overturn the prevailing consensus. For such liberal forerunners, there's an element of altruism at work.

In contrast, one supports the dignity movement against rankism to secure one's *own* dignity, and soon realizes that one's dignity is only as secure as the next fellow's.[22] As self-interest and altruism come into alignment, the Golden Rule is self-enforcing and the transition from a predatory to a dignitarian world becomes irreversible.

## The Human Potential Movement (1960–present).

> Man is a creature who makes pictures of himself and then comes to resemble the picture.                        — Iris Murdock

In its insistence that *everyone* has untapped mental, physical, and spiritual faculties, the Human Potential Movement goes beyond identity politics. No one has done more to midwife this movement than Michael Murphy, co-founder of Esalen Institute,[23] pioneer citizen diplomat, and visionary author. Murphy is an artist who has presented us

---

[21] See, for example, www.huffingtonpost.com/robert-fuller/what-is-rankism-and-why-d_b_465940.html

[22] www.openleft.com/diary/3593/

[23] See *Esalen: America and the Religion of No Religion* by Jeffrey J. Kripal (The University of Chicago Press, 2007).

with a new picture of ourselves, and, slowly but surely, we are coming to resemble the picture.

Each of the milestones mentioned above marks a curtailment of the potential for rank-based abuse, and so a strengthening of individual human rights. Establishing a human right doesn't guarantee it, but it does shift the burden of proof from victim to perpetrator, and that makes officialdom more accountable and therefore less likely to abuse the power inherent in rank.[24]

These milestones provide *empirical* evidence for Martin Luther King, Jr.'s claim that the arc of the moral universe bends toward justice. The arc's curvature, however, is still indecipherable to many. Indeed, no one who witnessed the horrors of the 20th century can be faulted for thinking that the curvature is bending *away* from justice.

To determine the curvature in spite of the arguable historical record, we need a theory.

## From Predation to Dignity: The Paradox of Force

Without a theory the facts are silent.          — Frederic Hayek

Since World War II there have been scores of wars, millions of casualties, tens of millions of refugees; fighting continues today in many parts of the world.

Since the Holocaust, and despite the world's determination that it not happen again, genocides have occurred in Cambodia, Rwanda,

---

[24] *Abuse* of the power attached to rank is *rankism*. I use "abuse" to signify the persistent misuse of power once it's clear that power is being used not to serve the group but to advance the personal interests of its high-ranking members. This explains why dictators and monopolists go to such great lengths to avoid competition. By the time rivals win a chance to challenge their monopoly, the institutions presided over by dictatorial rulers are usually far weaker than the alternatives they've been suppressing, and they crumble quickly. Transitions to more dignitarian governance, once they begin, often occur almost overnight, as in Romania, the Soviet Union, Indonesia, and Serbia.

Bosnia, Darfur, and elsewhere. Persistent poverty enshrouds one-third of the world's six billion people and many fear that population pressure and/or climate change will pit us against each other in a struggle for scarce resources.

In this light, it's not unreasonable to argue that man's predatory practices continue unabated, and many so argue. But, an analysis of the social dynamics of power provides a sliver of hope. Martin Luther King, Jr. did not prophesy quick or easy passage to justice, only that over the long haul the moral arc was bending in our favor.

Successful predation depends on a power advantage. Humans have an edge over the other animals and, from time to time, often as a result of a technical or organizational breakthrough, they may gain an edge over other humans as well. To the extent that we can put people down and keep them there, we can take what's theirs and force them to do our bidding. To the extent that we can't credibly do so, we become vulnerable to *their* predations.

One reading of the human story emphasizes war, domination, rapine, pillage, slavery, colonization, and exploitation. Wealth and leisure for the few and a subsistence living for the many.

Another telling of history, as illustrated in the milestones cited above, highlights overthrowing tyrants, expelling colonizers, and, by marshaling the strength in numbers, progressively emancipating ourselves from domination, slavery, and exploitation.

A "paradox of force" lies in the fact that a group's competitive success vis à vis other groups depends on limiting the use of coercive force *within* the group. Why?

If a ruler is too cruel to his subjects, morale will deteriorate to the point that the group's will to fight is impaired. Unjust leaders do not command loyalty and, when push comes to shove, their people turn on them. On the other hand, if members know their place in a group is respected and secure, this assurance is in itself an asset when competing with other groups.

This means that societies have had to seek a balance between two postures—a *predatory* stance (consisting of some mix of aggressive and defensive capabilities) looking outwards, and a *dignitarian* stance look-ing inwards.

Not to complement outward-directed predatory capability with a modicum of dignity for those within the group has been to lose out to groups whose stronger social bond enabled them to field a superior force. In sum, the predatory capability of a group vis à vis other groups depends on developing dignitarian policies *within* the group.

For this reason, the principle of equal dignity is more than an admonition to be "nice." A policy of equal dignity enhances the strength of groups that practice it. None do so consistently, of course, but some do so more than others and this gives them a competitive advantage stemming from group solidarity. This suggests that, on a millennial time scale, the Golden Rule is self-enforcing. We were too quick to judge it toothless. Rather, it simply took a few thousand years to grow teeth.

As we realize that dignitarian societies have, over the long haul, a competitive advantage, and as less dignitarian groups are absorbed by more dignitarian ones, we operationalize the Golden Rule.

Within a group, it's not just "top dogs" who abuse power. Power abuse is a tempting strategy at any rank because everybody is a some-body to someone and a nobody to someone else. Accordingly, a preda-tory posture can be assumed towards underlings no matter where one stands in the hierarchy.[25]

Because societies predicated on equal dignity are more stable, pro-ductive, creative, and are more strongly committed to their common cause—be it aggressive or defensive—they are, on average, fitter. This does not mean that dignitarian groups win every contest with more predatory ones. Factors other than social cohesion are at play. But it does mean that, with starts and fits, organizations that tolerate power abuses

---

[25] Unless, of course, you are at the very bottom. But even then, you can resort to kick-ing the dog. Much cruelty to animals is a result of indignation that humans feel towards other humans who have humiliated them, but whom they dare not confront because the abusers are shielded by rank.

effectively de-select themselves.[26] Over a long enough time period, the circle of dignity expands more than it shrinks.

The paradox of force is that, statistically, and over time, dignitarian societies gradually absorb more predacious ones until finally there is no longer a significant likelihood of inter-group predation. Indignant, disgruntled outliers may resort to terrorism, but they will not be viable unless they are serving as proxies for a group large enough to harbor and fund them.

A selection process governed by the same dynamic unfolds among organizations. For example, more dignitarian companies will, on average, serve their customers and employees better, and will outperform less dignitarian ones. In the end, equal dignity becomes the norm.

While such an evolutionary trend may sound Pollyannaish, it is revealed as a logical consequence of the free play of power within and between competing groups. The paradox of force—that in the long run, right makes might, not vice versa—provides a causal explanation for Martin Luther King, Jr.'s observation regarding the curvature of the moral universe. Despite the relentless drumbeat of bad news, and barring a major catastrophe (such as one resulting from nuclear war, pandemic, famine, climate change, or collision with an asteroid) denizens of the 21st

---

[26] Whenever a "survival of the fittest" argument is invoked, a question of circularity arises: Can "fittest" be defined independently of "what survives"? In this case, the question takes the form: Can "dignitarian" be defined independently of "what prevails"? If not, the argument is circular, a mere tautology and it can tell us nothing about the curvature of the moral universe.

Indeed, Darwin's theory was initially attacked as circular. Critics maintained that the only way we could gauge fitness was to look and see what survived. Fortunately for the theory of natural selection, it is possible to state independent conditions that give organisms an advantage, or handicap them, in the struggle to survive and reproduce. Similarly, there is by now a long list of practices that are known to undermine dignity. The de-selection of rankist organizations that tolerate rankism is analogous to the de-selection of relatively unfit organisms in the struggle for reproductive survival. Darwin's principle is not circular (fitness criteria *can* be defined independently of survivability), and since it can be foreseen that the inefficiencies attendant to rankism handicap organizations burdened by them, the notion that rankist values are recessive—and dignitarian values dominant—is not circular either.

century could find themselves witness to the phasing out of our age-old predatory strategy and its replacement by a dignitarian one.

## Predation, No; Competition, Yes

The majority of our human ancestors have suffered lives that, as seventeenth-century English philosopher Thomas Hobbes famously put it, were "nasty, brutish, and short." A great many still do. But we're at a critical juncture beyond which lies the possibility of an epochal shift to a post-predatory era. Predation has taken us this far, and for that we must give it its due. But as a survival strategy it can take us no further without undermining what any strategy is meant to do—ensure our survival. We can take heart from the fact that we've already disallowed several broad categories of predatory behavior (e.g., those referenced in "Milestones"), and go on from there to disallow predation itself.

First, however, there's one more make-or-break issue that must be addressed. Removing the traces of predation from our treatment of others is analogous to the reeducation now underway around issues of race, gender, sexual orientation, and disability. It's not a quick or easy process, but a start has been made and there's no going back. For those of us who grew up within a social consensus that condoned the familiar "isms," we can change our overt behaviors, but not entirely eradicate attitudes to which we were exposed as children. What can change, what in fact *has* changed, are the attitudes that one generation models for the next. For the most part, baby boomers did not pass the prejudices of their parents on to their own children. With each successive generation, bigotry attenuates. Over the course of several generations, prejudice and discrimination may diminish to the point where the young wonder what all the fuss was about.

But, in addition to overcoming temptations to put others down and advantage ourselves at their expense, there's a conceptual barrier to putting our predatory past behind us. Disallowing predation sounds impossible because we haven't figured out how to forego it without inhibiting competition. Although it's natural to see competition as the culprit (because it is so very often unfair, and because many competitors interpret winning a particular competition as an excuse for demeaning and exploiting those who lost), no society that has hamstrung competition has long endured. As libertarian ideology confuses predation with competition and may find itself an apologist for the former, so egalitarian ideology confuses competition with predation and may advocate killing the goose—competition—that lays the golden egg. To this dilemma—how to allow competition and disallow predation—dignitarian governance provides a possible solution.

Competition is an integral part of our past and fair competition is indispensable to a robust future. To delegitimize gradations of power is not only impossible, it's a recipe for dysfunction and anarchy.

From the natural selection that drives the differentiation of species to the marketplace that refines products and ideas, competition determines fitness and viability and protects us from rankist tendencies inherent in monopoly. To abolish competition is to invite economic stagnation, and eventually to fall behind societies that maintain their competitive edge.

The difference between predation and competition is that predation knows no rules. In contrast, competition can be made *fair*. Making sure that it is—by disallowing rankism in all its guises—is the proper role of government.

At every point in our social evolution, power rules. Power is neither good nor bad, it just is, and objecting to power differences is like complaining that the sun is brighter than the moon. Abuses of power persist until the individuals or institutions perpetrating them find themselves confronted with greater power. This would be grounds for cynicism were it not that when power is abused, it is misused; and when it is misused, there eventually surfaces a more powerful alternative. The long-term trend of this evolutionary process is the discovery of ever more effective forms of cooperation, successively out-producing, outperforming, and finally displacing rankist organizations, institutions, societies, and states.

## The Dawning of a Dignitarian Era

As Mo Tzu tried to tell us, we are one big extended family. The simultaneous advent of globalization and dignitarian values is no coincidence. Predation isn't working as well as it used to. In addition to the reasons given above, greater exposure to "foreigners" is making their demonization untenable.

Another factor in the demise of the predatory strategy is that victims of rankism have gained access to powerful modern weapons and can exact a high price for humiliations inflicted on them. Thus, the victims themselves are increasingly in a position to make the cost of predation exceed the value of the spoils. Weapons of mass destruction seize the imagination, but even if we do manage to keep them out of the hands of terrorists, non-violent "weapons" of mass *disruption*, employed by aggrieved groups, can so disrupt modern, highly interdependent societies as to render them dysfunctional. This represents a fundamental shift in the balance of power in favor of the disregarded, disenfranchised, and dispossessed.

Given that predation has been a fixture throughout human history, it's not surprising that when one form of predation has ceased to pay we devised alternative, subtler forms to accomplish the same thing. Although slavery itself is no longer defended, poverty functions in much the same way—by institutionalizing the domination of the poor by the rich. In the 21st century, the largest group of people that can still be taken advantage of is the poor. We should not be surprised if, using techniques of mass disruption (tactics of non-violent civil disobedience), they acquire the organizational skills to make their ongoing exploitation insupportable.

Something new is afoot, and it marks a change fundamental enough to define an era. Opportunistic predation—the survival strategy that we've long taken for human nature—has reached its "sell-by" date. Even wars by superpowers against much weaker states are proving unwinnable. Military domination is no longer the profitable business it once was.

Rankism is the residue of predation. As predatory uses of power are revealed as counterproductive, we leave predation behind, like the toy soldiers of childhood, and create a world in which the uses of power are limited to those that extend and enhance dignity.

Democracy's next step is to build a dignitarian society. Humanity's next step is to inhabit a post-predatory world. Knowing that the moral arc of history does indeed bend towards justice gives reason to hope that this may just be possible.

# The Evolution of
# Experiential Education

*Esalen and the Human Potential Curriculum:
the Relation of Countercultural and
Mainstream Cultural Forms[1]*

GORDON WHEELER

When Esalen Institute was founded in 1962, with an explicit agenda of offering a forum to "everything that is excluded from the Academy," certainly its youthful founders, Michael Murphy and Richard Price, did not have in mind to reinvent "experiential education"—much less to revolutionize the fields of adult education, lifelong learning, and a number of related areas in education. The truth is, they did not have a very clear idea of how they might go about achieving that ambitious and rather loosely defined agenda. What they did have in mind was that they would simply invite the teachers, philosophers, writers and practitioners who interested them, and whose work was outside the mainstream of academic thinking (or outside academic thinking altogether). The result, they imagined, would be not an academic course but some kind of conversation—something that they were missing in their formal university educational programs, but finding, oftentimes, in their exploratory studies of Zen and other meditative forms and trainings, in the coffee houses and informal gatherings in San Francisco and other centers of the "beat" generation of the times, and in some emergent radical approaches to psychotherapy and group process studies.

---

[1] Based on an article published in translation in the Korean journal *Here & Now*

To their pleasure and surprise, in the words of Esalen co-founder Michael Murphy, "everybody came." "Everybody" meant the now-iconic names in the West, in the broad fields of consciousness studies, human behavior, psychotherapy and somatics, and philosophy—names such as Aldous Huxley, Fritz Perls, Gregory Bateson, Alan Watts, Ida Rolf, R.D. Laing, Abraham Maslow, Joseph Campbell, Buckminster Fuller, Arnold Toynbee, B.F. Skinner, Karl Rogers, and on and on. Today this list includes well-known teachers and presenters such as Daniel Siegel, Paul Ekman, Galway Kinnell, Jim Kepner, Sharon Olds, Michael Lerner, Sam Keen, Gabrielle Roth, Rupert Sheldrake, Amory Lovins, Bert Hellinger, Deepak Chopra, Jean Houston, Dean Ornish, Jeffrey Kripal, together with scores and scores of others equally prominent.

Word spread, and interested and curious students came too. The question quickly became, what to *do* with these people, how to structure these "conversations" and other encounters. Some people lectured, some just "hung out;" but many—teachers and students alike—began to push for something more active, more experientially exploratory or "hands-on," more practice-focused. They wanted something more like what many of them had experienced in their first encounters and trainings with yoga and meditation, with new forms of psychotherapy—or for that matter (looking more interpretatively, because this was not necessarily in their own awareness) in the "progressive education" movement that had left a strong mark on early childhood education in the United States and Western Europe before the War, and was now stirring again especially in England and the US. Or, if they had never encountered various kinds of explorations in "holistic" educational forms directly, then they might have read about them in the histories of philosophy and religion, in certain much-mythologized academies and religious communities of the more-distant past.

Looking back now, we can identify clearly these strains in the new educational forms that began to emerge, at Esalen and elsewhere, in the 1960's and beyond—all those forms which we now group loosely under the umbrella term "experiential education."

1) From the yogic and meditative disciplines and practices of "the East"—especially the Vedantic forms introduced and popularized in the US by Swami Vivekananda around the turn of the 20th Century, and the tradition of Japanese Zen brought in the 1950's by Suzuki Roshi—came the idea that a change in consciousness, a new idea or way of understanding the world at a deep level, was the consequence, not the cause, of a change in sustained praxis. Such change might be sustained by a "*sangha*" or community of fellow seekers, practitioners, and students. Rather than the power of some abstract idea alone to reorganize one's thinking and behavior (the model of much academic/intellectual teaching), these ways of learning and knowing emphasized something closer to the "conversion experience"—a kind of learning where one had to give oneself over (even if only for a circumscribed time) to a new way of behaving and possibly of being, together with others, so as gradually to "inhabit" (rather than to "master") a new idea.

Psychoanalysis was of course one such "conversion practice" that was familiar and widely influential in the Euro/North American culture of the time; and certainly it was an "experiential practice" leading intentionally to a different worldview, and a different self. But psychoanalysis, which had been part of a radical fringe a couple of generations earlier, was by 1960 very much associated with the mainstream establishment and mainstream conformist values. But the idea of a psychotherapy without coercive authority, and without the assumptions of psychopathology, was strongly motivating to the progressive generation at the time.

As the example of psychoanalysis illustrates, in the individualistic culture of the United States any such "immersion" or "conversion" approach to education came with deeply ambivalent feelings and associations. Particularly in the immediate wake of a World War with the various fascist movements of Europe and the emperor/deity ideology of Japan, and at the height of the Cold War which pitted Western liberal/individualistic humanism against Communism, any signing over of personal authority and responsibility for one's own life and behavior to a teacher or "guru" had to be regarded with deep misgivings. The very separation of the spheres of science and religion, "knowledge" and "experience" (with the former typed as powerful, male, and reliable, while the latter was "soft," female, and "only a feeling") might be seen as offering a kind of solution to this kind of personal/cultural dilemma. A separation of the spheres (science/fact, and personal practice/feeling) answered the question of how to transmit authoritative teaching (science) in the realm of "hard facts," while still preserving a realm of personal autonomy (values) for the exploration of personal growth and transformation. That these two spheres were ontologically, irreconcilably separate was a bedrock principle of the post-Enlightenment technological age in the West, with all its achievements and all its then-recent horrors.

But if the separation of "knowledge" and "experience" functioned as a solution to the authority/autonomy problem in the West, that solution was, by 1960, deeply unsatisfying to a new generation. Not only had that cultural paradigm been badly discredited by the sobering technological horrors of the War and the nuclear shadow hanging over the world at the time, but it also seemed to have contributed to the mood of "alienation" or loss of felt meaning captured in mid-century Existentialism. However ambivalently, the generation of 1960 was moved and driven to experiment with forms of learning that addressed and placed demands on the "whole person"—behavior as well as thinking, feeling as well as analysis, "experience" as well as ideas.

2) From the Progressive Education movement came the notion of *learning as spontaneous play*, driven by natural curiosity. Long championed in the States by pragmatist philosopher John Dewey, the Progressive Education movement had roots in Europe in a long tradition of early-childhood education dating back at least to Pestalozzi in 17th Century Switzerland, and more recently in such reformers as Maria Montessori and Rudolf Steiner. According to this movement, human development followed a natural arc of hands-on experience leading to attitude and theory, not the other way around. Maria Montessori, for instance, was dedicated to what we might call a Victorian ethic of disciplined self-application, clear resolution of life into tasks through analysis, neatness,

and thorough accomplishment and completion of those tasks. But she didn't sit 4- and 5-year-olds at desks in rows and lecture them to inspire them with these values and capacities; she gave them tasks that were naturally interesting and challenging (sweeping is one classic example), and guided them to acquire these skills and internalize these values through their own experience.

What was radically new here, in drawing (somewhat unconsciously) on this legacy of progressive education in the 1960s, was the idea of applying "play learning" and "hands-on learning" not just to children, but to adults of all ages. In retrospect, this step, integrating "playful and serious," seems one of the most revolutionary leaps the founders of experiential education would take. Today we see lifelong development, self-directed learning, and adult education as universal, even normative ideas. But things looked very different a half century ago, under the dominance of a classical Freudian model that posited adolescence as the last significant developmental transition of the lifespan.

One model for making this leap was the image of the creative artist. In the aftermath of the World Wars, the artist archetype, with its freer access to embodiment, pleasure (including erotic pleasure), non-conformity, and play, gained in appeal and romanticized glamour. It was not artists, after all, but scientists and "corporation men" who had given us mass civilian bombings, mass death camps, and doomsday weapons. In the culture of the United States, which had glorified business and technology almost to the exclusion of other dimensions of life, the time was ripe for a transvaluation of social roles and archetypes.

3) For the religiously or academically inclined, there was the appeal of various iconic intellectual communities of the past. Some of them were plainly more "holistic" than our universities and professional schools in addressing and valuing more dimensions of human experience than our own educational institutions seemed willing to do. These learning communities of the past ranged as far back as Plato's Academy, and up through various monastic enclaves of medieval Europe, Ficino's academy in Renaissance Florence, and alternative religious or other intentional communities of 19th Century North America. Some included

Western notions of yogic or meditation communities of Asia as well. Michael Murphy himself spent a year in the 1950's at the ashram of Sri Aurobindo in India. Both Murphy and Richard Price, the other founder, were very much involved in the early activities of the nascent San Francisco Zen Center founded by Suzuki Roshi, one of the prime figures in bringing Japanese Zen to awareness in North America and Europe.

Thus we can say that there were at least these three main streams of influence that went into the emerging notions of experiential education at the time: the yogic and meditative traditions of the East, with their emphases on learning/practice in community; the American tradition of progressive education, including the powerful notion of play learning, now applied across the lifespan; and the romanticized (and often eroticized) images of philosophical and religious learning communities. To this we can add as negative red flags or pitfalls to be avoided: psychoanalysis with all its authoritarian overtones, inevitably stirring echoes of fascist (and communist) authoritarianism and conformism, and the "grey flannel suit" of Sloan Wilson's 1950's America. These influences would be the cultural ground and context out of which a new birth of experiential education would emerge.

### The (Re)Birth of Experiential Education

And so Esalen Institute was founded, to offer a space to "what was excluded" from formal higher education of the time. This realm of things excluded would intentionally include the whole arena of consciousness and spiritual explorations and disciplines, which were marginal indeed in American education at the time, and largely cut off from the worlds of politics, business, technology, science, and medicine (which included psychotherapy at the time). That these spiritual explorations sometimes involved psychedelics and the study of "extreme states of being" only made them all the more marginal in a culture that associated everything "spiritual" with the feminine and the "primitive."

The cultivation of the body was regarded with almost as much mistrust as the cultivation of spiritual experience. The only area excepted was vigorous competitive sport, and even here, sports heroes, like the other battle heroes they were associated with in the popular mind, were notorious for their neglect and abuse of their own bodies. To be sure, great athletes had their own private experiences of the exceptional states of consciousness often associated with those disciplines, and Esalen founder Michael Murphy would make this study of exceptional consciousness experiences in athletes a particular focus of his own research in the years to come. But all this was marginalized: there was little public discussion of these experiences. Body practices and body cultivation, even minimal care, beyond a youthful athletic stage, was regarded as vanity; and physical vanity was emphatically typed as feminine. As for "feminine" itself, the boundaries of nearly everything that was valorized and power-typed in the culture were policed by a rigid, reductive, and shame-charged cult of narrow masculinity.

And then of course there was the study of *body experience* itself—what later came to be called "somatic studies" at Esalen and beyond,—inextricably tied up, then as now, with erotic exploration and sexual liberation. It was this heady mix—the physical, the mystical, the psychedelic, the healing, and the erotic, all with greater or lesser degrees of awareness and integration—that marked the explorations of embodiment at Esalen and other centers of the day. The countercultural tradition of radical and alternative sexual communities was also a lively influence, even if that tradition had died out or gone further underground in the repressive years between and after the two World Wars.

The next area officially excluded from traditional educational forms of the times was of course the emotional. Again, the realm of "feelings," like the realm of spiritual experience, was gender-typed as "soft" or feminine, and thus seen as disempowering in an aggressively masculine-typed technological world. Feelings simply had no place in intellectual inquiry and learning, which was seen as taking place in a completely separate domain. In the mainstream world of the day, the emotions were to be "risen above" and "not given into." If this was not possible, then "the problem" was seen as was one for psychotherapy, a medical intervention to correct a pathological disturbance. And psychotherapy itself was also charged with associations of dependency, "feminine" regression to "primitive" states and feelings, and shame.

The exploration and expression of the emotions would be part of the alternative educational agenda from the start. This was especially true at Esalen where Richard Price felt himself to be a victim/survivor of the sometimes violent and destructive methods of psychological treatment of the times: electroshock therapy and heavy psychotropic medications. Price would be an early leader in breaking down the barriers between what was typed as pathological and what he and others saw as healthy, even essential personal and spiritual development and self-exploration.

Explicitly intellectual studies were not meant to be excluded from the new program of study. What was meant to be different was the particular content focused on in alternative education. Common themes that were felt to have been neglected in the universities included the history of mysticism and spiritual studies, the scientific study of consciousness and the effects of meditation, the new quantum physics and its implications for philosophy and self-understanding, philosophy itself (particularly the philosophy of consciousness, blended with psychotropic experimentation), and certain areas of social history (particularly the history of social radicalism and the application of that history to social action today).

Finally there were community, politics, and social action themselves. The European tradition of a link between radical politics and humanist intellectual study had never really taken root in the more anti-intellectual culture of North America. Now, with the repressive political atmosphere of the Cold War, the universities had generally grown even more conservative and conformist, more focused on turning out the technocrats/engineers who would fill the needed roles of a technological, business-oriented, corporate bureaucracy. Meanwhile the old agendas of social and racial justice, women's rights, and other civil liberties, which had been deferred and then buried in the West during the World War and then the Cold War, lay unaddressed.

At the same time, the isolation of American families into a nuclear-family, suburban living pattern, and the breakdown of old community structures of religion and small-town secular organizations, had left a powerful hunger for community in the generation of the 1950's and 60's. Community living, with all the relational/political challenges that would imply in a highly individualistic culture, would be part of the experiential education movement of the times.

But if this was the emerging curriculum at Esalen and other nascent centers—spiritual studies, the body, the emotions, the unrestrained creative mind, and the realm of relationship/community/politics,—how were they to go about studying these things? What would be the educational forms and procedures for such a study? To this question, most of the early leaders of this counter-cultural "movement" had not given much thought.

If there was a clear intention or plan, it was mostly a negative one: avoid the forms and structures of traditional mainstream education. In their place was a more intentionally "ad hoc," spontaneous notion more like: "make a space, invite the people, get out of the way—and see what happens." Once the people—teachers and students—got there, then what they would *not* do, for the most part, would be to sit in chairs or at desks in rows and listen to an expert lecture. There would be discourse, lecture, and discussion of course; but the mood of the students, once they arrived, was emphatically experiential, emphatically "hands-on."

If we're talking about meditation or expansion of consciousness, then give us an experience of meditation, teach us how and let us experience it—and then let us share those experiences, and learn from each other and our own "authentic data," as well as from the "expert." If it's altered states of consciousness that are the curriculum, then give us the tools for those altered states: psychedelics (many still legal in America at the time), as well as instructions for practice.

If we're talking about the body, then let us put our hands on each other, and explore embodied practices. If the emotions, then take us into emotional exercises and self-exploration—right here, not off in the formal and authoritarian privacy of a psychiatrist's office. If the content is more mental/intellectual, then let us see the "real-life" implications of the ideas on our worldviews and our behavioral repertoire—and let us experience the interplay between and among those new ideas and the realms of spirit, body, emotions, and relational life.

And if we're talking about relationships, community, politics, then let us explore and experiment with our own relationships, our own community right here and now—or directly bring in the socially marginalized "other" for encounter—and then *use* those explorations to stimulate our political and social-action projects out in the "outside world."

Such were the implicit and explicit demands that students and teachers alike brought to Esalen and soon to other emerging centers of those times. Out of these felt needs and demands, in a way that was often more spontaneous than planned, began to emerge a new educational methodology, and with it, a new philosophy of education. The new philosophy would be marked by holism (the idea that each of these areas had implications for the others), optimism (creative growth was possible and natural, for individuals and societies, all through their lifespans), the attitudes of philosophical existentialism ("here and now" focus on present experience), *anti-authoritarianism* (the felt experience of the individual, in interaction with the group, would "trump" traditional authority), *experimentalism* (don't just talk about it—*try* it), and a deep faith in human creativity (new forms are possible, and our human nature is to seek and find them). The method would be pragmatic/experimental. To questions of truth, the answer was often the pragmatic: "try it out." Comparative, empirical, individual subjectivity would be the final authority—as opposed to the authority of tradition, positional prestige, or other forms of official power.

It seems obvious that any such "movement," founded in anti-authoritarianism, spontaneity, and the primacy of personal experience over official forms, would resist definition or reduction into anything like a "curriculum" in the traditional sense. Yet in retrospect we can see that the outlines of a clear curriculum of experiential education did emerge and take on a thematic resolution into "faculties," or thematic clusters. We may call those faculties and that curriculum the "Human Potential Curriculum." The clusters of that curriculum will be examined briefly below, in turn.

### The Emergence of the Human Potential Curriculum

This new social/educational "movement" soon acquired a name, bestowed on it by the popular press out of the themes and slogans of many of these explorations: the "human potential movement" (an expression midwifed by Murphy himself in conversation with George Leonard). The term carried in it the radical assumptions of this new educational methodology: optimism, openness to new creative possibility, holism, and an accent on "the human," meaning life *as lived*, not life in a textbook; life here and now, in the full and felt exigencies of the present situation.

With its spirit of holism, in opposition to the fragmentation of academic training then and now, and building on experiential, exploratory methods and forms, the core curriculum of the movement had soon organized itself into five coherent basic areas or "faculties," in the dual sense of that word. One sense is "faculty" meaning a facility, a capacity or dimension of skill or experience; and the other is "faculty" in its sense of meaning a "department of studies," as in the "faculties" of a university. This duality of usage is relevant here: the whole point of experiential education as a movement was that those two senses of the word had become separated in academic studies, and must be reintegrated with each other, as related dimensions, not atomized elements, of human inquiry and experience.

The five faculties of the Curriculum (see Figure 1), in the order they are often found :

**1) "mind"—the cognitive realm:** This is of course the faculty of the Curriculum that most resembles mainstream traditional education. The differences here, as discussed above, have to do first with the particular topics concentrated on, which are generally those currently excluded from traditional academic institutions (particularly consciousness studies, in the early days of the Curriculum). And second are the particular differences of method introduced by the Curriculum: in place of the passive, expert-model learning that still characterizes much traditional education, we find an emphasis on participatory learning, active experiment, and interpersonal enactment.

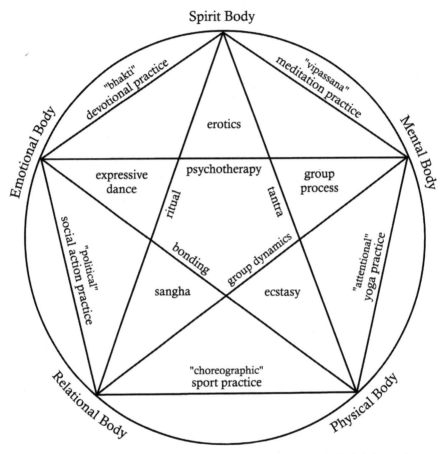

Figure 1. The Human Potential Curriculum as a visual whole: the labels on the connecting lines and within triangular spaces of the diagram represent possible locations for integrative practices, combining two or more dimensions of the holistic Curriculum.

**2) "body"—the somatic or psychosomatic system:** Along with this recognition of the indivisibility of the "mind/body" system comes as well a renewed celebration of embodiment and the life of the body "for its own sake." Topics such as expressive movement, touch therapies, the "inner world" of sport, and a new valorization of the erotic dimension of life (long marginalized or even demonized in the puritanical cultures of the West) are expressions of this dimension of the Curriculum.

**3) "heart"—the life of the emotions:** The "faculties" focused on the life of the emotions have been both the inspiration and the result of the collapsing of the old separation between "psychotherapy" and "lifelong personal growth and development." The transformational insight has been that human development and transformative, empowering change do not come to a standstill in early adulthood. Rather, those deep changes are normally ongoing throughout life. Most importantly for the Curriculum is the insistence that the meaning, quality, and social impact of an individual life are directly related to the ongoing cultivation of this human faculty on a lifelong basis.

**4) "spirit"—the transpersonal dimension:** It has been a central part of the agenda of the Human Potential to put spiritual exploration and spiritual experience back into the center of human life in a holistic way. Characteristically for the action-oriented flavor of the human potential movement, the answer of the Curriculum to the mid-century malaise of Existentialism was more experiential than theoretical/systematic. To a mood of meaninglessness or existential despair about purpose or place in the cosmos, the Curriculum's answer tended to be: Wake up, pay attention to your body and your feeling states, engage with your world and those around you, and explore consciousness through meditative practices. Rather than trying to exit the cul-de-sac of philosophical "Individualism" with purely verbal or cognitive/philosophical tools, the Curriculum insisted that the problems in one domain (in this case, the domain of "mind") cannot be usefully addressed without drawing on the other dimensions. Again, the Curriculum is holistic.

**5) "the social"—the domain relationship, community, and political engagement:** Here we come to what we might call the "shadow" dimension of the Curriculum—always there in practice, yet slower to come into focus and clear discourse in the extreme individualistic ideology of the mid-Century Western world. The entire spirit of the Western liberalizing bourgeois tradition of the past half-millennium had been based on the glorification and exploration of the individual, in opposition to the oppressive social and political tyrannies of church, state, and society. Both the articulation of psychological interiority and the advance of human rights in the West were fruits of this individual- istic thrust and legacy.

Often lost in this emphasis was the inherent social relatedness of our human natures. By mid-20th Century, that very relatedness could look like our most dangerous enemy, in a Western world that had somehow produced Nazi and Communist tyrannies, both of which glorified the communal over the individual. For all these reasons this faculty of the Curriculum tended to get left out of the discourse. "Holistic" educa- tion itself was often summarized as addressing "mind, body, heart, and spirit"—period. At times the entire world of social relatedness, all the way from deep personal intimacy to community life to macro-politics, was assumed to have been squeezed into the realm of "heart," or "com- passion." At other times this entire dimension of irreducible, insepara- ble human experience was simply left out of the discussion altogether.

And yet it was always central to the Curriculum in the enactment. Holistic or experiential education, to state the obvious, has always taken place in groups: the learning community, the *sangha*, was at the heart of the movement, one of the three chief inspirational sources dis- cussed at the outset of this essay. Group dynamics and group process have always been both basic tools and also productive outcomes of the Curriculum. Progressive political activism as well has been a prime characteristic of experiential education. Yet in discussion, the "holistic" picture of human nature that the Curriculum was founded to express and explore could often seem "monadic," in the sense of being made up of a universe of utterly separate selves floating around in a world of separate self-exploration and self-expression. Thus do the trailing roots of the old paradigm carry on, nearly always, in the first formulations of the new.

Today, as we feel more acutely the social and personal costs of the loss of meaningful community in mainstream life, and as the unmet holistic needs of the world political environment loom ever more menacingly, we can see more clearly the social and personal costs of marginalizing this dimension of the Curriculum.

## Conclusions—Alternative Education in Relation to Mainstream Culture

This then is a way of looking at the sources, the composition, and the legacy of the "Human Potential Curriculum" as it has developed at Esalen and the many other centers that have arisen in Esalen's wake. Noteworthy here is how closely this holistic organization of dimensions of humanness expresses and in a sense mirrors the holistic philosophy of Sri Aurobindo, the Indian philosopher, mystic yogi, and radical political revolutionary whose teachings and influence Michael Murphy brought back with him from India. Indeed, we can regard both Esalen, the evolution of experiential education, and the Human Potential Curriculum alike as expressions in the West of Aurobindo's magisterial integrative vision, itself a synthesis of Eastern and Western influences.

The Human Potential Curriculum is a way of organizing, viewing, and prioritizing the components of experiential education, and the curriculum of an alternative educational program. The five "faculties" of the curriculum—mental, embodied, emotional, relational, and spiritual—comprise a way of conceiving and organizing the dimensions of human development and human living. Taken together and looked at in this way, they help us to see the curriculum of experiential education as a whole, and to know where and when we are offering—or not offering—what is needed in the larger culture that surrounds and contextualizes our "alternative" institutions.

Alternative education institutes exist, after all, always in relation to a wider cultural environment and context, which is by definition "mainstream." This is why we undertake an alternative educational project in the first place: because something is missing in our surrounding cultural setting—and because that something is something essential for the ongoing progress and development of our societies and our world. Thus the content and priorities of the offerings of a particular alternative institution will change over time, as the culture around it changes.

At Esalen Institute, for example, which is now rounding out its fifth decade of life and influence, the focus and priorities have shifted and evolved—but always within the context of this larger, holistic vision. Thus in the 1960s and 1970s, when disembodied mental development (and aggressive sport) were dominant influences in Western education and culture, Esalen and many other institutions pioneered the exploration of spiritual studies as part of human development, emotional exploration, somatic experiment and development, and interpersonal dynamics. What still often lay "in the shadow" of this work, relatively less developed and brought out at the time, was the extension of the other dimensions into the world of community and social/political action. To be sure, Esalen and many other centers were themselves living communities with community dynamics and processes; but a direct focus on the "outside world" was often missing in this period, especially as the dynamic student movements of the late 60s faded into a period of greater political discouragement and apathy.

As this political apathy and withdrawal often tended to increase into the 1980s, one reaction at Esalen was to develop a new political initiative and outreach to the Soviet Union. After more than a decade of sponsoring conferences and gatherings that included Soviet scientists, writers, economists, cosmonauts, artists, and eventually highly placed politicians, Esalen had built a network of cooperation, within the context of mainstream division and enmity between the Euroamerican and Soviet blocs. This story—including Esalen's sponsoring of Boris Yeltsin's first encounter with the West, his emotional conversion from Communism, and his role soon thereafter, as Mayor of Moscow, in blocking the attempted coup in Russia in 1991—has all been recounted elsewhere, but serves here to illustrate the disproportionate influence a small countercultural or alternative project may at times have on the larger mainstream environment. What matters for us here, in relation to the Curriculum, is that it illustrates what may happen as centers like Esalen, with a holistic vision of what is needed for full human and social evolution, may themselves evolve and focus on different issues at different times. Always the "alternative" agenda is what is in "the shadow"—what is being marginalized and neglected in our wider social context.

Today more than ever, our world culture—and especially perhaps our hyper-individualist Western culture—suffers from a lack of a truly holistic perspective. True, we have shone a light on the neglect of the body, the emotions, and the spirit over the decades of the second half of the 20th Century in the West. But on a cultural and political level, holism today has to mean the whole political world. No more can we focus on the development of "the individual," without equal focus on the social, cultural, economic, and political surround. Our world today is one global economy, rapidly integrating; one global ecosystem, integrating and cross-influencing faster than we know how to deal with; one system of biology, health, and epidemics; one system of security and social order; one integrated demand for social justice and the decent conditions of human life that will permit and foster health, development and welfare for all. As the American pan-disciplinary spirit and revolutionary patriot Benjamin Franklin put it over two hundred years ago, at this point we will either find the way to all "hang together"... or we will surely all hang separately.

Holism is now not just an idea or a perspective but an urgent political imperative. The work of developing the full individual human being through focus on what is neglected in mainstream society is our shared mission in our shared field of alternative education in the widest sense. By undertaking this work in a consciously holistic way—a way that keeps in mind the full context of the Curriculum for human development, even as we focus on the particular themes that appeal to our different institutions and projects at different times—we ensure that the development of the individual is also the transformation of the social whole. This work of transformative individual and social development is ultimately a spiritual quest. Its ultimate meaning is transpersonal. This is politics in the highest sense. In the transcendent, deeply revolutionary spirit of Esalen's founder Michael Murphy, let us all dedicate and rededicate ourselves to this great work.

# Love Letters

# Dear Michael

### NANCY LUNNEY-WHEELER

D ear Michael,
I'm writing this from a hotel room in Princeton, NJ, where I spent last evening attending the first preview of our friend David Shire's new musical, so far from Esalen, yet so much a part of me, a piece of what set me apart and got your attention right from the beginning. I'm not sure I accurately remember the first time we actually met, actually spoke, but I remember clearly the first time I ever saw you and Dulce. It was a few years before Dick invited me to come live at Esalen with my kids, and I was just visiting. There was a party happening in the Far Inn, and I was there with Beverly Silverman, and I even remember what I was wearing, which is only significant because I know I wasn't dressed in the hippy, free form style that was de rigueur at Esalen in those days. Across the room was this amazingly attractive, magnetic, twinkly, kinetically alive man and a stunning woman. "Who is THAT? I asked Beverly. "That's Michael Murphy, and Dulce, his wife."

(Cue in Ezio Pinza singing "Some Enchanted Evening.")

And with that began a kind of love story, not of romance, but a love story nevertheless, more familial, filled with devotion and connection and shared sensibilities and so much laughter, mutual love, and respect.

A couple of days later, Beverly told me that you and Dulce and she and Julian had gone to Ventana for dinner, and that you had asked about me, asked who I was. She told you a bit about me, but according to her at that time, the part that she told you that really captured your interest was the fact that I knew Dom DeLuise and Mel Brooks!

This, from the charismatic, complex, spiritual, brilliantly accomplished author and co-founder of Esalen!

Ultimately it was first Janet Lederman, then Dick who recognized my talents in Gestalt and music, and he brought me in under his auspices. Now I knew who you were, out there, somewhere, bringing conferences to Esalen once a month (those were the days!), but it was Dick's Esalen that we all lived at "down there."

And those were also the days of Julian, and Jenny and the Nine, and people walking around with pyramids made with what looked like wire hangers sitting on their heads, and too many other people and images to recount or recall. Not your favorite time down there, I'll bet. But if it hadn't been for Jenny and the Nine acting as OD consultants to Dick and Julian, Rick Tarnas might have stayed a gate guard rather than been anointed programs manager (manager was the big title in those days), and there might not have been a new position called catalog editor that he hired me to fill. And our relationship might never have been developed beyond strangers across a crowded room. But it was, and they did, and he did, and ultimately Dick tired of Jenny and the Nine and they moved on, and Rick went on to write his first book and become famous, and almost 30 years and many regimes later we are among the last ones standing, sometimes bruised and bloodied and frustrated, sometimes proud and excited, sometimes maligned, sometimes ignored, always passionately involved and engaged, and deeply committed to Esalen, to what it is, to what it was, to what it could be, to what it can be.

"Once you have found her, never let her go."

Okay, so it's a love song to you *and* to Esalen.

And there would be no Esalen without you. You provided us with this most magical, majestic, overwhelmingly magnificent living lab, and you've insisted that it continue to be focused not just on the wonders that happen here on the property for the thousands who have come here as though it were Lourdes, to be healed, to be made whole. You've insisted that we must also have profound influence on the culture at large, in both the inner worlds and on the world's stage.

My love and gratitude for you are boundless. Through you I found my life's work, and ultimately even my wonderful Gordon. You wrote of my "grand curiosity about the mysterious tides that ebb and flow through the larger culture in which we swim." But it is your wondrous curiosity, brilliance, and passion that has forced the culture to at least look at and consider possibilities that were doomed to lie dormant, unexamined, until you turned your own light on them and forced us all to reexamine our beliefs and what we are so sure we know. You are the one who has been the catalyst that brought about more cultural change than can be measured, and you continue on! What an inspiration you are. Your ability to wonder is only part of what keeps you so young, regardless of your numerical age. It is your spirit, your zest for always looking at the bigger picture, and the love, support, and respect that we always had for each other that kept me here in the times that I felt so discouraged that I wanted to run screaming back to New York to try to regain my sanity! You are my inspiration, my brother, my friend, my partner in crime, and frequently my reality check! I love you forever.

Finally, I want to also offer great appreciation and love to Dulce, my "sister-in-law." You two had better keep taking very good care of each other! We want you both around as long as possible.

*Nancy*

# Homage to the
# Youngest Octogenarian

## STAN AND CHRISTINA GROF

Dear Michael,
I find it surprising and remarkable that your indomitable spirit and élan vital has not succeeded to stop the calendar from running! But here we are and this auspicious anniversary gives me an opportunity to take a trip down memory lane and explore the places where our lifelines touched and intersected. It also gives me a chance to do something we don't usually do: to tell you how important your friendship has been for me and how profoundly you have influenced my life.

I already felt very deep connection with you during our very first meeting in May 1965, when Virginia Satir took me to Esalen for the weekend. After we met in the Big House and had lunch in a beautiful Asian-style mansion down the coast, looking at white and black swans gliding by in a little pond, you took me to Point 16, which was at that time for sale. Something extraordinary happened there: in a moment approaching a rapture, I felt that my heart connected deeply with the Big Sur Coast and a passionate wish arose in me which—considering my life circumstances in the mid-1960s—seemed utterly silly and unrealistic: "If there is one place in the world where I would like to spend my life, this is it!"

You were not only instrumental in igniting this dream in me, but helped me to realize it, something that at the time seemed impossible. When I returned to this country and started working at the Maryland Psychiatric Research Center, I used every opportunity I could to go to Esalen and conduct weekend workshops. While my initial enthusiasm about the Big Sur Coast and Esalen was directed to the incredible natural beauty of the place, I was now witnessing the unfolding of the amazing vision you and Dick were bringing to the world. And during my many weekend visits to Esalen, I was experiencing in small increments my dream: to live in Big Sur.

My dream came to full fruition in 1973 when we met at a party in Bob and Lenny Schwartz's house and you proposed that I come to Esalen to write two books for which I had a contract with Viking Press. I feel deep gratitude for the fourteen years that followed; they represent without any doubt the highlight of my life. It was not just the luxury of living in a house on the Big Sur Coast with a broad view of the Pacific Ocean, with breathtaking sunsets, and whales and Monarch butterflies passing by, but also the incredibly rich intellectual stimulation provided by Esalen workshops and visiting teachers. During my first year at Esalen, I also connected with Rick Tarnas, who has remained one of my closest friends and a source of major intellectual inspiration ever since.

Before coming to Esalen, I had spent seven years in Baltimore, doing psychedelic research at the Maryland Psychiatric Research Center and teaching part-time at Johns Hopkins, one of the foremost educational facilities in the world. At Johns Hopkins, we had every Wednesday a seminar featuring prominent guest lecturers from the academic circles. In retrospect, these seminars were sterile and boring as compared to the constant influx of new ideas happening at Esalen on a daily basis. In addition to the rich program of Esalen workshops with various guest teachers, Christina and I had the luxury of organizing many month-long workshops; this gave us the opportunity to choose a theme we were interested in and invite guest faculty of our choice. These were true intellectual feasts featuring a stellar faculty including Fritjof Capra, Karl Pribram, Rupert Sheldrake, Jean Houston, Gregory Bateson, Joseph Campbell, Huston Smith, Michael and Sandra Harner, Ralph Metzner, Angie Arrien, Tibetan lamas, Indian spiritual teachers, native American and Mexican shamans, Christian mystics, and many others.

The month-long workshops made it possible for us to be with and listen to pioneers of transpersonal psychology, consciousness research, and new paradigm science, spiritual teachers, philosophers, and artists in an informal setting, spend time with them in the baths, and forge deep friendships with them. These personal connections were very important when Christina and I started organizing International Transpersonal Conferences. They helped us to create extraordinary programs, since all the presenters in these conferences were willing to come to these meetings in different parts of the world—from India, Australia, Japan, and Brazil to Prague—without receiving any honoraria beyond having their traveling expenses covered.

I have to mention a few more things from a long list of my thank yous. When I was facing the task of creating the International Transpersonal Association (ITA) and found out that it required three "founding members," you and Dick Price offered your participation and signatures without any hesitation and thus made this organization possible. There were others who were reluctant to do it because of their concerns about possible legal and financial responsibilities. And you and Dulce also offered your help when I was receiving my US citizenship and needed two witnesses and signatures. And last but not least, I thank you and Dulce for starting the Soviet-American Exchange Program, which played a crucial role in establishing the close connections we currently have with the transpersonal movement in Russia.

Dear Michael, many thanks for everything that you have done and are doing for a better future of all of us and, more specifically, what you have done for enriching my and Christina's life, only a small fragment of which I have managed to capture in this letter.

*Happy Eightieth, Michael!*

With much love and deep appreciation,
*Stan*

Dear Michael,

I second everything that Stan has said above: the spectacular beauty of Esalen, the great fortune of living there for 12 years, and most especially, the broad, rich vision that you and Dick Price created and carried, giving life to your dream for so many years. And since Dick left us, you continue to fashion new ideas and exciting endeavors in spite of the challenges brought by Mother Nature and by being the patriarch to such a visionary place.

If you had not created Esalen and set the standard so high, my favorite Sarah Lawrence College teacher and friend, Joseph Campbell, would not have suggested that I travel there to meet Stan Grof during a rough part of my life. Thirty-five years later, as a long-married couple, we continue to find new avenues to explore and continue to feel grateful to you for providing the atmosphere in which our partnership and our work could flourish.

Within the intellectual, physical, thoughtful, sensitive, and creative milieu that you and your team shaped, Stan and I had ample room to develop ourselves, our thinking, and our work. We were inspired to invite exciting, often paradigm-shifting faculty to our month-long seminars, workshops, and Wednesday nights. We had the chance to develop Holotropic Breathwork from its infancy to its mature form, and we have presented it worldwide. And, with Stan's support, in 1980, I founded the Spiritual Emergency Network at Esalen, and it has continued to grow internationally.

None of these work projects or books could have been realized and nurtured without you and Esalen. We also enjoyed the good-hearted competition of the Esalen softball team, the freezing cold "hot" tub float in one Big Sur Fourth of July parade, and the genuine hilarity of summer Kids Days involving parents and children and games and silly residents dressed up as mythic characters. Our now-adult children remember those days with wide grins.

There are many times and situations during which our paths have crossed, whether at Esalen or Marin or Moscow or somewhere in between, and each time you have welcomed us with your irrepressible smiles, enveloping hugs, and at least one good story or two. You may not know this, but when we bought our house in Marin, we only looked in Mill Valley because we had been to yours and Dulce's house on Hillside and we liked what we saw there. So Mill Valley it is, and we are glad.

*Happy Birthday, Michael!!!!*

*Go Forty-Niners!*

With my deepest gratitude and love,
*Christina*

# Dear Baba

## KEN DYCHTWALD

Dear Baba,
I have struggled with what to say to you on the occasion of your eightieth birthday. There are so many things to say, and so many potential angles to the saying. And so I have decided to take the simplest path and express to you my deepest and most heartfelt feeling toward you—"gratitude."

First, *thank you* for your smile. It is my favorite of all your qualities. Whenever I encounter you,—walking across the lawn, or holding court on the deck, your wondrous, boyish, knowing smile never fails to touch me, never fails to bring out my best....and never fails to cause me to smile back.

*Thank you* for the life you are living. In your own way, in your own style and on your own terms, you have crafted a truly unique and wondrous life. There are so many facets to you, it's hard to even track them all: avatar, spiritualist, philosopher, mystic, bed-and-breakfast manager, humanitarian, athlete, visionary, advanced teacher, beginning student, writer, film-maker, conversationalist, diplomat, motivator and, of course, loving husband, father, brother and friend.

*Thank you* for discovering (and opening wide) a gateway to a way of being, seeing and knowing that has directly and indirectly shaped and transformed our world in the least mechanized and most organic of ways—one person at a time, one feeling at a time, one thought at a time, one epiphany at a time, one breakthrough at a time, one breath at a time, one birth at a time, one death at a time.

*Thank you* for selecting—and maintaining—a social artist's palate with such a fantastic sampling of colors/flavors/ingredients: waves, cliffs, galaxies, butterflies, psychics, psychotics, artists, sensualists, therapists, sages, goofballs, elders, infants, seekers, knowers, progressives, regressives, beauties, uglies, hippies and billionaires.

*Thank you* for creating a physical and social institution/environment whose inkblot "constitution" is presciently sturdy, yet whose boundaries remain alive and resilient enough to withstand testing while continuing to evolve every minute of every day—by all comers (and quite a few goers as well).

*Thank you* for conceiving a dining room where garden workers, toilet cleaners, gurus and students all break bread (and bus their plates) together as equals...a rare and beatific expression of humanity's best self.

*Thank you* for unleashing your personal machete and clearing an ancient/modern/futuristic path through a thick and gnarly jungle of dogmas. More than any "guru" or teacher who has graced our era, your personal vision with all its range and complexity (and occasional mixedupedness) stands as the most extraordinary of all the teachings I have encountered.

*Thank you* for your ageless, unrelenting enthusiasm. I don't know how you do it! Regardless of what knocks you down, or stalls your gears, you always find a way to jubilantly pick yourself up and advance toward what you believe and care about.

*Thank you* for the impact you have had on me, my family, my life and my work. Encountering Esalen forty years ago let loose a vortex of personal awakenings, anxieties, passions, insights and commitments that have mobilized my nature to create an intersection of biography and history that I am fully proud of.

And, last, *thank you* for allowing the love, respect, playfulness and friendship to roll back and forth between us over the years. Our dance of friendship means so much to me! You are the only being I have ever—and will ever—refer to as Baba.

With deep love and great respect,
*Ken*

# Mother Mike

CHRIS PRICE

Partnership is not always easy, whether in business or personal relationships. I first knew Mike through his partnership with Dick and, when I think of the miracle that is Esalen, I often think of that collaboration. Considering their essential maleness, it may seem odd that I see Mike and Dick as the mothers of the place. They brought their life experience and their innate passion to the job. They invested their resources—financial, physical and intellectual—so that new ideas and practices could be born and nurtured to independence. They stayed through all the developmental stages and growing pains. Through ups and downs, their partnership held, with overlapping vision and lots of laughter as the glue. What a fertile situation they shaped. Ideas that were once incubated in Big Sur are now part and parcel of the common culture. Approaches that first found footing through Esalen programs are now answers to crossword puzzle clues. *A seven-letter word for deep muscle massage...*

Although Esalen and Mike have been the catalyst for many significant movements and major changes, I will testify to the aspect I know best. This small, exquisite property on the edge of the cliff has given me and thousands like me a sanctuary, a safe place to come to terms with our personal lives and to rediscover the heart of what it means to be a human being. We leave here a little more alive, a little kinder, a little more ready to exchange something wholesome with others we meet. Some of us return often and deepen that discovery. Some of us make a pilgrimage every 10 or 20 years to replenish and remember what is possible. Through the alchemy of the land and the traditions that have been renewed and developed here, most leave the experience more awake than when they arrived.

Thank you, Mike, for saying yes to being used for bigger purposes, over and over again. We have all benefited because of your willingness to work hard and play hard and stay curious.

Love,
*Chris*

# Dancing Mind Embodied

## CHUNGLIANG AL HUANG

It is easy to be seduced by Michael Murphy's quick intelligence and mega-wattage charisma; but truly getting to know the man with his many dimensions has taken me nearly half a century.

Compared to the spontaneous ease of knowing Dick Price, initially I found difficulty connecting with co-founder Mike. But I was deeply intrigued with his searching mind and high-flying spiritual intellect. Starting a conversation with Michael was like unleashing an inexhaustible fountain of flowing ideas. When I took my time to simply absorb his often brilliant expressiveness, it was always inspiring and worthwhile.

Unlike my effortless kinship with Dick Price whenever I came to teach at Esalen, meetings with Mike throughout the years seemed to have been always on "special occasions," with other luminaries, having to be equally brilliant within our "Mutual Admiration Society." It was a totally different Dance! My first meeting with Michael was when I came to visit Alan Watts one evening at Esalen. Alan enticed me to get everyone Tai Ji-dancing right away. Most of the seminarians were obviously left-brained intellectuals, a bit awkward with their bodies. While Alan Watts was a ham when he was in the spotlight, readily showing off, Michael, although athletically kinetic, was not naturally as free. But I appreciated that he tried, and wished that he would soon trust and own his "thinking body" to match his "dancing mind."

Throughout the years, the dance between Michael and me has remained mostly verbal and intellectual; but I have always felt his genuine appreciation and support of me as an intuitive and emotional, body-centered teacher. He knew well of the importance of having this

Yin/Yang Tai Ji balance, in order to fulfill the full potential of being truly human.

As we grow older and become more at ease in being ourselves, I have found increasing trust and comfort in our friendship. I have enjoyed seeing Michael loosening up with his subtle wit and I've appreciated his increasing humility in his self-awareness. When a longtime good friend and admirer, Josephine (Mrs. Walter Landor), confessed to Mike that it was too difficult to digest his monumental magnum opus, *The Future of the Body*, and teased him by saying that she had found a good use for it as a doorstop, I could feel the genuine "sharing a laugh on oneself" comfort in Mike. Another time, when Sam Keen, provocative as always, challenged Mike on being contradictory to the Esalen philosophy of endorsing the "Body Sensory" bath and massages, his immediate response was completely self-deprecating and all in fun.

Michael is now clearly comfortable to be who he is, the way he is and always has been, the super-intellect who is a perennial searcher for higher consciousness and expanding human potentiality. For nearly half a century, Michael has unrelentingly committed to forging ahead, guiding Esalen in the Institute's continuous evolution.

During the first weeklong Sino-American Forum at Esalen in the autumn of 1987, I remember fondly how we were all struggling to come up with a succinct mission statement to satisfy our Chinese guests. On our last day, after we took them for a round of beer and double-cheese burgers (specific request from the Chinese!) at Nepenthe, we came back to the Big House for our last exchange. I will never forget the warm feeling of harmonious "East/West" congeniality in that room. When the senior member of the Chinese delegate beamed at Michael and said to us, "We think we know what Esalen is all about. It is the same as so many of us feel now in China. We are all together in this world, searching for our SOUL!" At that precise instant, Michael, and all of us there, realized what Esalen was truly all about: heart-full of humanity, constantly evolving and transforming, transcendent beyond words. Kudos to you, dear Michael! From that magic moment on, in my heart and mind, you had become, and will continue to be the "sagely" founding leader of Esalen!

A Post Script:

Twenty years after that initial success of our Sino-American Forum on "Science, Technology and Social Change" at Esalen, I have joined again with Michael and Dulce Murphy, Jay Ogilvy, Sam Yau and Xiao Qiang, to finally resume this important "people to people" exchange at Esalen with the "Potential China" project, since April of 2008. For the past three years, we have continued with this NGO gathering with focuses on Journalism, the internet, and the environment. Each year we are re-affirmed of this timely, important work we have committed to share. More than ever, my admiration, respect and affection for my "elder brother" Michael continue to deepen and broaden. At our farewell dinner concluding our week of "Potential China" forum this year, I toasted to Michael to express my deep appreciation and added, "I love you, my brother!" I meant it and felt totally at ease declaring it.

Confucius, on his 70th birthday, exclaimed that he could finally follow his heart's desire, without going astray. For Michael at 80, surely, you are now able to joyfully follow your heart's desire all the Way, along the "Watercourse Way" of Tao!

# To Be Continued

## ALLAN BADINER

Michael Murphy brings it all down to Earth. Long before we formally met, I would see him, and sometimes overhear him on my intermittent visits to Esalen in the 70's and 80's, before I moved next door in 1990. It took me a while to integrate the many facets Murphy presented. For years I was amused by his aside to some friends overheard outside the lodge—that for all the vast array of cutting edge modalities under his nose, he was still finding it challenging to lose 10 pounds.

I remember hanging out with self-help guru Werner Erhard, and a smattering of Russian scientists on the Esalen lawn. Again I overheard Michael, this time in a conversation about Werner who was at the peak of his notoriety. I was struck how much was said in the pauses of Michael's speech, and his grins. No matter how much fine wine he may have enjoyed, Michael was masterful at tracking conversation and shining his light of humor and humility when and where it was needed most.

While Esalen was connecting the different worlds of our time, Michael was himself representing the most oppositional of dichotomies. Here is a former frat boy who goes to India to study meditation; an affable socializer who is an impressive athlete on the golf course; a contemplative ascetic who runs a facility known to facilitate free love. Michael's authenticity, humor, and compassion prepared him to be the field where opposites meet and know one another as themselves.

Michael Murphy's insights are penetrating, and the boundaries of his inquiries unrestrained, and yet he is so gentle. His smile is at once knowing, yet kind, and when he is looking at you, you feel unmistakably seen—even enjoyed. As each new social or psychological movement found it roots, or its climax or both on the Esalen green, Michael was there to both celebrate its success and keep it humble. "No one captures the flag here," he would say, even as whatever the latest scene was seemed poised to conquer not only Esalen, but the world.

One movement that almost seemed to have triumphed at Esalen was the psychedelic revolution. In the 80's, and continuing into the 90's, Esalen hosted a series of conferences on psychedelics that attracted serious researchers and leaders in the field. The baths, at times, became the venue for a kind of new age baptism, with healing waters massaging the body while new empathogenic substances from the Shulgin lab rebooted the mind.

Yet, as I interviewed Michael about the *Zig Zag Zen* of Esalen: being a place where Buddhism and psychedelics meet, Murphy would admit having what he called "a powerful allergy to hallucinogens." The lodge would often be populated with tripping seekers, but Murphy cut a conservative semblance decked in a cashmere sweater with orderly short hair. Esalen, as Newsweek once called it, was the Harvard of the human potential movement, and Michael Murphy was properly the dean.

In recent years, eyes will sometimes roll when Michael talks about exploring the potential to survive bodily death. Yet he is always convincing and inspiring when he points out how small a percentage of our physical, mental and paranormal capabilities are known.

Mostly, the impression of Michael that stands out consistently over the years is his optimistic spirit. He exudes a relaxed certainty that the mysteries of life are within our grasp; that the tools of personal salvation are there for the using; and that the possibility of our lives changing dramatically is real in every moment. It is the way he looks forward that makes Michael such a compelling presence. Genius isn't needed to recognize all the misery and tragedy of life. But Michael is focused on how there is so extraordinarily much that is right. "To be positive," Michael says, "is to be a realist."

If Michael is anxious about how little time there may be left in this mortal coil, it doesn't show. As he walks the property, and greets teachers, staff, and seminarians alike, he maintains an infectious but subtle smile. For such a heavenly place, there are so many dramas. As the stories swirl about him, he moves along gracefully with a familiar and reassuring refrain: "To be continued!!"

# Once More with Feeling

MARY ELLEN KLEE

Dearest Michael,

Is it possible that 45 years have passed since I ran across the then parking lot with arms outstretched to introduce myself and bring a hug from Jim Fadiman? Certainly that was a well-placed hug and one that I enjoy giving and receiving to this day.

Is there anything I can tell you now that I haven't already over the years? Perhaps you don't know that you have been and remain one of the giants in my life. My mind boggles when I think of the doors you have opened for me to the most fascinating people and opportunities. CTR is without doubt a graduate school worthy of any renaissance mind or reincarnating soul. Where else could I have been exposed to brilliant minds from all over the world exploring topics too diverse to itemize or quantify? Just writing this puts me back into the excitement I feel every time I have attended a conference in the Big House; the thrill of being in the presence of such dedication, expertise and vitality and then to be able to look across the room and enjoy the non-verbal exchanges that occur when our eyes meet.

Is there anything I can say about our travels together as the Board has evolved from a once-a-year chaotic circle of disparate souls all wondering to some extent or other exactly why they were there, to our current merry little band (of disparate souls) struggling to adhere to "good governance" practices as we carry on "once more with feeling"?

Yes, for all this and for so much more, I can once again say "Thank You" from my heart to yours. I cannot imagine what my life would have become if I had not run across the parking lot that sunny day in May, 45 years ago.

I am SO grateful to still be able to see your sparkling eyes and devilish Irish smile and to exchange hugs after all the twists, turns, travels and travails. And, just in case you don't know, I love you!

Happy, Happy.

# The Religion
of No Religion

# Tribute to Michael Murphy

HUSTON SMITH

For starters, Michael Murphy vies with the University of Chicago's President Robert Maynard Hutchins as one of the two handsomest men I have known. In Mike's case it isn't just his features, noteworthy as they are; it's the expression on his face which always seems to token eagerness and enthusiasm, as if to say, "What's next? What's coming over the horizon now?"

I suspect that I may have known Michael longer than any of the other contributors to this volume. Our first meeting was at the Aurobindo Ashram at Pondicherry, South India, and Mike told me the reason he was there. His favorite professor at Stanford was Professor Spiegelberg who would always mention in his courses that the most transforming moment in his life was the thirty seconds in which (after Spiegelberg had worked his way to the head of a forty-minute long line) it came his turn to receive *darshan*, the spiritual transfusion that occurs when a disciple gazes into the eyes of a realized Master. By the time Mike arrived, the Master had 'dropped the body,' as the Indians say, but his tomb was the centerpiece in the ashram's courtyard, and Michael had had it in view for two years.

In the course of my two-day stay at the ashram, Michael and I became friends, and he told me that before he left the States he had learned that the property that is now Esalen Institute had been bequeathed to him by his parents, and Michael was pondering whether he might use it to found an American ashram along the lines of Aurobindo's. I told him that it sounded like a good idea, and took my leave.

Let me now fast-forward a couple of years to a midnight when the telephone rang incessantly. It was Michael—he had overlooked the fact that it was three hours later on the East Coast where I was teaching at MIT. He said he had been offered a fabulous sum for his Big Sur property by a real estate developer who wanted to build high rise apartments on it. I had been awakened from a sound sleep and said, "Don't sell," and stumbled back to my bed. When we next met, Mike told me that those two midnight words turned the trick.

Fast forward again, now to the next time we were together. He told me that he was thinking of proposing marriage, but was hesitating out of fear that in time he might find marriage boring. He said that I had acknowledged that possibility, but had added that I suspected that with Dulce and him, as it had been with my marriage, the opposite was more likely to occur—that the greater overlap in their lives would provide more occasions to discuss and cross-reference their experiences. In short, "Boring? Hah!" Later Mike told me that that those words helped to persuade him.

Mike seems to drip with talent—early on he wrote a gem of a book that was titled, *Golf in the Kingdom.* By my lights, though, he has made one mistake: His enthusiasm for pushing the limits of excellence has led him to compile a huge compendium (as of now unpublished) that reads like a *Guinness Book of Records.* The mistake is that only physical achievements can be clocked and tabulated. Kindness, creativity, and people-skills don't lend themselves to statistical analysis.

Happy Birthday, Mike,
*Huston*

# Michael Murphy,
# A World of Friendship

## Zentatsu Richard Baker

Michael—The name is already for me a figure of friendship and compassion! The Friend: "In this tangled world, what is there other than the friend." (Rumi)

It is strange to be writing what is obvious in the living. Does the right hand need to write to the left hand? Friendship is the living of it, and for Michael and me it was also the meditating of it. My life is meditating and Michael is the most natural meditator I know. It just happens to him. He says that, in his twenties, he regularly sat for eight hours a day—while also holding a job as a bellhop. And his life presently feels like he did put in those kind of hours meditating. It's a bit like flight-time for a pilot.

For Michael, meditation is simply an immediately accessible form of being alive, as natural as sleeping is for most of us.

The word 'zen', translated as meditation, actually means something more like 'absorption'. And I have seen Michael just sitting, absorbed, while workers worked around him fixing something in his house. I think a ladder could have been leaned over him and a wall painted above without his meditation being disturbed.

Sometimes he put the phone beside himself about dawn and later, while still sitting, he would take a couple of mid-morning calls and then disappear again into the absorption of meditation.

When he had the big house in Mill Valley, I would often stay over and we would sit in the mornings. When I wasn't there, my cushion stayed as if I might show up at any time. It made me feel like I was always sitting beside him. It still does!

This 'always beside him' is not just because we meditated together; Michael's openness, unsidedness, to others is legendary. The many who know him, the many I know anyway, all feel their connection with him is just there. It doesn't go away. Whenever you see him again, his greeting eliminates intervening time. For many, Michael, is 'The Friend'. What a genius for friendship he has!

Michael, too, can make the phone disappear in conviviality. Being with him on the phone is being with him. Sometimes I was the mid-morning call, and Michael would say, "I knew it was you." And we would talk about many things, including meditation, which is not easy or usually even wise to talk about, but with him it was a musing together, almost as if with oneself.

Of course, there were many subjects and discussions on the phone, in person, in meetings, on trips together. Russia, the Soviet Union, poems, philosophy, transcendentalism, evolution, reincarnation, mind, the founding of America, love, charisms, siddhis, the paranormal, ESP, remote viewing, spoon bending, the 49ers, sports, the gardens at Esalen and Green Gulch, communal administration, and the particular hazards of institutions which explored and conveyed values, practices, and worldviews.

Michael saw all the world as friends (already as friends or soon-to-be friends). He could see no reason why friendship should not be how the world is put together!

He would take all the sides and no sides. However, when he did take sides for what he thought should be the case, he was the most supportive of supporters and the most considerate, but resolved of adversaries.

Where the world was the most unfriendly, Michael would decide to do something about it. Where there was ignorance, intellectual stagnation, a lack of vision, spiritual benightedness, Michael would do something about it. He is fearless, and he also saw nothing to fear.

With Dick Price, he turned his family's summer place on the Big Sur coast into the first "growth center", mixing traditional philosophy, new philosophy, traditional psychology, new psychology, science at the edges (Bell's Theorem, for example), new concepts of body and mind, yogic awareness, massage, and communal living. It was the right moment and the right time for America and soon also Europe.

In this way, Dick and Michael initiated the 'human potential movement' as a concept, a practice, and a program. And they gave it a name and a location, Esalen Institute on a Big Sur cliff on the Pacific rim. When I began to go to Europe every year from the '80s on, I found Esalen was a well-known catalyst in psychology circles.

Michael is not alone in envisioning the world as potentially a world of friends, but he decided to do something simple and surprisingly consequential about it: just invite everyone to Esalen who had something new to contribute to our view and practice of the world.

For Michael the new is also the not yet realized potentials of mind and body. He thought each of us could extend our potential in athletics, in wisdom, in compassion, in realization. He believed, he felt from his meditation practice, he intuited, that we could extend reality itself, reach into, live into, meditate into the hiddenness of reality. The plasticity of mind (now a recent topic of neuroscience), for Michael was a yogic given from his years of meditation. And for him it was not just a plasticity of mind, but also of body, of phenomenal immediacy, and of reality itself.

If no one else knew it yet, he was going to find those who did, or might know, and he was going to show all the rest of us, let us know the news, and he meant, let the world know too. Thus the "human potential movement" was not just a casual or contemporary idea. For him it was born from his meditation practice, born from an inner request of himself, and born from his vision of how the world could be, how each of us could become. His vow was to reconceptualize the world through Sri Aurobindo's teaching and through his own experience. My vow was to reconceptualize the world through Buddhist practice and my own experience. This was friendship!

With his wife Dulce, he founded the Esalen Soviet American Exchange. It was the beginning of what came to be known as "Track

Two Diplomacy." I joined them on several trips to the Soviet Union. We met people we had heard about or persons someone suggested we meet. One thing led to another. We wandered around the streets. Went to meetings with officials and also to almost hippy parties with people as crazy as us to think that there could be an opening in Soviet American relationships, under the shadows of the Wall, the KGB, and the trigger-ready nuclear arsenal. It was idealistic, but instrumentally so. With scientists, writers, broadcasters, healers, diplomats, telepaths we had conversations with an intensity that felt like a raging fire that well might have consumed us if the conversation had not kept it at bay. The motive was great curiosity, not political this or that. But the result was political, for we found we were meeting and finding out about things, alternative movements and interests, that the more formal diplomatic circles did not know about, or did not realize how influential they were about to become.

On one of the early trips, I asked a head of the Institute of the U.S.A. and Canada, "Why do you think the Esalen Soviet American Exchange is so successful in opening up relationships between Soviets and Americans?" He paused, leaned back, thought for a moment, and said, "It's Michael's smile."

A contemporary French philosopher I enjoy reading, Jean-Luc Nancy, states that being is always being-with, 'I' is not prior to 'we', and existence, of course, is co-existence. Michael actualizes this view everyday.

Although Michael's practice is rooted in Sri Aurobindo's teachings, his practice might as well be Buddhist. One of the most universal and basic Buddhist teachings is called the Four Sublime Attitudes, or the Four Immeasurables. Unlimited Friendliness/Loving-Kindness: this is certainly Michael. Empathetic Joy: I have never seen Michael not take immediate joy in a friend's success or find, in a friend, some success in which to take joy. Equanimity: Michael is unflappable. Takes all in stride. Is sure everything can be worked out, and if not, he will make that work out too. Compassion: Anything that can be done to lessen anyone's suffering anywhere, Michael will do.

These teachings, these attitudes, are understood to actualize the present in ways that can transform the future through our potentials. They are practices to discover happiness in yourself and with and through others. Each attitude radiates out from yourself to each person you meet and hopefully through each person to every sentient being. In Zen practice this conception of the equalness and potential of each person is held continuously in the flow of mind-moments. These teachings perfect us in their practice and they perfect others through our practice with them.

You, whoever you are, reading this, may say I am taken over by affection and admiration for Michael. Maybe so, what is wrong with that? Or you may say no one could be this good. Perhaps that's true, but I want to live in a world where there are persons like Michael, and I do.

Michael is certainly one of the most accomplished, visionary, and especially effective Western meditation adepts, I know. This is called enlightenment, and there is no need not to call it enlightenment.

Buddhaghosa's Visuddhimagga, The Path of Virtue (430 CE):

The inner tangle, the outer tangle —
This whole generation, entangled in a tangle,
Who will untangle this tangle?
When a person of Wisdom, established in Virtue,
Who through Vows and Vision, ardent and sagacious,
Develops Awareness and Understanding,
Such a person will untangle this tangle.

Thank you Michael!
*Zentatsu Richard Baker*
*Crestone Mountain Zen Center*

# An Exemplary Human Being

KEN WILBER

I have written elsewhere that nobody is more responsible for enlightening more people's lives than Mike Murphy, if for no other reason than the spaces he created for them to do so. As the co-founder of Esalen Institute, Mike really is the grandfather of the Human Potentials Movement in this country, and there hasn't been a more important or influential growth movement in America than the Human Potentials Movement—of which Mike himself is a radiant, shining member and example. At one point there were over 300 Esalen-like growth centers in this country, where thousands of human beings explored the further reaches of human nature, many of them awakening or being enlightened in the process. His many books have pushed the boundaries of what is possible for the human being-in-the-world, none more so than *Future of the Body*, a monumental overview covering human potentials—their meaning, evolutionary roots, evolutionary future, theories, and practices. The *Life We Are Given*, co-authored with longtime colleague George Leonard, is the historically-groundbreaking, first-ever outline of a fully Integral Transformative Practice (a type of spiritual cross-training that astronomically speeds up transformation and awakening). Of course, his novels (e.g., *Golf in the Kingdom, Joseph Atabet*) have done the same thing in novel form—novels that are still best sellers to this day!

And if one wanted a radiant example of what living Human Potentials is actually like, one need look no further than the character of Mike himself, who is brilliant, kind, compassionate, caring, athletically well-developed, genuinely knowledgeable of the entire field, incredibly creative, and, to repeat—at 80—a shining example of what living the Integrally Integrated life can do for you. Mike is somebody whom you meet and immediately fall in love with. The terrific integrity of character combined with a relentless twinkle of the eye makes him somebody impossible not to. And Mike has put all of these talents together for one major benefit—to help all sentient beings everywhere awaken to their true being, their true nature.

In short, this is an exemplary human being, in every sense I can think of. I have been proud and honored just to know Mike, and to call him my friend. Looking back over his 80 years, it's hard not to be awed in the presence of such a one. For, make no mistake, these types of human beings are rare, my friends, truly rare. With a heartfelt bow, big hug and kiss, I send all of my love to this extraordinary human being and the life he has been given.

# Michael Murphy in the Land of Oz

© 2010 Jeffrey J. Kripal

> At times, and with increasing frequency now, I experience a kind of clarity that I've never seen adequately described in a football story. Sometimes, for example, time seems to slow way down, in an uncanny way, as if everyone were moving in slow motion. It's beautiful.
>
> — Quarterback John Brodie in the *Esalen Catalog*, 1974

It is difficult for me to express what I feel about Mike, about our friendship and what amounts to his decade-long spiritual and professional mentoring of me—"difficult" not because I do not know what to say, but because I know far too much to say. I gather, however, that this occasion does not call for another 600-page book, so I will keep this relatively brief and more or less concise. I will tell a story.

I want to tell this particular story because I think it displays in an unusually clear way how Mike holds himself in the world, how he laughs, how he teaches, how he relates to people from all walks of life, who he *is*. The tale involves a trip that Mike took to my hometown the fall of 2005 in order to meet my family and to attend a college football game.

## The Land of Oz

I grew up in a little farming community called Hebron, Nebraska (population: 1800, or so). Already we are in the realm of a cultural fusion, in this case the fusion of biblical and Native American histories.

The original town of Hebron, of course, is on the West Bank in Israel. It is most famous for the Cave of the Patriarchs, where Abraham and much of his family are said to be buried. Nebraska, on the other hand, is an Omaha native word for "Land of the Flat Water," or what the French called the Platte River, quite literally, the Flat River. The Platte, as they say, runs a mile wide and an inch deep. And that's not much of an exaggeration. Hebron sits about one hundred miles below the running Flat Water and about eleven miles from the Kansas border in the southeastern part of the state.

My memories of childhood are many and various and reflect, as one might expect, the land and its people. And its violence. Hebron happens to sit in the Little Blue River Valley, otherwise known, by the locals, as Tornado Alley. The town, which is also the county seat of Thayer County, was pretty much leveled in 1953 by a monster tornado. It took out most of main street, the movie theater, the Catholic church, and the high school, and it shaved the roof off the county court-house building like a crazed boy dismantling his little sister's doll house. Both of my parents were adolescents and remember the event well. So does anyone else there who happened to be alive at the time—it is difficult to forget the back of your car lifting off the ground as you try to escape town on a Saturday night; or your church reduced to rubble with your priest hanging, still very much alive, by a rafter; or the fact that you attended, as I did, a high school building that was the third built that century, the other two having met their end in the winds.

I was not alive in 1953, but I have very distinct memories of fleeing to Grandma and Grandpa Kripal's storm cellar at the threat of a similar storm (disturbingly, storm cellars were dug out away from the house, so you had to run *through* the storm to get out of the storm). I also remember being scared out of my wits as a little boy watching *The Wizard of Oz*. The 1939 movie starring Judy Garland is an adaptation of L. Frank Baum's children's book by the same name, which first appeared in 1900. The movie begins with a farm and a tornado (both of which were very familiar to my little psyche). Although I never would have put it this way as a boy, space and time both morph from those opening scenes into one long altered state of consciousness or tech-nicolor dream. As Dorothy famously describes the situation to Toto, "We're not in Kansas anymore." Or Nebraska. And then there was that green, pointy-nose witch and those damned flying monkeys. God, I *hated* those monkeys. They scared the shit out of me. Finally, there was the bumbling, deceptive, and yet somehow still beloved Wizard. Interestingly, I played the Wizard, not very well I might add, when my elementary school decided to stage the play. I've been playing him ever since, trying to teach young people that things religious are never what they seem, that there is a bumbling but profound human nature behind the red curtain.

There is an important side-note here. Frank Baum, it turns out, was a Theosophist. Theosophy was an important religious movement that was founded in 1875 in New York City to help create a "universal brotherhood" without distinction of race, creed, sex, caste, or color; to encourage and promote the comparative study of religion, philosophy, and science; and to investigate the unexplained laws of nature, or what the founders called "the powers latent in man." Baum was introduced to Theosophy through his wife, Maud Gage, whose mother was none other than Matilda Joslyn Gage, the fiery feminist and famous early activist for women's rights. Frank deeply admired his mother-in-law, who often lived with them and was herself a committed Theosophist, largely because of its insistence on the equality of men and women.[2] When Baum's family lived in Aberdeen, South Dakota, they held séances in their home, and after they moved on to Chicago, they joined the Ramayana Theosophical Society, on September 4, 1892. While still back in South Dakota, Baum even wrote a piece for the Aberdeen *Saturday Pioneer* on the powers of clairvoyants in which he discussed the existence of elementals or nature spirits. Later, he would fill his fairy tales with similar subtle beings. Indeed, according to Michael Patrick

---

[2] Katharine M. Rogers, *L. Frank Baum: Creator of Oz* (New York: St. Martin's Press, 2002), 11-12.

Hearn, "Baum drew freely on this traditional occult cosmography in inventing his own secondary world."[3]

Baum did more than invent subtle worlds, elementals, and parallel universes, though. He also believed in them. "The spiritual was a living experience" for Baum. He believed, in the words of his biographer Katharine Rogers, that "this visible world is one of many, that life on earth is only one stage in the progress of a soul, and that the good and evil one does in one's lifetime here returns in future reincarnations."[4] He also was convinced that he and Maud had met in previous incarnations. In the end, it seems that Baum was something of a nature mystic or pantheist. Hence Baum summed up the basis of his own understanding of Theosophy in the notion that, "God is Nature, and Nature God."[5] In a similar spirit, he portrayed magical powers in his stories as real forces of Nature that we do not yet understand, but will someday, after which we will be able to work true wonders. This, of course, was also the basic understanding of the British and American psychical research traditions that were so active in Baum's time and that eventually would flow into a place like the Esalen Institute. Nature is hidden God, and the supernormal powers we witness in the history of psychical phenomena are entirely natural, if still ill understood, extensions of evolution and its actualizing potentials.

In a similar theosophical spirit again, Baum rejected traditional religion, seeing in belief systems like his family's Methodism little more than intolerance and an over-reliance on the Bible. There was certainly revelation in the world for Baum, but it now flowed through the fantasy writer. When asked how he came to write his first Oz book, he replied that, "It was pure inspiration. It came to me right out of the blue. I think that sometimes the Great Author has a message to get across and He has to use the instrument at hand. I happened to be that medium."[6]

---

[3] Patrick Hearn, Introduction, in *The Annotated Wizard of Oz: Centennial Edition* (New York: W. W. Norton, 2000), xc-xcv. See also Rogers, *Baum*, 96, 100-101.

[4] Rogers, *Baum*, 50.

[5] Hearn, Introduction, xcii.

[6] Ibid., xcv.

Frank Baum, in other words, understood *The Wizard of Oz* as a kind of channeled revelation.

Well, it certainly worked on me. I used to have a very distinct kind of lucid dream around the time I was being initiated into the terrors and wonders of the land of Oz on the television screen. Alas, I was always being chased in my dreams by this or that monster (or those damned flying monkeys, no doubt). Oddly, I knew perfectly well that I was dreaming inside the dream, but it was no less scary, and, worst of all, I couldn't get out. Until, that is, I figured out how. Eventually, I learned, still in the dream now, to cover my body with a sheet and tap my shoes together three times. With that, the vision would end, the monster would disappear, and I would wake up in my room, "back in Kansas." Okay, Nebraska. Believe it or not, it never occurred to me where I had learned this little bit of dream magic. Which is all to say that all this tornado and *Wizard of Oz* stuff was not just about weather and Hollywood. It was also part of my little psyche and soul. I may have lived in Nebraska just north of Kansas, but I also lived in that parallel universe called Oz.

Then there was the highly symbolic location of the land with respect to American history and literature. I lived about forty-five miles west of where Willa Cather grew up. As kids, we knew about Cather and her tales about life on the Nebraska prairie, vaguely. We were much more certain about the Oregon Trail. The trail ran just north of town. There was a stone memorial to that effect about two miles out, and we were told that one could still see the ruts in some of the pastures around town. Century-plus ruts? That sounds a bit incredible, but those were the stories, and that was the place I grew up—just "where the West began," as Nebraskans like to say. I found it somehow meaningful, and more than a little amusing, that I was bringing to this little town a man who grew up "where the West ended."

## The Family Visit

It didn't start out so well. I flew up from Houston and was there, faithfully, at the Omaha airport to pick up Mike in my rental car. Which was fine, except for the fact that he was flying into the Lincoln airport. Oops. After a few calls to Jane Hartford and a bit of speeding between Omaha and Lincoln, I managed to finally locate him. An hour and a half later we were driving into Hebron.

My family is divided between farmers and townspeople. Family members on my mother's side are mostly farmers. Family members on my father's side are townspeople, mostly small business owners. We lived in town. Mom and Dad ran one of the local hardware stores for forty years. Indeed, as I write this, they are selling the "Kripal True Value" in order to retire.

We wanted Mike to meet as much of the family as possible, so we had different people over to Mom and Dad's house at different times. During one of these many visits, we happened to be drinking beer and eating popcorn on the back porch when Mom decided to tell Mike the story of how she once was an unknowing accomplice in a bank robbery. A man in a wheel chair, a local known to many, came into the store wanting to buy a hunting knife. No big deal. Mom sold him a hunting knife. The man then wheeled out of the hardware store and went next door to the bank, where he proceeded to hold the place up with the knife, in a wheel chair. Pat, the banker (who, by the way, is married to my cousin Carlece), was on the back porch that night when Mom told Mike this particular story. He was happy to add more detail, explaining how the robber rolled around in his wheel chair chasing the female bank tellers, trying to corner them and demanding a bag of money. They did the reasonable thing: they gave him a bag of money, and he "escaped" down the street, right down the middle of the street, actually. Pat and the bank tellers then did the next reasonable thing: they called the Sheriff. The Sheriff drove down the street (he did not have to drive very far) and arrested the man in the get-away wheel-chair. He was eventually sent to the state penitentiary in Lincoln, which is probably exactly where he wanted to go all along. There, after all, he could get three warm meals and a solid roof over his head, rent free no less. All good things come to an end, though. He was eventually released and came back to Hebron. Mom is not so happy with him.

Between such true tall tales, Mike and I also walked the town (which does not take long) and paid a visit to The Brand X, the local bar, where we chatted at some length with a young man who claimed that he was a special ops pilot for some branch of the military (I forget which), and that he had just finished a duty in the Middle East hunting for Osama bin Laden. He was in Hebron, hunting pheasant, now. That seemed a lot easier. I'm sure he could have killed us both with a spoon.

We also took a trip out to Grandpa Wiedel's farm. Grandpa Wiedel is what we affectionately call a "character." His real name is Cornelius, but most people just call him "Corny" (which rather adds to his character). His family emigrated from Germany to Nebraska in the second half of the nineteenth century. Grandpa lost most of his right hand in a farming accident back in the 1980s. He was working with a baler (an immense machine that pulls in sheaths of hay and transforms them into hay bales). The baler caught Grandpa's hand and pulled it in, mangling it to shreds in the process. All that they could finally save was the forefinger and thumb. It was all very traumatic, but now the odd limb just adds to his character.

That and the fact that Grandpa is the kind of person who just assumes the world is really, really small, and that we are all just a handshake, or a story, away. He once came with Dad and Mom to see my family in western Pennsylvania. Shortly after they arrived, he insisted that Dad drive him out into the countryside, "to meet some Amish," he explained (the Amish, by the way, are not too keen on this). Dad drove him out to the countryside. Grandpa stopped one of the first Amish wagons that he saw and struck up a conversation with the bearded man. A few minutes into the conversation, Grandpa asked, "Say, didn't I see you in a magazine?" Then came the reply.

"Was it *Country* magazine?"

"Yes, I believe it was," Grandpa answered, "I thought I recognized your mules."

It was indeed the same man and the same mules that he had seen in a magazine article about the Amish in a dentist's office back in Hebron. Of course.

Corny and Wilma, now deceased, had four children: Roger, Diane, Idonna (my Mom), and Lonnie. Lonnie gave Mike a special tour of the family farm. Lonnie and Mike climbed into one of those immense tractors, and Lonnie drove around the farm, showing Mike the cattle—hundreds of them—that he raised and sold with pride. Then we drove out to another of Lonnie's farms, where he was growing turnips. We picked a few turnips and tasted them (okay, they did, I didn't). Like Grandpa Wiedel, Lonnie really liked Mike. He had only one serious problem with him—Mike's opinion about college football coaches.

If you live in Nebraska, the Nebraska Cornhuskers are veritable deities. There is not a single professional team, of any sport, anywhere in the state. So the incredible energy of sports fandom generated by the hundreds of high school athletic programs that dot the countryside tends to concentrate on one, and only one, team—the Cornhuskers football team. The program enjoyed a legendary status in the college football world from the early 1970s (originally under Bob Devaney), through the 70s, 80s, and 90s (under Tom Osborne, 1973-1997), as they racked up one of the most impressive records in the game and National Championship after National Championship (1970, 1971, 1994, 1995, 1997). Indeed, only the University of Miami has won more National Championships, and only one more at that. The Huskers are, to put it quite simply, the pride of the state.

There are also all sorts of jokes about the Cornhuskers, most of them involving a spouse missing the funeral of his or her partner on game day. Hey, people have priorities. Another revolves around the single "N" on the football helmet, which, or so it is said, stands for "Knowledge." Then there is the earlier name for the team—the Nebraska Bug Eaters. That happens to be a historical fact, not a joke. Or perhaps it is a joke that just happens also to be a historical fact. Mike loved that one.

Tom Osborne retired as head coach in 1997, and the program began to wobble a bit. In response, the Athletic Director hired Bill Callahan, an NFL coach from the Oakland Raiders who brought in something called the West Coast Offense (read: lots and lots of passing). This is what Lonnie worried about. Nebraska, after all, had become the legendary home of power running and something called the option, which is another form of running. Mike was effusive about Callahan and the West Coast Offense. He assured Lonnie that all would be well. Lonnie was not so sure.

## Game Day

November 12, 2005. Game day. The University of Nebraska Cornhuskers versus the Kansas State Wildcats. Dad, Mom, Mike, and I drove up to Lincoln. As we approached the capital, I explained to Mike what some Nebraskans call the state capitol building that was now appearing on the horizon: the Penis on the Prairie. It is not difficult to see why. The building features an immense, 400-foot tower with a golden dome on top. The dome is said to represent the sun. On top of this "sun" is perched a nineteen-foot bronze figure called "the Sower." The Sower is a shirtless man facing northwest, that is, the direction of Nebraska from Lincoln, holding a bag of seed tied around his waist. He is quite literally, "sowing his seed" over the entire state.[7] Who needs Freud when you grew up in Nebraska?

If we would have visited the inside of the Penis, uh, I mean the capitol building, Mike would have been delighted. The floor tiles, created by mosaicist Hildreth Meiere, recreate the history of biological evolution in the state, from the time the prairie was an ancient ocean filled with ammonites, through the age of the dinosaurs, to the age of mammals and, eventually, us.

We arrived at the stadium early in order to walk through the various tail-gating parties. Since we seemed to know someone, or lots of someones, at almost every other corner we turned, Mike grew more and more flabbergasted. He began to think that we were either (a) related to, or (b) knew pretty much everyone in the state. We let him think that. Our plan was made even easier when we were driving home after the game and turned on the radio to a channel that was broadcasting

---

[7] Such state symbolism also, of course, has implications for the unconscious meanings of "cornhusking" (which basically involves stripping the husk of a phallic plant back to reveal the bright yellow seed underneath), but I'll let that one go.

a state high school football play-off game—my cousin Kurk was the announcer.

The game itself was marvelous. We had seats about half way up the stadium on the fifty-yard line. A perfect view. Lincoln Memorial Stadium is one of those classic college football stadiums that hugs the field tight and so provides a unique communal, ritual, or "tribal" experience. There you are, with 85,000 other screaming fans, all focused on a bright green stage below, where a kind of ritual battle is taking place. Everyone is dressed in red and white, except for the opposing team fans, who are crunched into one corner of the stadium with one of the worst views in the place.

Mike was in heaven. He beamed. He marveled at the precision steps of the band. He expounded on the "occult theatre" that is modern sport and the supernormal abilities that occasionally manifest on the field or court. He kept comparing this experience to his college experiences at Stanford in a similar football stadium. It was the last home game of the year, which meant it was also the last time the senior players would play in Lincoln Memorial Stadium. This added a certain poignancy to the event, particularly after the game when all the senior players walked over in front of the band, removed their helmets, and thanked the band members with gestures and salutes for all they had done over the last four years: the gods bowing down to the choir. Mike was ecstatic.

The Cornhuskers beat the Kansas State Wildcats that crisp fall day, 27-25.

## Playing the World Game

This story is not just a story. It is also an allegory of sorts, an allegory about who Mike is. Certainly this was no accidental trip. He chose to take it, and he chose to organize it around a college football game.

I have learned a great deal from Mike over the years, but few lessons have been more lasting and more life changing than Mike's approach to life and the world as a "game" that we choose to play, or choose not to play. Mike speaks often, and passionately, of "playing the world game," and athletic analogies are constantly appearing in his conversation.

Recently, for example, he warned me of the danger of "metaphysical hernias" when I overcommitted myself to too many writing projects (I couldn't tell him that this was one of them).

This is the point at which I believe many people misunderstand who Mike really is and what he is about. The simple truth is that Mike thinks, imagines, and envisions big. *Really* big. He is not particularly interested in advancing a particular career, or writing another book, or holding another conference, or whatever. He is interested in *changing the world*—literally, profoundly, and permanently. One might call him a visionary, or a charismatic leader, or an activist mystic, or any number of other things, but all of these, I believe, miss that unique combination of complete seriousness and ironic playfulness that defines his spirit or soul. A "game," after all, is played in all seriousness, but one also knows that, at the end of the day, it was "just a game." There is, if I may put it this abstractly, a certain transcendence in Mike's immanence, a way of committing himself completely to the here and now, while always knowing, somewhere back there or up there, that he is not completely determined or defined by this particular moment and project, in short, that he is not the game.

He is also completely convinced that truly profound things happen when one commits, completely and totally, to playing the world game. His own life, as is well known, is riddled with synchronicities, magical moments that might give even the harshest skeptic reason to pause. In two recent interviews I did with parapsychologist Dean Radin and philosopher Stephen Braude, both men explained to me that one of the best places to look for real-world psychical functioning is in highly successful, extremely "lucky" people.[8] Dean and Steve both suspect that paranormal processes are generally covert or hidden, and that, indeed, they work most effectively precisely when they are not seen or detected. They also believe that these paranormal abilities serve very practical needs, that they have their own natural history (in other words, they

---

[8] See (really listen to) the "Impossible Talk" podcast I host with Scott Jones of XL Films at www.authorsoftheimpossible.com/podcasts.html.

are products of evolution, like everything else), and that we should expect to see them woven, imperceptibly, into daily life, particularly in people who are highly successful and accomplished. This is exactly true in Mike's case. Entering his orbit feels a bit like entering a magical vortex—things just *happen*.

But there is more. For Mike, the game of life is also a ritual designed to invoke and employ these same supernormal capacities, and athletic games in particular invoke them. Mike often tells stories about John Brodie, the Stanford quarterback star who went on to play for the San Francisco 49ers. Drawn to each other's occult or paranormal understanding of sport, Brodie and Mike wrote an essay in *Intellectual Digest* together in January of 1973. In it, Brodie explained how sometimes time slowed way down in the midst of a game, how he would acquire a most unusual lucidity in the midst of, and no doubt because of, the game.[9] He wrote the same thing again in the *Esalen Catalog* in the fall of 1974. Hence my opening epigraph. This Murphy-Brodie collaboration has always meant a great deal to me, and for one simple reason: what happened to Brodie happened to me too. Just once, mind you. But that is all it takes to open one up to these sorts of potentials—one then *knows* that they are possible.

I played safety on my high school football team, back in Hebron now, on the same field Mike and I walked on during his visit. The safety is the "last man" on the defense, the guy who defends against the pass, but also comes forward to tackle any runner who gets through everyone else. It was a good position for me to play, since I hated getting hit, much less hitting, and I was really good at reading a quarterback's eyes (perhaps because I myself was the quarterback on the offense). In any case, on this particular night, the ball was snapped and the opposing quarterback went back to pass. I saw him look my way and throw the ball. As I ran toward the trajectory of the ball, suddenly, everything went silent—completely and utterly silent. The screaming crowd, the band, the grunting, colliding players—they just all disappeared as

[9] *Intellectual Digest*, January, 1973.

sounds. And everything slowed down—*way* down. It was really weird. And really wonderful. I could see the football floating, very slowly, through the air. I could feel my body leaping and twisting as it propelled itself, somehow knowingly, toward the ball. But everything was floating in slow motion, everything except my state of consciousness, which was crystal clear, hyper-alert, and "moving" at regular speed. Because of this radical disjunction or difference between my altered state of consciousness and the experienced, very slow flow of time, I could jump just at the right time, twist just as I needed to twist, put my right hand exactly where it needed to be, and pluck the ball out of the sky before it reached the opposing receiver. It was perfect. But not for long. The moment I hit the green turf with the ball tucked in my arms, time sped up again, and the screams of the crowd were back in my brain. Everything was moving at regular speed again.

It was a little, tiny experience, but quite enough to convince me that Mike is exactly right about sport as one of the premiere places to actualize human potential and enter any number of altered states of consciousness and energy. I have come to see, through a thousand events, that he is also right about "playing the world game," and I have done my best to play the same game with him, with the same double sense of utter seriousness and ironic humor. He was wrong about one thing, though. Coach Callahan and his West Coast Offense proved to be a veritable disaster in Nebraska. Uncle Lonnie was right about that one.

# And More,
# Always More…

# Appreciating Mike

## A. LAWRENCE CHICKERING

My connections to the human potential movement and to Esalen are, at best, thin; and such connections as I have are entirely through Mike. I have an unusual right-of-center political background—William Buckley and Milton Friedman were two of my closest friends; but the tensions that were obvious whenever the three of us were together were a constant reminder of conflicts *within* the right and *within* the left that continue to mock our political vocabulary and its pretense that there is such an animal as a "conservative" or a "liberal" ("progressive"?). This is hard for many people to accept because it pushes them to see truths in places where at present they only see falsehood.

Mike and I have been friends for thirty years because we share this understanding. We met in 1980 at a mutual friend's home in San Francisco. Our first real connection, however, was in 1984, when I was preparing to go to the Soviet Union for the first time, and he had just returned from a couple of months there. While there, he had an interesting opportunity to see the dark side of Communism. He got the news full in the face when the U.S. Ambassador took him up into the secure embassy "cage" and broke the news that the KGB had tried to recruit him. He reported that he was as close to totally nuts as this even-tempered soul had ever been. At that moment he also came as close as he ever would to becoming a full-blown supporter of Ronald Reagan.

I had written about our ideological connection a couple of years before that when I wrote an article on the conservative revival in America and laid an important reason for it at Esalen's doorstep. I argued that Esalen and the Human Potential Movement were searching for a new understanding of order (obligation, virtue) through freedom. That, I argued, was precisely the purpose of modern conservatism, trying to integrate Bill Buckley's traditional (order) conservatism with Milton Friedman's libertarian (freedom) conservatism. Mike reported to me, gleefully, that when the article appeared, important apostles of the Human Potential Movement concluded that "Murphy is finished." Whoever thought this did not have the faintest clue about Mike's powerful and enduring presence as a giant among us. Mike told me he carried the article around with him for several years. (I need to add, as a footnote, that ten years later, in *Beyond Left and Right*, I argued that integrating freedom and order is also the principal purpose of the modern left.)

So, I think I am safe in saying that Mike's and my central concern— what connects us intellectually and spiritually—is the same thing that connects all modern people: conservatives, progressives, and the Esalen community.

Seeing us all as connected frees us from the stultifying *moral* vocabulary, reeking in judgment and blame, that contaminates the modern intellectual debate. When I am with Mike, I know that our wide-ranging conversations will never be debased by the moralism and scolding that one is forced to listen to everywhere. The perspective we share is therapeutic, and that is the idiom that I understand informs the best of the human potential movement. (The worst of the movement comes with judgment as intense and obnoxious as the worst of religious extremists.)

I cannot talk about Mike without mentioning other enthusiasms. Among these, the 49ers during the Walsh period ranks very high. I *grieve* at the passing of this period, which Mike used to say was a powerful manifestation of Northern California's "cultural dominance."

The concept of "aging" and Mike Murphy sounds like an oxymoron—a conceptual mistake. Yet approaching 80, he recently shared his growing sense of mortality and the many things he still wants and needs to do. For me, I am not buying it. I know he will outlive *all of us*—as he has since he left the ashram in the early fifties.

# Michael Murphy:
# The Person, The Legacy

RICHARD TARNAS

When people who know Michael Murphy think of him, I imagine they generally think of two things. One is his immense charm. A conversation with Mike, with or without wine and dinner, is an experience *sui generis*. The ever sparkling eyes and smile, the wonder and delight in life, the curiosity and laughter, the play and volley of ideas, the seemingly limitless font of extraordinary stories and memories along with the innumerable luminaries who populate them, not to mention one's own experience of personally being, at that moment, the focus of not just Mike's radiant attention but somehow of cultural significance generally—there is no experiential equivalent to a conversation with Mike.

And the second thing one associates with Michael is, of course, that astonishing phenomenon called Esalen. Yes, Esalen has had a life of its own far beyond the control or even the imaginings of its founders Mike and Dick nearly fifty years ago. But the reality remains that Mike brilliantly intuited the deep pulse of history and then initiated, on his family's spectacular land in Big Sur, one of the great cultural experiments of our time. I don't have to recount or even allude to the pantheon of major figures that found in Esalen a place to disseminate and develop their seminal ideas and innovations—that has been done elsewhere many times; and anyway, to name ten or twenty such figures is to leave out another fifty of equal significance.

It is true that many times Esalen must have seemed to Mike like an unruly teen-age scion, embarrassing him with its excesses and notoriety. Yet its actual achievements and charismatic beauty always far outweighed the sensationalist side-stories. And the fact is that Esalen's underlying polarities, held in constant creative dialectic—East and West, body and spirit, evolution and eternity, culture and counterculture—all existed a priori in Mike himself, and then unfolded outside him with autonomous creative force, as great progeny are wont to do.

Scholars of cultural history have often observed that the winds of epochal intellectual and spiritual change generally do not emanate first from within the established centers of cultural authority, but do so rather from adventurous communities peripheral to the respected mainstream. The great cultural transformation of the Renaissance and even certain elements of the Copernican revolution which mediated the birth of the modern age were not gestated in the universities of the late Middle Ages, which by then had become sclerotic and ingrown, but rather in Ficino's Platonic Academy in Florence—small, dissident, excited, inspired, attracted to the esoteric, the ancient, the eastern, the exotic, the mystical, the multicultural, the heretical, the prophetic. Comparing Esalen in twentieth-century California to the Platonic Academy in fifteenth-century Italy might seem inflated, but in fact, in sheer quantity and range of great thinkers, innovators, teachers, and visionaries, the historical record of Esalen's actual contribution to the transformation of our cultural landscape will, I suspect, hardly seem inferior to that of its illustrious predecessor.

For conceiving and watching over this miraculous, precious, irreplaceable vessel of awakening that has affected so deeply so many, and also just for being his remarkable self, let us raise our glasses and an affectionate salute to Mike on the occasion of his 80th birthday, even if he looks a full twenty years younger.

# Your Legacy

## RIANE EISLER

Dear Michael:
I want to wish you a happy birthday and join in honoring you for your many outstanding contributions.

As co-founder of the Esalen Institute, where I have had the pleasure of speaking as keynoter of Esalen fundraisers as well as by giving weekend workshops, you have greatly enriched the lives of many thousands of people.

Through your social and environmental initiatives, you have helped further a better future for us.

Through your writing, especially your book *The Future of the Body*, you have enriched both our consciousness and our culture.

Your legacy will last for generations to come, and we all owe you a debt of gratitude.

I am delighted to be able to join in wishing you, Michael, a very happy 80th birthday, and many more to come...

With affection and appreciation,
*Riane Eisler*
President, Center for Partnership Studies
Author, *The Chalice and The Blade, Sacred Pleasure, Tomorrow's Children, The Power of Partnership,* and *The Real Wealth of Nations*

# Acknowledgement

STEPHAN SCHWARTZ

Michael, you are 80 years old, a most apposite time for a man to be acknowledged explicitly by his friends:

More than anyone I know you have birthed, often behind the physician's mask, psychological movements, international programs, and a cultural genre. This has touched the lives of millions in compassionate and life affirming ways. I respect and admire you.

*Stephan*

# Eleven Theses on Murphy[1]

## JAY OGILVY

Leadership takes many forms, some individual, some institutional. And leadership is exhibited in many domains: not just in business or the military, but also in culture and religion. Michael Murphy, cofounder (with Richard Price) of Esalen Institute is a leader, as is Esalen. To assess the innovativeness of their contributions, we need to situate them within their time and place. In order to see how Murphy and Esalen led, we need a sense of how religion and psychology stood in California in the 1960s and 70s.

Murphy and Esalen staked out new possibilities for the human spirit. But the boundaries of the new were in part determined by the borders of the old. Murphy and Esalen ventured into outlaw country. But in order to assess the measure of their leadership, we need a sense of the order they transgressed.

My initial assessment will be purposefully rough rather than carefully crafted. The point is not to prove the *real* condition of religion and psychology in California in the sixties by citing statistics on church membership or numbers of visits to different schools of psychotherapists. Instead my aim is to state what was *obvious*, what was taken for granted, what "everyone knew." For it is precisely in its challenge to the commonplace that Murphy and Esalen had their greatest impact.

What was obvious in the 1960s? First, that God transcended man. Religion was a matter of belief, not practice or action. To be a believer was to go to church and worship a deity at a distance, the Lord of lords

---

[1] An earlier version of this essay was initially written for a meeting of Esalen's Center for Theory and Research. It was then modified for publication in *ReVision*, Summer, 2010, and is modified yet again for this volume.

who loved mankind, but a Lord who dwelt at a distance, remote from the affairs of men and women; a transcendent God whose essence could be seen only through a glass darkly.

Second, psychology was mainly Freudian. It supplied a map of the human condition that was based on the pathologies most evident in Freud's Vienna, namely, the neuroses, psychoses and hysterias produced by the Victorian repression of sexuality.

Third, to the youth of the sixties, the bloom was off the rose of post-WWII economic growth as manifested in the suburbs of America. Sociologist Kenneth Keniston wrote a book about the young entitled *The Uncommitted*, and followed it up with an article in the *New York Times Sunday Magazine* entitled, "You Have to Grow Up in Scarsdale To Know How Bad It Really Is." The kids were alienated from bourgeois America so, following the beatniks of the late fifties, they started tuning in, turning on, and dropping out.

Then along came Michael Murphy and Richard Price, two smart young men schooled in philosophy and the practice of meditation, and suddenly what seemed obvious to most of California's *haute bourgeoisie* seemed stale and in need of revolutionary reframing.

I begin with the obvious before moving on to some subtleties because the significance of subtler refinements will be lost unless the larger context is clear. To put it fairly crudely, Esalen provided a school for kids who were tired of a desiccated scholasticism that was irrelevant to their experience, and a church for those to whom mainstream religion was a dead letter. All those religious rituals, the (un)likely stories about virgin birth, crucifixion and resurrection, the miracles, the God of Abraham to whom Jews prayed, the mumbo-jumbo...it was all so patently implausible to bright young students raised on a diet of post-Enlightenment science.

The dominant paradigm in psychology was as suspect as the reigning orthodoxy in religion. The very idea that the talking cure of

Freudian depth psychology represented the best we could do in culti-vating the psyche…talk about a glass half empty! Abraham Maslow was already articulating a theory about a psychology of health rather than a psychology of sickness. All that remained was the practice.

The religion of the day was too 'idealistic'—too preoccupied with the divine, a distant God in whom one should *believe*, but never actu-ally *experience*. The psychology of the day was too mechanistic—too preoccupied with drives and instincts, resistances, displacements and other processes of plumbing in the unconscious, rather than *experience as experienced*. And the social mores of the day seemed stilted, artificial, phony. For those too young to remember, or too eager to forget, see the movie *Far From Heaven* to get a sense of the values and the inhibitions of those decades.

Then along came a community where people walked their talk; where a ruthlessly honest gestalt psychology flourished in the work of Fritz Perls and his followers; where members of the world famous mas-sage crew joined with visiting gurus like Ida Rolf, Charlotte Selver, George Leonard and Don Johnson. Esalen advanced the field of somat-ics far beyond where the likes of Wilhelm Reich last left it. As for reli-gion, the word wasn't much used. People preferred 'spirituality.' What's the difference?

Religions have doctrines—dos and don'ts, articles of faith, dog-mas, catechisms. And more often than not, religions push scientifi-cally implausible stories about how the world came to be and where it is going. Spirituality tends to be less concerned with some sacred high society *out there* in the cosmos. Spirituality is all about what's *in here*—subjective, experienced, immanent rather than transcendent.

To scholars of religion, this recital of what was obvious in California in the sixties is less likely to sound revolutionary than all too familiar. Weren't the Gnostics more concerned with what was *in here* rather than *out there*? Can't we find precursors to a psychology of health as far back as the neo-Platonic ascent up the Great Chain of Being? Yes, we can, and Michael Murphy found himself pursuing some of that literature under the mentorship of Frederic Spiegelberg in the graduate department of philosophy at Stanford. But that department was dominated by positivists like Patrick Suppes, who vowed "to bury the metaphysicians." So in order to pursue his studies of the past, in preparation for a new future, Murphy traveled to India to study in an ashram founded by Sri Aurobindo. Like many others on a spiritual path that deviated from the western, Judeo-Christian tradition, Murphy made his journey to the East.

Returning home to California, however, Murphy did something different. Rather than simply bowing down to a new orthodoxy, eastern rather than western, he looked for a new synthesis. Still speaking crudely and simplistically before getting into subtler refinements, Murphy and his colleagues at Esalen saw the extent to which the journey to the East led *up* rather than *down*. Beyond the tremendous respect Murphy paid to the intellectual and spiritual paths of his teachers, beyond the discipline to which he dutifully and thoroughly subjected himself, beyond the hours of meditation, Murphy realized that there was something missing in a tradition that paid too little attention to the body, too little attention to the psychology of the unconscious, to sex and to the sensuous realities of this world. *And so Michael Murphy and Dick Price set out to found an institute where the wisdom of the world's spiritual traditions could be wed to the materiality of this-worldly, bodily existence.* They would join the sacred to the mundane, at times by way of the downright profane. *Esalen was outlaw country!*

Here again, to students of the history of religion this taste for the mundane is not altogether new. Isn't the very essence of Christianity about the *incarnation* of the Holy Spirit? And as for dabbling in profanity, there is a tradition going all the way back to the *Song of Songs*, the *Confessions of St. Augustine*, and the erotic art gracing Hindu temples. So what's so new? Perhaps not that much. To those who are convinced that there is never anything new under the sun, it's not that hard to find precedents for what Esalen is all about. It's possible to tame the outrageousness of outlaw country by placing Esalen in traditions that go clear back to pagan rituals. It's possible to lend legitimacy to Esalen by locating and describing earlier precedents. But when you try to do so, by seeking out precedents among pagans and Gnostics for example, you find yourself quickly in the company of people and practices regarded as heretical if not scandalous. How orthodox or legitimate can you be if you're located in a tradition of heretics?

So much for the simplistic and obvious. In order to take a more refined cut at just how Esalen has wed the sacred and the mundane, the spiritual and the material, I would like to call up two voices from the past and attempt a kind of scholarly mixed-track sampler like the songs that kids create by sampling swatches from different tunes and then adding their own riffs. The songs I'll conjure up are those of Marx and Feuerbach, specifically Marx's *Eleven Theses on Feuerbach*. Why this choice? Because the more I think about the innovative leadership of Michael Murphy's Esalen Institute, the more I am reminded of both the innovative leadership of Feuerbach and of his critical appropriation by Marx. Beginning at the end, with the most famous and oft-quoted of Marx's *Theses*, how does this sound as a characterization of Esalen's difference from most academic institutions? "Heretofore philosophers have only interpreted the world in various ways; the point, however, is to change it." And this last of the eleven theses is only a beginning.

Feuerbach was a so-called "left Hegelian." Born in 1804, he was raised on Hegelian philosophy, and taught Hegel's system for several years. But as his thought matured he found himself critical of Hegelian idealism. Feuerbach's feet were planted firmly on the ground of this-worldly existence and he found the philosophy and theology of his day flying too quickly aloft toward the ideal and a distant divinity.

Feuerbach's main contribution to philosophy and theology consisted in redirecting attention to the importance of *sensuous* existence. He scandalized the theologians of his day by interpreting the main features of Christian dogma as projections from the features of material human existence. Feuerbach is the original author of that saying emblazoned on the walls of health food stores everywhere: "You are what you eat"—in German, closer to a pun, *"Man ist was er isst."*

In addition to materializing Hegel's idealism, Feuerbach also anticipated Marx in his use of the concept of *alienation*. In Feuerbach's philosophy, humanity was alienated from its own highest potential precisely to the extent that it projected that potential onto a distant divinity.

Marx was much taken with the way Feuerbach stood Hegel on his head, stressing the primacy of the material to the ideal. As Engels put, "The spell was broken; the 'system' was exploded and cast aside.... One must himself have experienced the liberating effect of this book [Feuerbach's *Essence of Christianity*] to get an idea of it. Enthusiasm was general; we all became at once Feuerbachians."[2] Marx was particularly influenced by Feuerbach's portrayal of man as alienated from his own highest potential. The concept of alienation was absolutely central to the young Marx's philosophy.[3] But Marx was not entirely happy with the rest of Feuerbach's philosophy. Nor should we be entirely happy with the rest of Marx's philosophy. The fall of communism in the Soviet Union and Eastern Europe—a chapter in history with which Esalen was influentially involved—should teach us something about the shortcomings of Marxism, even in the philosophical, humanistic form it took in Marx's early writings. So in the following variations

---

[2] Frederick Engels, "Feuerbach and the End of Classical German Philosophy," in *Karl Marx and Frederick Engels, Selected Works*, International Publishers, New York, 1968, pp. 602f.

[3] The concept of alienation figures centrally in Marx, *Economic and Philosophic Manuscripts of 1844*, Foreign Languages Publishing House, Moscow, 1961; this text first became available to American readers in Erich Fromm, *Marx's Concept of Man*, tr. T. B. Bottomore, Frederick Ungar Publishing Co., New York, 1961. A vast literature on Marx's concept of alienation soon followed: Cf. *Revisionism*, ed. by Leopold Labedz, Praeger, New York, 1962; Robert Blauner, *Alienation and Freedom*, University of Chicago Press, 1964; *Marxism and Alienation: A Symposium*, ed. by Herbert Aptheker, Humanities Press, New York, 1965; *Marx and the Western World*, ed. by Nicholas Lobkowicz, University of Notre Dame Press, Notre Dame, Indiana, 1967; Fritz Pappenheim, *The Alienation of Modern Man*, Monthly Review Press, New York, 1959; Gajo Petrovic, *Marx in the Mid-twentieth Century*, Garden City, New York, 1967; Bertell Ollman, *Alienation: Marx's conception of man in capitalist society*, Cambridge University Press, 1971.

on themes from Marx and Feuerbach, there are themes and counter-themes, dialectical dances that will allow us to find greater subtlety behind the statements of the obvious with which we began.

The strategy of this essay is similar to that described by Louis Althusser in his essays on Marx and Feuerbach. Althusser describes a "double rupture" between Marx and Hegel in which Feuerbach provides a crucial link:

> What is at stake in this double rupture, first with Hegel, then with Feuerbach, is the very meaning of the word philosophy. What can Marxist 'philosophy' be in contrast to the classical models of philosophy?...The answer to this question can largely be drawn negatively from Feuerbach himself, from this last witness of Marx's early 'philosophical conscience', the last mirror in which Marx contemplated himself before rejecting the borrowed image to put on his own true features.[4]

Here we are looking at Murphy's double rupture with traditional psychology and religion through his break with a California culture that was itself breaking away from what was then prevalent in religion and psychology. Althusser's words may be as true of Murphy as of Marx: "If it is true that we can learn as much about a man by what he rejects as by what he adheres to, then a thinker as exacting as Marx [or Murphy] should be illuminated by his break with Feuerbach [or Murphy's break with his predecessors] as much as by his own later statements."[5] But here we are entertaining not just a double, but a triple or quadruple rupture: Murphy breaking with received wisdom in 1960s California, which was breaking with traditional religion, society and psychology; but further than that, traditional religion, society and psychology breaking with Marx's break with Feuerbach's break with Hegel. If Marx was fond of describing his relationship to Hegel as one of standing Hegel on his

---

[4] Louis Althusser, *For Marx*, tr. Ben Brewster, Vintage, New York, 1970, p. 48.
[5] *Ibid*, p. 47.

head, then here we are contemplating a sequence of somersaults off the high dive of history.

Why such scholarly contortions? Because the body being flipped consists of many more than just one binary opposition between head and feet, right-side-up and upside-down. Both in Marx's relationships to Feuerbach and to Hegel, and in Esalen's relationships with California and Vienna and India, a whole series of binary oppositions call for sorting into a whole series of possible constellations. Consider the following binary pairs:

Theory/Practice
Subjective/Objective
Internal/External
Ideal/Material
Individual/Social
Abstract/Concrete
Mystical/Naturalistic
Esoteric/Literal
Contemplative/Engaged
Passive/Active

While it may be tempting to clump all of the elements on the left as features of a contemplative, quasi-Hegelian, philosophical pursuit of enlightenment, and all of the elements on the right as features of an engaged, concrete social practice...life isn't that simple. And neither is the history of philosophy, psychology or religion. So we will proceed more slowly toward a more subtle appreciation of Murphy's leadership by starting, first, with a review of Feuerbach's philosophy; then turn, second, to Marx's famous *Theses on Feuerbach*; and then, third, through another half gainer by way of a critique of Marx, to a set of similar-yet-different Theses on Murphy and Esalen.

### Feuerbach's Break with Hegel

In his *Principles of the Philosophy of the Future* (1843), Feuerbach paid his respects to Hegel before criticizing him: "The culmination of

modern philosophy is the Hegelian philosophy. The historical necessity and justification of modern philosophy attaches itself, therefore,
mainly to the critique of Hegel."[6] In his best known and most influential work, *The Essence of Christianity* (1841), Feuerbach had already made
a case, impressive in its anticipation of both Marx and Murphy, for
bringing the lofty ideas of Hegelian philosophy down into the everyday
practice of embodied human beings:

> This philosophy does not rest on an Understanding *per se*, on an abso-
> lute nameless understanding, belonging one knows not to whom, but
> on the understanding of man;…it declares that alone to be the true
> philosophy which is converted in *succum et sanguinem* [in flesh and
> blood], which is incarnate in Man.[7]

The radicalism of Feuerbach's views, and the subtlety of his thinking, are both evident in the following passage that touches on both
his humanism and his understanding of how religion alienates man's
humanity by projecting it onto the divine:

> When religion—consciousness of God—is designated as the self-
> consciousness of man, this is not to be understood as affirming that
> the religious man is directly aware of this identity; for, on the con-
> trary, ignorance of it is fundamental to the peculiar nature of reli-
> gion. To preclude this misconception, it is better to say, religion is
> man's earliest and also indirect form of self-knowledge. Hence, reli-
> gion everywhere precedes philosophy, as in the history of the race, so
> also in that of the individual. Man first of all sees his nature as if out-
> side of himself, before he finds it in himself. His own nature is in the
> first instance contemplated by him as that of another being. Religion
> is the childlike condition of humanity; but the child sees his nature—
> man—outside of himself.[8]

---

[6] Ludwig Feuerbach, *Principles of the Philosophy of the Future*, trans. Manfred H. Vogel,
Library of Liberal Arts, Bobbs-Merrill, Indianapolis, 1966, p. 31, Aphorism #19.

[7] Ludwig Feuerbach, *The Essence of Christianity*, trans George Eliot [yes, *the* George
Eliot, the famous English novelist], Harper & Brothers, New York, 1957, p. xxxv.

[8] *Ibid.*, p. 13.

Religion, it seems, is esoteric psychology. Lacan's essay *On the Stage of the Mirror in the Formation of Consciousness* reads remarkably like this last passage. But Feuerbach uses the term 'anthropology' rather than the term, 'psychology'. He does so in a way that differentiates his reduction from a critical debunking: "While reducing theology to anthropology, I exalt anthropology into theology, very much as Christianity, while lowering God into man [in the person of Jesus], made man into God."[9]

Feuerbach does not dismiss religion any more than Freud dismissed dreams. Instead he interprets religion as the dream-work of the human spirit. "Religion is the dream of the human mind," writes Feuerbach. "Hence I do nothing more to religion—and to speculative philosophy and theology also—than to open its eyes, or rather to turn its gaze from the internal towards the external, i.e., I change the object as it is in the imagination into the object as it is in reality."[10]

Feuerbach's view of religion is thus very different from Freud's. To say that religion is esoteric anthropology is not to say that religion is an illusion, for, quite to the contrary of a Freudian reduction of religion to wish fulfillment, Feuerbach sees in religion an esoteric reading of the human spirit that features the role of love rather than that of Oedipal envy.

> The clearest, most irrefragable proof that man in religion contemplates himself as the object of the Divine Being, as the end of the divine activity, that thus in religion he has relation only to his own nature, only to himself...is the love of God for man...God, for the sake of man, empties himself of his Godhead! Herein lies the elevating influence of the Incarnation; the highest, the perfect being humiliates, lowers himself for the sake of man.... How can the worth

---

[9] *Ibid.*, p. xxxviii. See also the very first aphorism of his *Principles of the Philosophy of the Future, op. cit.* p. 5, #1: "The task of the modern era was the realization and humanization of God—the transformation and dissolution of theology into anthropology."

[10] *Ibid.*, p. xxxix.

of man be more strongly expressed than when God, for man's sake, becomes a man?[11]

Only when this high estimation of human potential remains central to the reading of Feuerbach can we appreciate why as rigorous and orthodox a theologian as Karl Barth would say of Feuerbach, "The attitude of the anti-theologian, Feuerbach, was more theological than that of many theologians."[12] And further, "Feuerbach wants, in the end, to help man secure his due. Therefore his philosophy begins with the sentence: 'I am a real, a sensuous, a material being; yes, the body in its totality is my Ego, my being itself.' His teaching aims to be a 'frankly sensuous philosophy.'"[13]

Does this not begin to sound like something close to what was said, in a different idiom, at Esalen?

## Marx's Break with Feuerbach

We'll have more to say about Feuerbach in the course of reversing some (but not all) of Marx's reversals of Feuerbach, but enough has been said to give traction to Marx's critique. Because Marx's Theses are, for the most part, relatively succinct, I'll begin by simply quoting all eleven of them. Where the first goes on at some length, I'll mark an omission with ellipses like so.... Only after quoting all eleven theses will I go back and add some commentary, and then suggest changes that give measure to both an appreciation of Esalen's leadership and a criticism of Marxism's failures.

The essay proceeds this way for three reasons: first, because Marx's theses are remarkably dense, an understanding of the earlier theses will benefit from a reading of the later theses. They reward several readings. Second, I want to give Marx his due by letting him speak for himself before "sampling" him into a more contemporary tune. Third, given the setup thus far, the overall strategy of this essay—the series of

---

[11] *Ibid.*, p. 57.
[12] Karl Barth, in *An Introductory Essay* to *The Essence of Christianity, op. cit.*, p. x.
[13] *Ibid.*, p. xii.

somersaults that will land us back on an appreciation for Murphy's and Esalen's innovative leadership—I encourage the reader to add his or her own riffs before I make mine.

Like a video game, I would like to think of this essay as interactive. In addition to reviewing Marx's double rupture with Hegel, and Murphy's double rupture with traditional religion and psychology, this essay should rupture it's own boundaries by breaking with didacticism to provoke the reader's own reading of Marx on Feuerbach on Hegel, as well as the reader's own reading of Ogilvy on Murphy on California on spirituality.

## Theses on Feuerbach
## By Karl Marx

### I

The chief defect of all hitherto existing materialism—that of Feuerbach included—is that the thing *[Gegenstand]*, reality, sensuousness, is conceived only in the form of the object *[Objekt]* of contemplation *[Anschauung]*, but not as human sensuous activity, practice *[praxis]*, not subjectively. Hence it happened that the active side was developed by idealism rather than materialism—but only abstractly, since idealism knows nothing of real, sensuous activity as such. Feuerbach wants the sensuous object really differentiated from objects of thought, but he does not conceive human activity itself as objective *[gegenständliche]* activity...

### II

The question whether objective *[gegenständliche]* truth can be attributed to human thinking is not a question of theory, but is a practical question. In practice man must prove the truth, that is, the reality and power, the this-sidedness *[Diesseitigkeit]* of his thinking. The dispute over the reality or non-reality of thinking which is isolated from practice is a purely scholastic question.

### III

The materialist doctrine that men are products of circumstances and upbringing, and that, therefore, changed men are products of other circumstances and changed upbringing, forgets that it is men that change circumstances, and that the educator himself needs educating. Hence this doctrine necessarily arrives at dividing society into two parts, of which one is superior to society [as in Robert Owen, for example, *Engels added*].

The coincidence of the changing of circumstances and of human activity can be conceived and rationally understood only as revolutionary practice.

## IV

Feuerbach starts out from the fact of religious self-alienation, the duplication of the world into a religious, imaginary world and a real one. His work consists in the dissolution of the religious world into its secular basis. He overlooks the fact that after completing this work, the chief thing still remains to be done. For the fact that the secular foundation detaches itself from itself and establishes itself in the clouds as an independent realm is really to be explained only by the self-cleavage and self-contradictoriness of this secular basis. The latter must itself, therefore, first be understood in its contradiction and then, by the removal of the contradiction, revolutionized in practice. Thus, for instance, once the earthly family is discovered to be the secret of the holy family, the former must then itself be criticized in theory and revolutionized in practice.

## V

Feuerbach, not satisfied with *abstract thinking*, appeals to *sensuous contemplation*, but he does not conceive sensuousness as *practical*, human-sensuous activity.

## VI

Feuerbach resolves the religious essence into the human essence. But the human essence is no abstraction inherent in each single individual. In its reality it is the ensemble of social relations.

Feuerbach, who does not enter upon a criticism of this real essence, is consequently compelled:

1. To abstract from the historical process and to fix the religious sentiment *[Gemüt]* as something by itself, and to presuppose an abstract— *isolated*—human individual.

2. Human essence, therefore, can with him be comprehended only as 'genus,' as an internal, dumb generality which unites the many individuals *naturally*.

## VII

Feuerbach, consequently, does not see that the 'religious sentiment' is itself a social product, and that the abstract individual whom he analyzes belongs in reality to a particular form of society.

## VIII

Social life is essentially *practical*. All mysteries which mislead theory to mysticism find their rational solution in human practice and in the comprehension of this practice.

## IX

The highest point attained by contemplative materialism, that is materialism which does not understand sensuousness as practical activity, is the contemplation of single individuals in 'civil society.'

## X

The standpoint of the old materialism is 'civil' society; the standpoint of the new is *human society*, or socialized humanity.

## XI

Heretofore philosophers have only interpreted the world in various ways; the point, however, is to change it.[14]

As stated earlier, these theses are dense. Don't hesitate to read them again, from the first to the last, and as you do so, consider how you might want to amend them to read as Theses on Esalen.

Before I make my own amendments, let me clarify the transform I will use: a quasi-mathematical operator, like a rotation function that

---

[14] Karl Marx, *Theses on Feuerbach*, the translation is my own blend of the version found in *Marx & Engels, Basic Writings on Politics & Philosophy*, ed. Lewis Feuer, Doubleday Anchor, Garden City, New York, 1959, pp. 243-245, and the version in *Writings of the young Marx on Philosophy and Society*, ed. and trans. By Loyd Easton and Kurt Guddat, Doubleday Anchor, Garden City, New York, 1967, pp. 400-402.

would torque everything clockwise 90 degrees. The transform derives from a critique of Marx based on the lessons of history read through a commentary on his texts. The main points are three: first, Marx placed too much emphasis on the social vis-à-vis the individual; second, Marx paid insufficient respect to the practice of contemplation. Third, Marx's theory of alienation was internally incoherent. Let me clarify these points by adding three qualifiers to each:

*Marx overemphasized the social at the expense of the individual.*

1. Consider Kierkegaard's critique of Hegel. The unhappy Dane objected to the way the life of the concretely existing individual got swallowed up and subsumed by the over-powering influence of The System.[15]

2. The practical expression of this theoretical shortcoming is evident in the insufficient protection of civil liberties in communist societies.

3. Creativity and innovation suffer when the rights of the individual are subordinated to the needs of the collective. As Harold Bloom argues in *The Western Canon*, "Social energies exist in every age, but they cannot compose plays, poems, and narratives. The power to originate is an individual gift, present in all eras but evidently greatly encouraged by particular contexts."[16]

*Marx showed insufficient appreciation for the practice of contemplation.*

1. Consider the testimony of tens of thousands of meditators, from ancient India to modern Esalen. From ancient Buddhism to the present, there is a tradition of centuries of inner empiricism, an inter-subjectively validated compendium of evidence whose

---

[15] Kierkegaard's resistance to the all-inclusive totality of Hegelian philosophy runs through virtually all of his writing, but is most explicit in his *Concluding Unscientific Postscript*, tr. David Swenson and Walter Lowrie, Princeton University Press, Princeton, 1941, pp. 99-113.

[16] Harold Bloom, *The Western Canon*, Harcourt Brace, New York, 1994, p. 46. But see for importantly dissenting opinions the several essays collected in two volumes edited by Alfonso Montouri and Ronald Purser, *Social Creativity*, Volumes I and II, Hampton Press, Cresskill, New Jersey, 1999 and 2001.

texts and oral teachings amount to an owners' manual for the human mind.

2. This *practice* of meditation is very different from the imperative to practice, practice, practice before you can perform in Carnegie Hall. The stress on the practice of meditation is actually quite close to the definition of *praxis* as a revolutionary activity that *changes* everyday reality.

3. Seen as inducing change rather than the mere contemplation of existing reality, the practice of meditation may be every bit as pragmatic and efficacious as the manning of barricades.

*Marx's theory of alienation was incoherent.*

1. In his early work, which some regard as humanistic to the point of being moralistic, Marx spoke of alienation as an estrangement (*Entfremdung*) from man's *essence*.

2. In his later work, Marx realized that morality based on an ahistorical essence violated the revolutionary historicism of his dialectical materialism.

3. The proof of his own realization of this incoherence shows up in the fact that in his later work, particularly the three volumes of *Das Kapital*, he says almost nothing about alienation.

So clarified, this *operator* called *What's-wrong-with-Marx* will render, when applied to Marx's *Theses on Feuerbach*, a series of slightly different theses that take us closer to Murphy's innovative leadership in religious, philosophical, social, and psychological thought. Let's have a look.

## From Marx and Feuerbach to Theses on Murphy

Take the first thesis. Once again:

The chief defect of all hitherto existing materialism—that of Feuerbach included—is that the thing *[Gegenstand]*, reality, sensuousness, is conceived only in the form of the object *[Objekt]* of contemplation *[Anschauung]*, but not as human sensuous activity, practice *[praxis]*, not subjectively. Hence it happened that the active side was developed by idealism rather than materialism—but only abstractly, since idealism knows nothing of real, sensuous activity as such. Feuerbach wants the sensuous object really differentiated from the objects of thought, but he does not conceive human activity itself as objective *[gegenständliche]* activity...

Feuerbach got the stress on materialism right, just as America surpassed India in the material realm of economics. But what Feuerbach missed was the *active* aspect of world-making, which idealism grasped in Kant's stress on the constitution of the object of knowledge by the activity of the human mind—Kant's so-called "Copernican revolution" according to which the object of knowledge had to correspond to the active constitution of the categories of understanding and the forms of intuition, rather than to a passively received impression of an external object.[17]

What Murphy and Esalen add to the spirituality imported from India is a similar stress on American materialism—spirituality incarnate in the body of the existing individual. And just as Marx chides Feuerbach for his insufficient attention to the moment of *activity* that was grasped by Kantian idealism but not by Feuerbachian materialism, so we can criticize Marx and the tradition of Marxism for giving insufficient latitude and liberty to individual activity in the form of artistic creativity and individual dissent. Dissident writers like Viktor Erofeyev, a frequent guest at Esalen, paid too high a price

---

[17] Immanuel Kant, *Critique of Pure Reason*, tr. Norman Kemp Smith, St. Martin's Press, New York, 1961, p. 22 (xvi-xvii) for his description of his Copernican revolution. For some sense of the momentousness of the significance of Kant's Copernican revolution, see the following commentaries: T.D. Weldon, *Kant's Critique of Pure Reason*, The Clarendon Press, Oxford, 1958, pp. 78f., 89-93, 202-4, 208-10; H. W. Cassirer, *Kant's First Critique*, Macmillan, New York, 1954, pp. 267f., 271ff., 302-308; Norman Kemp Smith, *A Commentary to Kant's 'Critique of Pure Reason'*, Humanities Press, New York, 1962, pp. 18f, 22-25, 478ff., 519f.; Nathan Rotenstreich, *Experience and its Systematization: Studies in Kant*, Martinus Nijhoff, The Hague, 1965, pp. 68ff., 122, 157f., 162-168; A. C. Ewing, *A Short Commentary on Kant's Critique of Pure Reason*, The University of Chicago Press, 1938, pp. 16, 208-27; Herman-J. de Vleeschauwer, *The Development of Kantian Thought*, tr. A. R. C. Duncan, Thomas Nelson & Sons Ltd., London, 1962, pp. 49-61.

under the strictures of Soviet Communism. The thaw at the end of the Cold War allowed a blossoming of individual expression of human potential.

So let us amend Marx's first thesis to read as follows:

1.  The chief defect of all hitherto existing materialism—that of Marx included—is that sensuousness is conceived only in the form of the object of political action but not as the object of meditative contemplation. Hence it happened that the active side was developed by Marxist materialism—but only politically, since Marxist materialism knows nothing of meditative practice as such. Marx wants the sensuous object really differentiated from the objects of thought, but he does not conceive meditation itself as objective activity. Murphy and Esalen brought meditation down out of the ether of pure contemplation and implemented an incarnate practice that helped change the world.

Consider the second thesis:

II. The question whether objective *[gegenständliche]* truth can be attributed to human thinking is not a question of theory, but is a practical question. In practice man must prove the truth, that is, the reality and power, the this-sidedness *[Diesseitigkeit]* of his thinking. The dispute over the reality or non-reality of thinking which is isolated from practice is a purely scholastic question.

It's not enough just to *think* the liberation of the human spirit. You must *act it out*. So workshops at Esalen are not like classes in universities. How often have gestalt workshop leaders said to those in the hot seat, "*Be* that locomotive you dreamt about...*Be* that limp dish rag..."? Acting it out, speaking the part, taking the appropriate body posture, feeling the associated feelings...these constitute a practice that is altogether different from just *talking about* different ideas, symbols, mere words.

Through its hundreds of workshops, Esalen pioneered in the field of *experiential learning*. (See above the essays by George Leonard and

Gordon Wheeler.) Unlike university classrooms where students listen to teachers pose scholastic questions seeking merely academic answers, Esalen's workshops called for movement, body contact, and real confrontations with the demons of the psyche.

Marx's second thesis requires very little amendment to apply to Esalen:

2. The question whether objective truth can be attributed to human thinking is not a question of theory but of practice and experience. In practice man must prove the truth, that is, the reality and power, the intentionality of his thinking. At Esalen you must put up or shut up or be called for the hollowness of your intentions. The dispute over the reality or non-reality of thinking which is isolated from practice is a purely scholastic question.

III. The materialist doctrine that men are products of circumstances and upbringing, and that, therefore, changed men are products of other circumstances and changed upbringing, forgets that it is men that change circumstances, and that the educator himself needs educating. Hence this doctrine necessarily arrives at dividing society into two parts, of which one is superior to society [as in Robert Owen, for example, Engels added].

The coincidence of the changing of circumstances and of human activity can be conceived and rationally understood only as revolutionary practice.

Here Marx is addressing the old nature vs. nurture dispute, and in a way that runs contrary to facile criticisms of liberals and lefties. Against those who believe that the left places too much emphasis on social conditioning rather than human nature, Marx places a plague on both houses. Neither circumstances, nor an innate human nature determine the course of human action. Instead, autonomous human beings who take charge of their own destinies can change the circumstances that in turn change men. As is said of great architecture, our buildings shape us…but we shape our buildings, sometimes even after they have been built and occupied by their initial tenants.[18]

Marx's famous phrase, "that the educator himself needs educating," applies especially to an education for the future—something that Feuerbach, the author of *Principles of the Philosophy of the Future*, as well as forward looking Californians care about. If Parmenides was correct in thinking that all change is illusory, if Plato was right in thinking that the true forms of things are eternal, if Aristotle was correct (contra Darwin) in claiming that the number and nature of living species remains fixed for all eternity, then society could be split into two parts: the gurus who are in contact with the eternal truths, and a vast unwashed student body awaiting the dispensing of those truths. Ever since Hegel and Darwin, though, we know that human consciousness develops. History is real. Things change, and sometimes the kids get the news before the elders. Hence the educators themselves need perpetual re-education.

Rather than the sage on the stage, the teacher becomes the guide on the side. Group leaders in Esalen workshops must mix it up with the workshop participants and make it up as they go along in real time. Maintaining a dynamic frontier at Esalen entailed, as Michael Murphy often put it, that no one "capture the flag." Esalen could have easily become the Fritz Perls Institute of Gestalt psychology, or the Ida Rolf Institute of Structural Integration. Any number of very strong personalities made bids to become the reigning guru, but Murphy and Price maintained a pluralistic culture very distinct from authoritarian cults. No one gets tenure at Esalen. While there is a community that has sufficient stability to maintain institutional memory, build expertise, and get all the necessary jobs done, the Esalen community is like a living body that is perpetually sloughing off old cells, taking in new energy, and re-generating new cells.

---

[18] For an original and profound account of the ways that the material realities of buildings can be shaped and repurposed even after they have been first occupied, see Stewart Brand, *How Buildings Learn*, Penguin, New York, 1995.

3. The leftist idea that men are products of circumstances and upbringing, and that, therefore, changed men are products of other circumstances and changed upbringing, forgets that it is men and women that change circumstances, and that the educator himself needs educating. The old guru approach arrives at dividing society into two parts, of which one—e.g. Fritz Perls or Werner Erhard—is superior to the rest.

   A truly progressive practice demands a self-reflexive cycling of changing personnel, changing circumstances, and changing human activity.

IV. Feuerbach starts out from the fact of religious self-alienation, the duplication of the world into a religious, imaginary world and a real one. His work consists in the dissolution of the religious world into its secular basis. He overlooks the fact that after completing this work, the chief thing still remains to be done. For the fact that the secular foundation detaches itself from itself and establishes itself in the clouds as an independent realm is really to be explained only by the self-cleavage and self-contradictoriness of this secular basis. The latter must itself, therefore, first be understood in its contradiction and then, by the removal of the contradiction, revolutionized in practice. Thus, for instance, once the earthly family is discovered to be the secret of the holy family, the former must then itself be criticized in theory and revolutionized in practice.

You can see why the Christian right went apoplectic over the threat of Communism: The Reds were against family values! "The earthly family...must be criticized in theory and revolutionized in practice!" Next thing you know we'll have lesbians raising kids conceived in Petri dishes.

Feuerbach saw that the holy trinity was a projection of Dad, Mom and Junior. Like Freud, Feuerbach understood the extent to which religious beliefs were scripted by secular realities. Marx accepted Feuerbach's insight into the dynamics of projection, but Marx was not content with stopping there. Rather than deconstruct the sacred as a projection of the secular, he wants to revolutionize the secular that is the source of the sacred.

This move is not unlike the radical challenge that Esalen poses to many ordinary lives. People come to Esalen, take part in workshops, and the next thing you know they want to quit their jobs, file for divorce, and start their lives over from scratch—as if their ordinary lives need to be "criticized in theory and revolutionized in practice." Where too much of Freudian therapy was aimed at getting people to "adjust" to their circumstances, as critics like Thomas Szasz and R. D. Laing pointed out, Esalen was ready to revolutionize the circumstances.

4. Freudian therapy starts out from the fact of religious self-alienation, the duplication of the world into a religious, imaginary world and a real one. Its work consists in the dissolution of the religious world into its secular basis. But Freudian therapy overlooks the fact that after completing this work, the chief thing still remains to be done. For the fact that the "politics of the family" (Cf. R. D. Laing's book by that name) projects itself onto a sacred nuclear family is really to be explained only by the pathologies of its origin in ordinary, alienated life. The latter must itself be understood in its alienation and then, by the overcoming of alienation, revolutionized in practice.

V. "Feuerbach, not satisfied with *abstract thinking*, appeals to *sensuous contemplation*, but he does not conceive sensuousness as *practical*, human-sensuous activity."

5. Americans, not satisfied with the other-worldliness of Indian asceticism, find themselves pumping iron at the gym. But they do not conceive of their body-building as part of a larger context of humane, social self-construction. They separate mind from body, and their body work is therefore mechanistic, like taking their cars to mechanics. They don't see, until they come to Esalen, the potentiality for an integral practice that harmonizes the development of body, mind, soul and spirit.

VI. Feuerbach resolves the religious essence into the human essence. But the human essence is no abstraction inherent in each single individual. In its reality it is the ensemble of social relations.

Feuerbach, who does not enter upon a criticism of this real essence, is consequently compelled:

1.  To abstract from the historical process and to fix the religious sentiment *[Gemüt]* as something by itself, and to presuppose an abstract—*isolated*—human individual.

2.  Human essence, therefore, can with him be comprehended only as 'genus,' as an internal, dumb generality which unites the many individuals *naturally.*

Here, as I have often heard Michael Murphy say, "we are getting into the high grass." I've never been quite sure whether this expression referred to the grass on some honorifically elevated plateau...or to grass so tall one could lose visibility and get lost in it. In any case, the plot thickens with the sixth thesis, especially with Marx's acknowledgement that human essence is not some ahistorical abstraction, but instead, "the ensemble of social relations," which are, of course, subject to historical change.

The problem is just this: If you want to make a moral case against current social conditions as somehow *alienated* from what they could or should be, you need a theory of human nature or essence *from which* we are alienated. But if you posit such a theory of human nature or essence, you deny the very historicity of humanity that was so dear to both Hegel and Marx—if not to Feuerbach, as Marx noted. In the end, Marx sided with Hegel on this point, and not with Feuerbach. Marx himself credited Hegel for acknowledging the historicity of humanity: "The outstanding thing [*die Grösse*, the greatness] in Hegel's *Phenomenology* and its final outcome—that is, the dialectic of negativity as the moving and generating principle—is thus first that Hegel conceives the self-genesis of man as a process, conceives objectification as loss of the object, as alienation and as transcendence of this alienation; that he thus grasps the essence of *labor* and comprehends objective man—true because real man—as the outcome of man's *own labor*."[19]

This is a powerful idea, and it is one that is at the very heart of what Esalen is about. Call it *the human potential movement*. Rather than simply repeating over and over again some fixed and ahistorical essence, we human beings continue to make it up as we go along. We make history. We evolve toward actualizing what in earlier times was only latent or potential. Hence Michael Murphy's very well documented argument in *The Future of the Body* to the effect that extraordinary human performances by athletes and mystics represent pre-figurations or presentiments of human capacities that will later become commonplace.

But there are problems, deep problems, theological and philosophical problems, with this concept of potentiality. E.g., how precisely—or dimly—is higher potential prefigured? If the pattern is as precise as that of the oak in the acorn, then we are back to the kind of ahistorical essentialism we find in a pre-Darwinian Aristotle. But if the potentiality is as broad as that of wet clay that can be shaped into any form whatever, then what sense does it make to say that higher potentials are prefigured at all? Further, if we are like wet clay, entirely plastic, then by what standard could one say that we were either alienated from our true nature, or falling short of some higher potential?

Marx wavered on these issues, as have Marxists ever since. At times, as in his honoring of the greatness of Hegel's *Phenomenology*, Marx seems to see alienation as a *good* thing—as the objectification or externalization (*Entäusserung*, or othering) of human potential through the medium of labor or constructive work in the world. This *positive* read of "alienation" has a long history. Nathan Rotenstreich notes the correspondence between the Latin term, *alienatio*, and the Greek term *ekstasis*. "Just as *'ekstasis'* connotes the state of being beside oneself or transported from one's self, so *'alienatio'* means the state of being of a man who, having been beside himself, is transformed into another."[20]

---

[19] Marx, *Economic and Philosophic Manuscripts of 1844*, trans. Foreign Language Publishing House, Moscow, 1961, p. 151.

[20] Nathan Rotenstreich, *Basic Problems of Marx's Philosophy*, New York, 1965, p. 144.

From this "ecstatic" sense of alienation as *Entäusserung*, there derives a more positive connotation than from the negative connotations of alienation as estrangement (*Entfremdung*). Throughout the neo-Platonic tradition, alienation is a state to be sought after rather than resisted. For Plotinus the aim of contemplation is a loss of consciousness of self in order to seek unity with the One, and "like Plotinus, St. Augustine conceived of alienation as a state of ecstatic contemplation in which the human soul or spirit is elevated."[21] And certainly we can say that this sort of ecstatic transformation is a consummation devoutly to be wished by many who come to Esalen.

This ambivalence between the positive connotations of alienation as *Entäusserung* and the negative connotations of alienation as *Entfremdung* are noted by the translators of the official Foreign Languages Publishing House edition of Marx's *Economic and Philosophic Manuscripts of 1844*.[22] Nicholas Lobkowicz has traced the use of both terms through the work of Fichte and Schelling.[23] I believe that this very same ambivalence can be traced all the way forward to R. D. Laing's claim that sometimes so-called "breakdowns" are really breakthroughs; also to the radical criticisms of psychotherapy as forcing people to "adjust" to circumstances that should themselves be changed;[24] and to J. D. Salinger's wonderful line, somewhere in *Franny and Zoe*, "This is the age of Kaliyuga, Buddy. If you're not schizophrenic you're part of the enemy."

High grass indeed. Sometimes real leadership requires one to be out of step, alienated from prevailing beliefs and practices. But how is one to know just which times? Certainly not by reference to some ahistorical essence. Hegel, Marx, and the evolutionary/developmental path toward higher potential at Esalen are all united on this point. But what other point of reference, what other criterion can serve as a norm or standard if *not* an ahistorical essence? If not some fixed and original *alpha*, then

---

[21] *Ibid.*, pp. 146-7.

[22] Karl Marx, *Economic and Philosophic Manuscripts of 1844*, Foreign Languages Publishing House, Moscow, 1961, "Translator's Note on Terminology," pp. 11-12.

[23] N. Lobkowicz, *Theory and Practice*, Notre Dame, Indiana,1967, pp. 301ff.

[24] See the works of Thomas Szasz; and Ken Kesey's famous portrayal of "big nurse" in *One Flew Over the Cuckoo's Nest*.

perhaps some eventual *omega*, e.g., the "omega point" posited by Teilhard de Chardin? The trouble with that sort of teleology is that it drives one toward the denial of history just as surely as does an ahistorical *alpha* essence. If the goal has already been set, the die cast, then time, as Plato put it in the *Timaeus*, is just "the moving image of eternity."

Murphy understands these issues. This is why he has sponsored a series of invitational conferences at Esalen on evolutionary theory. This is why he is so eager to find a third way between "intelligent design" or the Omega Point on the one hand, and on the other those advocates of a neo-Darwinian synthesis that sees no directionality or progress whatever in evolution. According to Murphy, the realization of potential is neither completely pre-scripted, nor is it a blind game of chance going nowhere in particular. As Murphy likes to put it, "Evolution meanders."

While there is neither *alpha* essence nor *omega* telos to serve as a standard for distinguishing breakdowns from breakthroughs, or destructive alienation from constructive ecstasy, the evolving, changing human body and soul seem able to find guidance in a spiritual practice that is monitored, checked, and shared with others on the path. Hence we can say…

> 6. Murphy resolves human essence into spiritual essence. But human essence is no abstraction inherent in each single individual. In its reality it is the ensemble of social relations.
>
> At Esalen, a community of practice makes it possible to avoid the renegade insanities of *isolated* ecstasies that veer into pathological alienation.

VII. Feuerbach, consequently, does not see that the 'religious sentiment' is itself a social product, and that the abstract individual whom he analyzes belongs in reality to a particular form of society.

At Esalen, to the contrary, there is a hyper-sensitivity to the diversity of social conditions behind different religious and spiritual beliefs. Yes, it is good to make sure that no one "captures the flag" in the name of some single orthodoxy. But at the opposite extreme a community so tolerant can lapse into what Ken Wilber has called "Boomeritis": the green meme run rampant. Rather than try to footnote and explain what may sound like jargon to some readers (though well known to others), let's just say…

> 7. At Esalen the degree of tolerance toward different religious and spiritual beliefs and practices runs the risk of allowing (to use a bit of distinctly Californian argot) *whatevah*…

VIII. Social life is essentially *practical*. All mysteries which mislead theory to mysticism find their rational solution in human practice and in the comprehension of this practice.

Here we need to grab hold of the *What-is-wrong-with-Marxism* operator and take issue very directly. Both Marx and Soviet Communism had a blindspot when it came to religion and mysticism. While Feuerbach was quick to say, "While reducing theology to anthropology, I exalt anthropology into theology," Marx accepted only the first half of that equation. He saw religion as esoteric psychology, or worse, as "the opiate of the people," and nothing more.

As Michael Murphy well knows, I myself claim very little by way of religious belief or regular spiritual practice. Yet even I regard the radical secularism in Marx and his heirs as deficient. While I am reluctant to subscribe to almost any known religious orthodoxy, I still find Marx and his heirs guilty of a hyper-rationalism that violates the test of experience. Apart from the official atheism, this hyper-rationalism shows up in two other obvious errors: the denial of the unconscious in Soviet psychology until well on into the 20th century, and the arrogance of central planning, as if a few smart minds in the Kremlin could figure out how to allocate resources without feedback from the market.

Think of religion as the social unconscious, somewhat the way Carl Jung and James Hillman speak of psychological archetypes using the names of the gods and goddesses to personify dynamics at work well below the radar of rational cognition. So-called myths, the narratives of the gods and goddesses, speak truths about our human condition that cannot be captured by the hyper-rationalism of Marxists, computer programmers, or philosophers of consciousness who preach "eliminative materialism."[25] A radical empiricism of the sort William James advocated forces us to recognize certain *experiences* that are best described as mystical. But rather than describe those experiences any further by clothing them in the garbs of any religious orthodoxies, I prefer to quote the famous last lines of Wittgenstein's *Tractatus:* "What we cannot speak about we must pass over in silence."

8. At Esalen, there is a healthy suspicion of attempts to eff the ineffable. There is no common creed, no orthodoxy. Murphy likes to quote a phrase he picked up from his teacher, Frederic Spiegelberg: "The religion of no religion."

IX. The highest point attained by contemplative materialism, that is materialism which does not understand sensuousness as practical activity, is the contemplation of single individuals in 'civil society.'

"Civil society" is a slippery phrase with a long and diverse history. Most recently it has been raised to a fairly honorific status to the extent that it refers to all of those non-governmental organizations (NGOs) like Greenpeace, unions, Amnesty International and the PTA that mediate in the vast and growing space between shrinking governments (the public sector) and growing markets (the private sector). This is not exactly what Marx had in mind. In the Marxist tradition, 'civil society' is code for the kind of society envisaged by the social contract theorists like Rousseau for whom the collective—society—is a result of implicit and explicit contracts drawn up and agreed to by *individuals* who, like Robinson Crusoe, somehow come to self-consciousness prior to their

---

[25] Cf. Dan Dennett, *Consciousness Explained*, Little Brown & Co., Boston, 1991; and P. S. Churchland, *Neurophilosophy: Toward a Unified Science of the Mind/Brain*, MIT Press, Cambridge, 1986. For a fuller survey of different approaches to consciousness, some of which are less uncompromisingly reductionistic, see *Explaining Consciousness, the Hard Problem*, ed. Jonathan Shear, the MIT Press, Cambridge, 1998; and *The Nature of Consciousness*, ed. Ned Block, Owen Flanagan, and Güven Güzeldere, MIT Press, Cambridge, 1997.

entry into these social contracts. Both Hegel and Marx found this story implausible. In the collectivist creation myth, mankind comes on the scene as a herd. Only later, through the process of alienation, are individuals alienated from the herd, cut away from the herd like so many cattle in a penning contest at the rodeo.

So individuated have we Americans become, we may find it difficult to comprehend social solidarity as prior to individuality. Communal life, if not communism, can serve as an antidote to our knee-jerk individualism. So can workshops at Esalen where the process encourages a "transcending of ego"…but the fact is that much of the process at Esalen has quite the opposite effect. Depending on the method, and the convictions and techniques of the group leader, much of the group process is actually very individualistic in its assumptions and in its outcomes. Much of the rhetoric is about getting in touch with your *real feelings*. What do you *really* want? Can you find your inner self?

To anyone familiar with Hegel and Marx, or to anyone steeped in oriental traditions, this rhetoric of Robinson Crusoe individualism is highly suspect, whether or not one embraces the equal and opposite abstraction of extreme collectivism.[26] Further, it invites ridicule of the sort that Tom Wolfe leveled in his essay about the 1970s entitled, "The Me Decade." I'm reminded of a friend who is fond of poking fun at those whose conversations can be glossed as, "Enough about me; now, what do *you* think of me?"

Marx's critical ninth thesis on Feuerbach therefore still has some bite:

9. The highest point attained by Esalen in its first several decades, is the contemplation of single individuals in 'civil society.'

---

[26] On this whole subject of the equal and opposite abstractions of individualism and collectivism, see J. Ogilvy, "Beyond Individualism and Collectivism," in *Revisioning Philosophy*, ed. Ogilvy, SUNY Press, New York, 1991, an anthology that compiles the highlights of four years of Esalen conferences under the same title. On the limits of individualism in the psychological literature, see Gordon Wheeler, *Beyond Individualism*, GIC Press, Cambridge, Mass., 2000; on the limits of individualism from a sociological perspective, see Robert Bellah, *Habits of the Heart*, University of California Press, 1985.

X.  The standpoint of the old materialism is 'civil' society; the standpoint
    of the new is *human society*, or socialized humanity.

Marx may have been right to criticize Feuerbach—and Esalen—for
being limited to the "contemplation of single individuals in 'civil society.'" But it does not follow that the socialism of "socialized humanity"
is a preferable alternative. One of the fruits of the decline and fall of
the Soviet Union has been a growing awareness of the dangers of totalizing too far and too quickly. The refrain, *No one is free until we're all
free*, sounds nice. It is so non-parochial, so expansive, so generous in
spirit. But in practice this lofty sentiment greases a one-way slide to
totalitarianism.

Herbert Marcuse summarizes part of the argument of the 1844
Manuscripts as saying, "Man is free only if all men are free and exist as
'universal beings.' When this condition is attained, life will be shaped
by the potentialities of the genus, Man, which embraces the potentialities of all the individuals that comprise it. The emphasis on this universality brings nature as well into the self-development of mankind."[27]
So, as philosopher Peter Singer puts it, even trees have standing. Next
stop, the Buddhist vow to honor and protect *all living things*. Again,
this sounds like a great idea. But as we increase the radius of solidarity
to include not only all human beings but also all living things, great
and small, from whales to microbes, we find ourselves, conceptually
speaking, in what Hegel called a night in which all cows are black. We
lose the ability to distinguish anything from anything else. Just as an
extreme individualism invites ridicule of ego-centric Yuppies from the
Me-Decade, so this extreme totalism invites ridicule of those chanting
over and over, *We are all One, We are all One, We are all One*...until, say,
a telemarketer calls.

In an important address marking the end of Esalen's first forty years
and the beginning of the next forty years, Gordon Wheeler and Keith
Thompson sounded a much-needed refrain: "From Me to We."[28] They

---

[27] Herbert Marcuse, *Reason and Revolution*, Beacon Press, Boston, 1960, p. 275.
[28] Talk given at Esalen Institute, November 2, 2001.

did not say, *From Me to Absolutely Everyone*. Nor were they trying to set up an antagonism between *Us* and *Them*. But they were acknowledging, with due humility, the need for expanding the radius of human potential from the individual self to a larger social and natural milieu. Ecological sustainability was part of the purview. But the move toward sustainability may have to take place one acre at a time.

In moving away from the preoccupation with the precious self toward a larger horizon of concern, Esalen will not make the Marxist mistake of totalizing too quickly. Just how far and how fast the radius of care can usefully and practically expand is very much up for grabs. A refrain I often sound goes, "Not one, not all, but some."[29] This is not about elitism, but humility. The point is not to protect *we precious few* against *them*, but to foster an intimacy and a community among as many living beings as can plausibly constitute a living and viable ecology. The length of the radius of concern varies depending upon the issue. Global warming is a global issue. Cultural integrity is not. Romantic love and the raising of a family may be best nested in a village, but not necessarily in an entire nation.

Part of what I find most remarkable about Esalen is its leadership as a *social invention*. We are all familiar with technological inventions. They happen all the time. Just look at the number of patents. But social inventions are extremely rare. If you start counting with your fingers, you may not need your toes: the nuclear family, the church, the university, democracy, the corporation…what else? Before 1962 there was nothing on the face of the earth that looked much like Esalen. Now there are dozens of clones incorporating experiential learning, group living, bio-dynamic gardening, financial viability, and an aspiration toward expanding human potential. It could be that Esalen's leadership has less to do with any particular theory, doctrine, or –ism and more to do with its unique incarnation of many spiritual traditions in a new

---

[29] J. Ogilvy, *Many Dimensional Man: Decentralizing Self, Society, and the Sacred*, Oxford University Press, New York, 1977, *passim*.

crucible, a new kind of social body, a new body politic—very old wines in a new wineskin.

10. The standpoint of Marxist socialism is equality for all: everyone will be equally poor. Esalen is neither a classless society, nor a tyranny, but an intentional community organized around principles of mutual respect, a shared mission, the development of human potential, and sustainability.

XI. Heretofore philosophers have only interpreted the world in various ways; the point, however, is to change it.

Esalen has changed the world in several ways:
1. By serving as the inaugural exemplar of a new social invention
2. By changing the lives of many who have visited Esalen
3. By introducing into our discourse the new meme of "the human potential movement" and all that implies
4. By helping to bring about an end to the Cold War.

Given the fact that Esalen's involvement in citizen diplomacy with the Soviet Union is less well known than its contribution to the human potential movement—as well as the play on (and with) Marx running throughout this essay—it may be worth saying a few words about this fourth point. First the facts: After reading the book, *Psychic Discoveries Behind the Iron Curtain*, Michael and Dulce Murphy made several trips to Russia in the 1970s as part of their research on paranormal phenomena. They met many people in Russia and established friendships and professional relationships. Then came the deep freeze in Russian-American relations when Russia invaded Afghanistan in 1979. Virtually all exchange programs between the U.S. and the Soviet Union came to an abrupt halt—except Esalen's.

Starting in 1980, Esalen hosted a series of annual conferences to which influential Russians were invited. These meetings, as well as a number of trips that some of us made to Russia, were part of a movement now known as "citizen diplomacy." Joe Montville, then serving in the State Department, coined the term "Second Track Diplomacy" at one of our meetings at Esalen. The idea was to identify profession-als from both countries who shared similar interests—health, psy-chology, energy, space exploration, future studies, philosophy—and then allow them to meet one another, talk shop with one another, further their shared interests, and eventually create friendships, all below the radar of the ideological differences and mutual suspicions of the official, first track diplomats and politicians. Fruits of those meetings included the creation of the International Society of Space Explorers that joined U.S. astronauts like Rusty Schweickart with Russian cosmonauts. Another participant in those meetings, philoso-pher Sam Keen, wrote a book of text and pictures called *Faces of the Enemy*, whose main point was to show how the unknown, un-experi-enced enemy gets demonized by projections from the fears of one side onto images of the other. The best way to combat such demonizing, and halt the deadly dynamics of projecting one's own shadow onto the image of the enemy, is to meet the other face-to-face. And so the practice of Second Track Diplomacy was born at Esalen and practiced through dozens if not hundreds of human and humanizing relation-ships throughout the 1980s.

We will never know for sure just how influential these relationships were. Some say that Gorbachev's decision to throw in the towel was primarily motivated by the Reagan administration's evil empire rheto-ric, America's immense arms build-up during the 80s, and Soviet fear of the Star Wars deployment—a new level of technology that Russia could neither master nor afford. Perhaps. But on the basis of my visits to Moscow and Tblisi in 1983 and 1985, I can bear witness to Esalen's influence on the climate of opinion and ideas in good favor in high places. When I went to the American Embassy to debrief toward the end of one visit, the officials I met were amazed at the access I'd been granted on the basis of my association with Esalen. "I've been here for four years and I haven't been able to get a meeting with those people," said one frustrated member of the diplomatic staff. This I took as a tes-tament not to my reputation or abilities, but to the level of friendship and trust that Michael and Dulce had generated by keeping the lines of communication open in the early 80s when all other avenues of communication had been shut down.

Esalen hosted Yeltsin's first visit to the United States. During that visit, Boris Yeltsin experienced an epiphany. In a supermarket in Houston he confronted shelves containing dozens of brands of mustard and, as he put it in his tearful revelation, he suddenly understood, "what seventy years of communism had denied the Russian people."

Esalen did not *cause* the end of the Cold War...but it nudged the wheel on the bridge of world history. It *helped* to bring an end to hostilities by melting some of the suspicions of our former adversaries. It exercised leadership in a benign direction.

Returning to Marx's eleventh thesis, it's now worth pondering the lines of a great scholar, a former Marxist, Manuel Castells. Toward the very end of the third volume of his magnum opus, *The Information Age,* he writes, with explicit reference to the eleventh thesis, "In the twentieth century, philosophers have been trying to change the world. In the twenty-first century, it is time for them to interpret it differently."[30] My point in invoking these lines is not simply to seek help in standing Marx on his head, but rather to temper and add measure and deliberation to the way Michael Murphy and Esalen have both changed *and* reinterpreted our world.

To the extent that spirit is incarnate, and not some ethereal essence at a distance from everyday life, then spiritual practice must manifest itself not only in meditation, but also in commerce, politics, *praxis* in all its forms. The greatness [*die Grösse*] of Esalen is thus first that Murphy conceives the self-genesis of man as a process, conceives breakdown as loss of an old self, as alienation and as transcendence of this alienation; that he thus grasps the essence of *practice* and comprehends incarnate man—true because real man—as the outcome of man's *own practice*.[31]

---

[30] Manuel Castells, *End of Millennium,* Volume III of *The Information Age: Economy, Society and Culture,* Blackwell, Oxford, 1998, Vol III, p. 359.

[31] This is a riff on Marx, *Economic and Philosophic Manuscripts of 1844,* trans. Foreign Language Publishing House, Moscow, 1961, p. 151.

11. Heretofore philosophers have only interpreted the world; the point, however, is both to reinterpret it and thereby to improve it.

After flipping Marx's reading of Feuerbach on its head to get closer to Murphy's leadership in the invention of Esalen, it seems only appropriate to give Feuerbach the last word—a word that is appropriate to that sacred land where salt water meets fresh water and the mineral water of the hot springs. At the very end of *Essence of Christianity*, Feuerbach has a few paragraphs about the sacraments. Then he concludes:

> Hunger and thirst destroy not only the physical but also the mental and moral powers of man; they rob him of his humanity—of understanding, of consciousness. Oh! If thou shouldst ever experience such want, how wouldst thou bless and praise the natural qualities of bread and wine, which restore to thee thy humanity, thy intellect! It needs only that the ordinary course of things be interrupted in order to vindicate to common things an uncommon significance, *to life, as such, a religious import.* Therefore let bread be sacred for us, let wine be sacred, and also let water be sacred! Amen.[32]

---

[32] Ludwig Feuerbach, *The Essence of Christianity, op. cit.*, pp. 277f.